# Programmer's Reference Guide to Expert Systems

# Related Titles

**Understanding Artificial Intelligence**
*Henry C. Mishkoff*

**Crash Course in Artificial Intelligence and Expert Systems**
*Louis E. Frenzel, Jr.*

**Mastering Expert Systems with Turbo Prolog**
*Carl Townsend*

**Expert Systems in AI**
*Thomas C. Bartee, Editor-in-Chief (forthcoming)*

**Understanding Expert Sytems**
*Louis E. Frenzel, Jr. (forthcoming)*

**Turbo Prolog Primer, Revised Edition**
*Dan Shafer (forthcoming)*

**Advanced C Primer++**
*Stephen Prata, The Waite Group*

**C with Excellence: Programming Proverbs**
*Henry F. Ledgard with John Tauer*

**MS-DOS® Bible**
*Steven Simrin, The Waite Group*

**Discovering MS-DOS®**
*Kate O'Day, The Waite Group*

**MS-DOS® Developer's Guide**
*John Angermeyer and Kevin Jaeger, The Waite Group*

**Tricks of the MS-DOS® Masters**
*John Angermeyer, Rich Fahringer, Kevin Jaeger, and Dan Shafer, The Waite Group*

**C Programmer's Guide to Serial Communications**
*Joe Campbell*

**C Primer Plus, Revised Edition**
*Mitchell Waite, Stephen Prata, and Donald Martin, The Waite Group*

**Turbo C Programming for the IBM**
*Robert Lafore, The Waite Group*

**Quick C Programming**
*Carl Townsend (forthcoming)*

# Programmer's Reference Guide to Expert Systems

♦ ♦ ♦

David Hu

HOWARD W. SAMS & COMPANY
*A Division of Macmillan, Inc.*
*4300 West 62nd Street*
*Indianapolis, Indiana 46268 USA*

*To Lise, Eileen, and Emily*



FIRST EDITION
FIRST PRINTING—1987



International Standard Book Number: 0-672-22566-2
Library of Congress Catalog Card Number: 87-61480

Acquisitions Editor: *James S. Hill*
Editor: *Marie Butler-Knight*
Designer: *T.R. Emrick*
Illustrator: *W. D. Basham*
Cover Graphic: *Visual Graphic Services, Indianapolis*
*Keith J. Hampton*, Designer
*Robert J. Pitcher*, Illustrator
Indexer: *Ted Laux*
Technical Reviewer: *Carl Townsend*
Compositor: *Shepard Poorman Communications Corp.*

Printed in the United States of America

# Contents

## *Appendixes*

# Trademark Acknowledgments

All terms mentioned in this book that are known to be trademarks or service marks are listed below. In addition, terms suspected of being trademarks or service marks have been appropriately capitalized. Howard W. Sams & Co. cannot attest to the accuracy of this information. Use of a term in this book should not be regarded as affecting the validity of any trademark or service mark.

GCLISP is a registered trademark of Gold Hill Computers
IBM is a registered trademark of IBM Corp.
Insight is a service mark of Whitney Educational Services
Intel is a trademark of Intel Corp.
LOTUS 1-2-3 is a registered trademark of Lotus Corp.
Macintosh is a trademark of Apple Computer Corp.
MS-DOS is a registered trademark of Microsoft Corp.
Personal Consultant is a trademark of Texas Instruments, Inc.
Q&A is a trademark of Symantec Corp.
Rulemaster is a registered trademark of Radian Corp.
Turbo Prolog is a registered trademark of Borland International, Inc.
VAX and DEC are registered trademarks of Digital Equipment Corp.
WordStar is a registered trademark of MicroPro International Corp.
ZETALISP is a registered trademark of Symbolics, Inc.

# Program Listings

# Tables

# Preface

This guide is written for two types of programmers who want to introduce into their programs a new and advanced software technology—AI (artificial intelligence)/expert systems. The first type of programmer is the casual user who wants to learn AI languages and the skills of building expert system shells as well as expert systems. The second type is the serious user who wants to develop fairly sophisticated expert systems for commercial use.

Expert systems can be explained in terms comparable to those that pertain to conventional software programs. An expert system generally includes a knowledge base (comparable to a program code), an inference engine (comparable to a compiler/interpreter), and user interface facilities. The knowledge base contains rules and facts, and the inference engine consists of search control and reasoning mechanisms.

AI/expert systems have come out of laboratories and begun to gain market recognition. Sales of AI (including expert systems) were estimated at more than $150 million in 1984 and are expected to increase to approximately $2 billion in 1990. DM Data (Scottsdale, AZ) anticipates a general trend in market growth for AI/ES of about 60 percent compounded annually. The expert system market has been the fastest growing segment of the artificial intelligence "industry." This market segment has grown from $9 million in 1982 to $74 million (estimated) in 1985, and is expected to reach $810 million (projected) in 1990. The number of new start-up companies pursuing the expert system market increased from seven in 1982 to twelve in 1983, to twenty in 1984, and to twenty-eight in 1985, for an average growth rate of 41 percent. The estimated 1000 percent increase in market size during the period between 1985 and 1990 presents an excellent employment opportunity for many programmers who seek advancement. Whether this forecast of growth can be sustained ultimately depends on the applicability of the technology to traditional programming and the availability of manpower and funds.

Out of approximately forty organizations that were contacted for information on future trends in the technology I have interviewed representatives of twenty-six. The organizations that agreed to interviews are centered in and around Boston, Pittsburgh, Washington, D.C., and San Francisco. Their experts' views on the future of expert systems cover a wide spectrum, with Edward Feigenbaum's *The New Wealth of Nations/ Knowledge is Power* at one extreme and Gary Martin's *Limited Usefulness/*

*Expert Systems Are Oversold* at the other. Most experts' views fall somewhere between these two extremes of optimism versus pessimism.

The majority of experts do not believe that expert systems will replace human experts. They believe that expert systems will take over certain functions of low-level specialists—for example, junior loan officers and computer system configurers—and free these specialists to perform more creative tasks. For some applications, expert systems are becoming useful tools to provide some level of expertise when an expert is not available. Expert system technology can bring to programming a new dimension in which rule-of-thumb or heuristic expert knowledge is encoded in the program. Expert systems may employ high-level programming languages (expert system shells) that enable the user to capture the judgmental knowledge of experts such as geologists, doctors, lawyers, bankers, or insurance underwriters.

Nevertheless, programmers equipped with extensive knowledge of AI/expert system languages, such as LISP, Prolog, and Smalltalk, are required to build and maintain robust working expert systems. Early successful applications include diagnosis systems such as MYCIN, geological systems such as PROSPECTOR, and design/configuration systems such as XCON. These expert systems are mainly applicable to scientific and engineering problems that are not well understood theoretically in terms of decision-making processes by their experts and therefore require judgmental assessment.

Profitable applications exist in almost every field from manufacturing to financial planning. Each expert tends to regard his/her field as the most useful and profitable. The three major areas that most expert systems concentrate on are manufacturing, military operations, and financial planning. However, some companies have explored such conservative markets as operation of electric utilities, with applications for use in nuclear power plants as well as load management of industrial and commercial customers. These applications have been confirmed through a grass-roots survey of 155 potential expert system end users. The survey was conducted by Mackintosh International (Saratoga, CA) in 1985.

In addition to their ability to encode the expert's judgmental knowledge, expert systems generally provide the user with a more convenient man-machine interface than conventional programs; provide an explanation tracing that displays many different aspects of the problem; and demonstrate how a decision has been derived. Many expert systems allow the user to ask why a decision is made or not made. Because of these convenient features, programmers who acquire expert system technology skills can expect to increase the user friendliness of their software products.

The most effective programming approach to building expert systems was confirmed by John Kunz of IntelliCorp and others to be rapid production of the expert system. In expert system rapid production, the user must be involved as early as possible to identify the user's real needs and to generate user enthusiasm. A crucial question is where to start rapid production. (You can start from specifying the problem.) The objective is to complete as many prototypes as needed for various aspects of the problem.

This book is thus written for programmers who are interested in artificial intelligence and want to integrate artificial intelligence techniques, particularly expert system technology, into their programs to enable these programs to perform as

- *Intelligent "users."* The program acts as a data base for other software packages. Interaction with the software package/data base is not its primary objective, but merely a convenient means to access data.
- *Intelligent "representatives."* The program uses mathematical logic to represent general facts about data in the software package/data base, to increase the usefulness of the package/data base in responding to queries.
- *Intelligent "probers."* The program supports browsing through a data base or program and also supports query modification to either narrow or broaden the scope of the request to make it more understandable to the user. For example, if `employ(X, john)`—that is, find all persons whom John employs—fails for the initial query the intelligent prober may try relevant queries such as `teach(X, john)` or `supervisor(X, John)`.
- *Natural language "interfaces."* The program provides natural language interface software packages and allows the user to search for and process information without having to learn the specialized command language of a software package.
- *Natural language text "analysts."* The program processes a user's natural language input text to produce appropriate responses to user queries. The capability of the expert system to understand natural language text in a given field permits the user to enter data in a relatively flexible form.
- *Knowledge "accumulators" and "disseminators."* The program extracts the expert's/specialist's expertise to advise or train junior personnel to perform a job at a level close to that of experts.

The text in this guide is written specifically for use with the IBM PC, XT, and AT and compatibles. It provides the programmer with core knowledge that can be used to build the functions listed above into conventional programs. This guide includes most material on AI languages, programs to build each component of an expert system shell, methods to develop an expert system, and approaches for expert system delivery. It attempts to list most software packages for AI languages and expert system shells/tools available for the IBM PC and its compatible environment. Its primary focus is on expert system technology.

This guide can be used for four purposes:

- To review the individual AI languages LISP, Prolog, and Smalltalk, refer to Chapters 2 through 6.
- To build an expert system shell/tool, refer to Chapters 2 through 8.

- To develop expert systems, refer to Chapters 2, 3, 4, 9, and 10.
- To develop and deliver expert systems for commercial use, refer to Chapters 2 through 10.

# Acknowledgments

I am indebted to those whose enthusiasm inspired me to write a series of expert system books and to those who contributed their ideas, cases, and reviews. These professionals include Mr. V. Daniel Hunt, Dr. Mark Fox, Dr. Rick Roth-Hayes, Dr. Frank Lynch, Mr. Richard Brimer, Dr. Craig W. Cook, Dr. Kenneth C. Hayes, Mr. Brad Netherton, Ms. Catherine Roy, Dr. Cordell Green, Dr. M. James Naughton, Mr. Mike Chamber, Mr. Eric J. Jacobs, Dr. Darryl F. Hubbard, Dr. John Kunz, Mr. Robert Fondellier, Dr. James R. Brink, Mr. Deva D. Sharma, Dr. Norman Neilson, Dr. John R. Josephson, Dr. Steven Rosenberg, Mr. Kit Sakamoto, Mr. Peter Hart, Mr. William R. Crisp, Mr. Bobby Johnson, Dr. Chee Yee Chong, Dr. Peter Hirsch, Dr. David Cain, Mr. Bob Iverson, Mr. Clark Dohner, Mr. Chuck McGowin, Dr. Pradeep Gupta, Mr. Gary Martins, Mr. Thomas R. Ruschbac, Dr. Emilio J. Navarro, Dr. Bill Sun, and Dr. Robert F. Nease, Jr.

Special thanks to Mr. Rob Ramero and Mr. Han (Frank) Tay for their assistance in software and hardware, respectively.

*David Hu*
*Hayward, California*

SECTION

# 1

# Introduction to Expert System Development in the Personal Computer (PC) Environment

This book introduces you to the idea of incorporating expert system technology into your daily programming work, by providing details on how to build each component of this innovative technology in the PC environment. Section 1 discusses in detail the major components and terminology—hardware and software—available for you to learn and develop expert systems. It also discusses the programming principles and approaches of expert system technology. The description of this technology draws heavily upon an analogy of the new technology to conventional programming techniques, to enable you to comprehend the new terms easily and quickly.

# I

# 1

# Introduction to Expert Systems

Expert system (ES) technology is an advanced programming technique that many programmers will have the opportunity to use in the near future. This technology provides a new programming capability for incorporating symbolic representation of articles and heuristic knowledge in conventional software packages.

Expert systems are different from conventional software programs, which provide access to computer capability in arithmetic power, and from decision support systems, which provide access to computer capability in distributing information. Expert systems capture and distribute the human expert's expertise in making judgments under various conditions. They "clone" experts by capturing knowledge that is perishable, scarce, vague, and difficult to apply, distribute, or accumulate. Expert systems afford cost-effective services in areas that require symbolic processing of knowledge and rule-of-thumb judgmental problem-solving methods. An initial application of expert systems was in the diagnosis and treatment of human physical disorders. The basic purpose of these systems was to determine what the symptoms indicated and what remedial treatment was appropriate.

Expert system technology is one of the most successful branches of artificial intelligence (AI). It focuses on expert systems and on natural or semi-natural language interfaces. Other branches of AI include robotics, voice recognition and synthesis, and vision. Expert system technology started to emerge as a potent force in 1977 when Professor Edward Feigenbaum of Stanford University presented an insight that the problem-solving power of a computer program comes from the knowledge of a given domain it processes, not just from the programming techniques and formalism it contains [1].* Experience indicates, however, that programming tech-

* Bracketed numbers indicate references at the end of each chapter.

niques and formalism may determine the eventual destiny of an expert system.

## Basic Concepts of Expert System Technology

As shown in Figure 1-1, the structure of an expert system resembles a conventional software program. The major components of an expert system are knowledge base, inference engine, user interface mechanism (including explanation facility), and data. Major components of conventional programs are data (or data base), code, interpreter/compiler, and sparse user interface mechanism, but the interpreter/compiler is not obvious to the user. Expert systems are capable of symbolic processing, inferencing, and explaining.

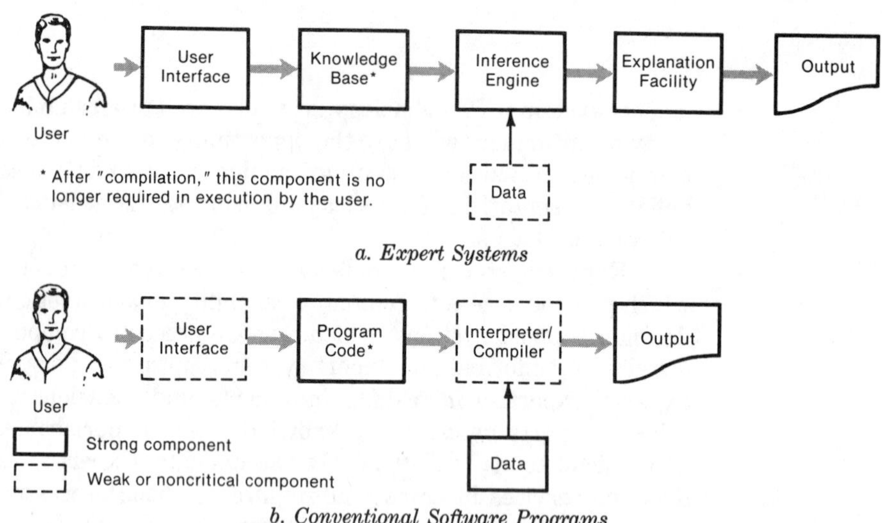


**Figure 1-1**
***Expert systems vs. conventional software programs***

In terms of terminology used, expert systems can be considered an advanced form of programming. As shown in Table 1-1, the terminology of expert systems can be mapped on a one-to-one basis to that of software programs. For example, the knowledge base of an expert system that contains rules (likely IF-THEN rules) and facts matches the program (code) of a software program. However, a knowledge base should not be confused with a data base. A knowledge base is executable but a data base is not. A data base can only be queried and updated. Like an interpreter that evaluates a program in the source code and executes the statements, the inference engine takes the statements in a knowledge base and executes them because it contains search control and reasoning mechanisms.

AI/ES languages such as LISP, Prolog, and Smalltalk can be used to build an empty package of the knowledge base, inference engine, and user interface or explanation facility. This package is called an expert system tool or *shell*. The "shell" defined here is *not* an extension to an operating system such as UNIX. It is a tool to facilitate the rapid development of an expert system. Expert system shells are high-level programming languages with unconventional conveniences such as explanation and tracing facilities.

**Table 1-1**
***Comparison of expert system and software program terminology***

| Expert Systems | Software Programs |
|---|---|
| Knowledge base | Program |
| Inference engine | Interpreter/compiler |
| Knowledge engineers | Software engineers/programmer-analysts |
| High-level programming tools (shells)—i.e., KEE | Relatively low-level programming languages—i.e., FORTRAN |

# *Knowledge Base*

The programmer can use two types of knowledge to build expert systems: (1) facts and (2) rules that state relations between facts. To represent these types of knowledge in the knowledge base, three methods are used:

- Rules to represent rules of thumb
- Frames to represent facts and relations
- Logic to represent assertions and questions

## Rules

Rules are conditional sentences expressed in the form:

IF (premise) FACT 1, FACT 2, . . .
THEN (conclusion) FACT 9, FACT 10, . . .

For example, if the rule of "starts per month" is

IF (the number of motor starts per month exceeds 20 times)
THEN (increase the operational potential of the motor)

this rule can be translated into LISP as follows:

```
(IF ((starts-per-month-of-motor ) >20)
 THEN (increase(operational-potential-of-motor)
      significantly))
 )
```

## Frames or Units

A *frame* (also called a *unit*) contains the hierarchies of objects (components) and the attributes of objects that can be assigned, inherited from other frames, or computed through procedures or other computer programs. The attributes are filled in the *slots* of a frame. The box below contains a sample unit.

**Sample Frame in ASD_Advisor**

Frame name: ASD Adjustable Frequency AC Drive
Installed to: Induction motor
Inherited from: ASD
Created by: 6-30-86
Modified by: 7-5-86

Slot: Capacity
Type: Real number, value: 0 to 1000 hp
Slot: Main component
Type: Alphanumeric, value: INVERTERS
Slot: Usage
Type: Alphabet, value: (Inherited from ASD it is a kind of ASD)
Slot: Economics
Type: Real number, value: (Computed from PROCEDURE = ECONOMICS)
Slot: Operation
Type: Logic, value: (Rule 5a)

## Logic

Logic expressions consist of predicates and values to assess facts of the real world. A *predicate* is a statement concerning an object such as

```
Kind-of (Adjustable-Frequency-AC-Drive, ASD)
```

The predicate in the above example may be interpreted as an adjustable frequency AC drive, a kind of ASD (adjustable speed drive). The object may be either a constant or a variable that can change over time. A predicate may have one or more arguments that are the objects it describes. In the example of ***ASD_Advisor***, the other kind of logic expression is appropriate for asking questions such as

```
? - (Indicator_Matrix, X) :- Company(X), ASD(X), Economics
(X, Excellent).
```

This question can be interpreted as: show me all possible ASD installations in a given company that can be implemented to induction motors only with excellent economic potential.

# *Inference Engine*

Once the knowledge base is completed, it needs to be executed by a reasoning mechanism and search control to solve problems. The most common reasoning method in expert systems is the application of the following simple logic rule (also called *modus ponens*):

> IF A is true, THEN B is true in a statement of
> "IF A, THEN B."

The implication of this simple rule is that:

> IF B is not true, THEN A is not true in the same statement.

Another implication of the simple logic rule is

| Given: | IF A, THEN B and |
|---|---|
| | IF B, THEN C |
| Conclusion: | IF A, THEN C |

In other words, IF A is true, THEN we can conclude that C is also true.

These three simple reasoning principles are used to examine rules, facts, and relations in expert systems to solve problems. However, to minimize the reasoning time, search control methods are used to determine where to start the reasoning process and to choose which rule to examine next when several rules conflict at the same point. The two main methods of search are *forward and backward chaining*. These two methods of chaining may be combined in an expert system for maximum efficiency of search control.

## Forward Chaining

When the rule interpreter is forward chaining, if premise clauses match the situation, the conclusion clauses are asserted. For example, in the rule of starts per month, if the real situation matches the premise (that is, the number of motor starts per month exceeds 20), the operational potential of ASDs to the motor increases. Once the rule is used or "fired," it is not used again in the same search; however, the fact concluded as the result of that rule's firing is added to the knowledge base. This cycle of finding a matched rule, firing it, and adding the conclusion to the knowledge base is repeated until no more matched rules can be found.

## Backward Chaining

A backward chaining mechanism attempts to prove the hypothesis from facts. If the current goal is to determine the fact in the conclusion (hypothesis), then you need to determine whether the premises match the situation. For example,

Rule One: IF you lose the key and the gas tank is empty,
THEN the car is not running.

Rule Two: IF the car is not running and you have no cash,
THEN you are going to be late.

Fact One: You lost the key.

Fact Two: The gas tank is empty.

For instance, if we want to prove the hypothesis that "you are going to be late," given the facts and rules in the knowledge base (Facts 1 and 2, Rules 1 and 2), backward chaining must be applied to determine whether the premises match the situation. Rule 2, which contains the conclusion, is tested first to determine whether the premises match the fact. Because the knowledge base does not contain the facts in the premises of Rule 2, "the car is not running" and "you have no cash," "the car is not running" becomes the first subgoal. Rule 1 is then tested to assert whether the premises "you lost the key" and "the gas tank is empty" match the facts. Because the facts (Facts 1 and 2) in the knowledge base match the premise of Rule 1, the subhypothesis is proven. However, the system still has to prove that "you have no cash," which is not contained in the knowledge base and cannot be asserted through rules for no rule is related to it. The system then asks, "IS IT TRUE THAT: you have no cash?" If the answer is "yes," then the second subgoal is also satisfied and the original hypothesis is proven, concluding that "you are going to be late."

## *Man-Machine Interface*

The man-machine interface mechanism produces dialogue between the computer and the user. The current expert system may be equipped with templates, "menus," mice, or natural language to facilitate its use, and an explanation module to allow the user to challenge and examine the reasoning process underlying the system's answers.

Menus refer to groups of multichoice options that appear on the computer screen. The user selects menu options by pushing designated buttons on a "mouse" or designated keys on the keyboard. The user does not have to type instructions. A natural or semi-natural language interface is more sophisticated than a menu interface. A natural language interface allows computer systems to accept inputs and produce outputs in a language close to a conventional language such as English (see references 2, 3, and 4 for detailed approaches). Several expert systems incorporate primitive forms of natural language in their user interfaces to facilitate knowledge base development. Explanation modules generate output statements of expert systems in language that can be understood by noncomputer-professional users.

## *Uncertainty of Knowledge*

Rules obtained from human experts are sometimes uncertain. Experts describe some rules or facts as "maybe," "sometimes," "often," or "not quite certain about the conclusion." You need methods to handle these types of probabilistic statements. Further, expert systems, like human experts, may have to draw inferences based on incomplete, unavailable, unknown, or uncertain information. Unavailable or unknown information is resolved by allowing rules to fail if the information needed is critical in evaluating the premise—that is, the information needed is in the condition (IF) statements connected by *and*. For example, in Rule 1 under "Backward Chaining," if the expert is not sure whether "the gas tank is empty," the conclusion of "the car is not running" cannot be asserted. When IF statements are connected by *or*, the absence of one or more statements does not affect the outcome of the rule.

Uncertainty of facts or rules can be represented by the use of probabilistic judgment such as the Baysian theory or the theory of belief function. The latter is also called the Dempster-Shafer theory of evidence in the AI community. Because of circumstances and assumptions regarding facts and rules, the two probabilistic judgment approaches are often modified to accommodate the circumstances. Two examples are

- The case of PROSPECTOR [5], in which a set of quasi-Baysian rules for combining probabilities is used.
- The case of MYCIN [6], in which an ad hoc set of rules for combining belief functions are established [7].

The Baysian and belief function approaches find their respective niches in the development of expert systems, and they fit only certain narrow kinds of problems. In general, the Baysian approach functions more efficiently in representing probability judgments in expert systems that are applied under constant conditions, so that solutions are determined randomly with known chances (such as in the diagnostics of physical, man-made machineries). Belief function designs, on the other hand, are more effective in representing uncertainty of knowledge involving personal experience in a specialty field such as medicine.

Modification of either approach is often required to fully represent the flexibility of human probability judgment. In any modification of the two probability approaches, you must carefully establish rules for the following issues:

- How uncertainty is represented
- How uncertainty probabilities are combined
- How premise clauses are connected and how they affect the joint probability

As long as these issues are resolved, the modification will serve the purpose of representing uncertainty in knowledge.

# Summary

- An expert system mimics experts or specialists in a specific field—for example, medicine or computer configuration.
- The power of an expert system lies in knowledge and how it is represented, not in programming technique.
- The principal components of current systems are knowledge base, inference engine, and man-machine interface.
- The knowledge base contains facts and rules that embody an expert's expertise.
- The three commonly used methods for encoding facts and relationships that constitute knowledge are rules, frames, and logical expressions.
- Inference engines are relatively simple. The most commonly used methods are backward chaining and forward chaining.
- User interface is a weak but critical element of expert systems. Many current expert systems are equipped with "menus" and explanation modules to allow users to query expert systems and examine their output statements.

# References


[1] E. A. Feigenbaum, "The Art of Artificial Intelligence: Themes and Case Studies," *Conference Proceedings of the International Joint Conference on Artificial Language* (1977), 1014-1029.

[2] Brodie Associates, "Language Workbench, a programmer's toolkit for developing natural language interfaces to application software," *Kurzweil AI* (Waltham, MA, 1986).

[3] G. G. Hendrix and E. D. Sacerdoti, "Developing a Natural Language Interface to Comp Data" (Technical report, Artificial Intelligence Center, International, 1976).

[4] G. G. Hendrix, "The LIFER Manual: A Guide To Build Practical Natural Language Interfaces" (Technical report, technical note 138, SRI, 1977).

[5] J. Gasching, "PROSPECTOR: An Expert System for Mineral Exploration," *Machine Intelligence*, Infotech State of the Art Report 9, no. 3 (1981).

[6] E. H. Shortliffe, *Computer-Based Medical Consultations: MYCIN* (New York: Elsevier, 1976).

[7] J. Gordon and E. H. Shortliffe, "The Dempster-Shafer Theory of Evidence," *Rule-Based Expert Systems: The MYCIN Experiments of the Stanford Heuristic Programming Project*, ed. B. G. Buchanan and E. H. Shortliffe (Reading, MA: Addison-Wesley, 1984), 272-292.

[8] DM Data, Inc., "AI Trends in '85" (Scottsdale, AZ, 1985).

[9] Randall Davis, "Expert Systems: Where Are We? And Where Do We Go from Here?" *The AI Magazine*, 3, no. 2 (Spring 1982).

# 2

# Hardware and Software Available to Programmers

This chapter examines the hardware equipment and software packages available in the personal computer environment to programmers for learning and building expert systems. Due to their sophistication and cost, an attempt was made to describe hardware and software separately for the casual and the serious programmer.

## Hardware Available

Personal computers are highly accessible to programmers and are appropriate for developing toy expert systems by the casual programmer who wants to learn AI language or expert systems. However, most personal computers are too slow and have insufficient memory for use in serious expert systems development. The IBM PC/AT and its clones do have sufficient capacity to allow a serious programmer to enter expert system development if the system is appropriately configured. The suggested configuration of the system is shown in Table 2-1. For a price of $4,350 this system provides the serious programmer with a dedicated workstation for use in developing expert systems.

## Software Available

Most available AI programming languages and tools are sufficient for casual programmers to develop toy expert systems. The three major expert system programming languages are LISP, Prolog, and Smalltalk, which are used to create shells/tools. The majority of tools available are written in LISP; only a few tools are written in Prolog and Smalltalk. These tools may

**Table 2-1**
***Suggested configuration for IBM PC/AT or compatible system for expert system development***

| Component | 1986 Price |
|---|---|
| AT clone system (8MHz, 1Mb) | $ 1,300 |
| Two 20Mb hard disks (half height) | 700 |
| EGA card | 300 |
| Color monitor | 550 |
| Printer | 600 |
| 1.2Mb floppy disk drive | 150 |
| Mouse | 150 |
| Extended memory card (3Mb) | 600 |
| Total | $ 4,350 |

provide some conveniences that are not available in conventional programming packages. Most AI languages and tools are readily available to casual programmers for use in sharpening their skills in building expert systems.

## *Languages*

Of the three most widely used ES languages—LISP, Prolog, and Smalltalk—LISP is the predominant language worldwide for expert system development that can be "hooked" to other programming languages such as C. LISP is well understood by the AI community even though various dialects exist. Prolog is more widely accepted in Europe and Japan than in the United States. Smalltalk is an emerging object programming language for building user interface packages. The three ES languages are not directly comparable. LISP is a pure language, whereas Prolog consists of a language, a basic knowledge representation structure, and a "backtracking" inference engine. Smalltalk is strong in user interface features such as windows and graphics.

### LISP

LISP is the acronym for *LIS*t *P*rocessing language and is the second oldest programming language still in use today. (FORTRAN is the oldest.) Its basic data structure consists of *lists* and *atoms*. An *atom* is an element that cannot be further subdivided—for example, an object, an integer, or a function. *Lists* are made of atoms and other lists. Lists and atoms can be made into functions and programs. LISP therefore offers generality and conceptual simplicity. This feature, in which programs and data are expressed by the same structure, accommodates the recursive nature of the language. It is relatively easy to write LISP programs that generate other LISP programs.

Various "dialects" of LISP have been developed in the past. A simplified diagram showing the relationship between these dialects in chronological order is given in Figure 2-1. Major dialects include INTERLISP, MacLISP, UCI LISP, Standard LISP, and FRANZ LISP. Common LISP emerged as a standard in 1984; it succeeded MacLISP and was influenced by other dialects, such as ZETALISP, SCHEME and INTERLISP. Documents for most dialects are cited in references 1 through 13. Common LISP thus serves as a common dialect to which various LISP implementations, such as MacLISP, ZETALISP, SPICE LISP, NIL, AND S-1 LISP, make necessary extensions.

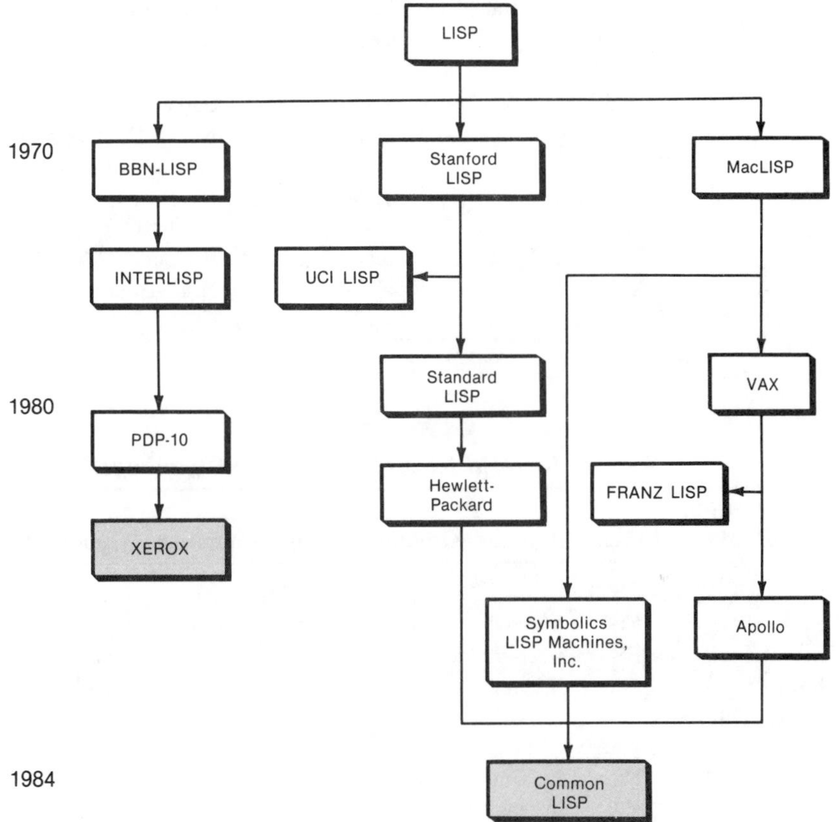


**Figure 2-1**
***Development of LISP dialects***

The features and speed of the PC LISP packages available on the market are summarized in Tables 2-2 and 2-3. Chapter 4 gives details on programming in LISP. Books available for LISP programming are given in references 22 and 23 at the end of this chapter.

# Prolog

Prolog (*Pro*gramming in *log*ic) was initially implemented by Alan Colmerauer at the University of Marseilles, France in 1972–73. Interest in Prolog seemed confined to the European AI community until October, 1981 when

**Table 2-2**
***PC LISP packages***

| Name of Package | Applicable PC | Developer | Telephone |
|---|---|---|---|
| BYSCO LISP | IBM AT | Levien Instrument | (703)369-3345 |
| CLISP | IBM | Westcomp | (714) 982-1738 |
| Cromenco LISP | Z-80 | Cromenco | (415) 964-7400 |
| Expert LISP | Macintosh/IBM | ExperTelligence | (805) 969-7871 |
| Golden Common LISP | IBM | Gold Hill Computers | (617) 492-2071 |
| 286-Developer | IBM AT | Gold Hill Computers | (617) 492-2071 |
| IQLISP | IBM | Integral Quality | (206) 527-2918 |
| LISP/80 | IBM | Software Toolworks | (818) 986-4885 |
| LISP/88 | IBM | Norell Data Systems | (213) 748-5978 |
| muLISP | all | Soft Warehouse | (206) 455-8080 |
| UO-LISP | IBM | Northwest Computer Algorithms | (213) 426-1893 |
| Waltz LISP | all | ProCode | (800) LIP-4000 |
| XLISP | all | N.Y. Amateur Computer Club | (603) 924-9820 |

**Table 2-3**
***General features of PC LISP packages*†**

| Manufacturer and Product | Editor | Numbers | Graphics | Debug | Compiler | Window | Assembly Interface | Factional (seconds) |
|---|---|---|---|---|---|---|---|---|
| BYSO LISP | FS | int | no | yes | no | no | no | — |
| ExperLISP | FS | int,real | yes | yes | yes | yes | yes | 0.79 |
| GCLISP | FS | int,real | yes | yes | no | yes | no | — |
| IQLISP | struct | int,real | yes | yes | no | yes | yes | 3.74 |
| LISP/80 and LISP/88 | struct | int | no | yes | no | no | yes | — |
| muLISP | FS | inf*/int | yes | yes | pseudo | no | yes | 3.11 |
| TLC-LISP | FS | int,real | yes | yes | yes | yes | no | — |
| UO-LISP | FS | inf/int | yes | yes | yes | no | yes | 0.97/6.58** |
| Waltz LISP | FS | inf/int | no | yes | no | no | yes | 2.26 |
| XLISP | no | int | yes | yes | no | no | C source | — |

*Infinite precision integers.
**The compiled version required 0.97 second, and the interpreted version required 6.58 seconds.
†Source: Modified from *Computer Language*, (July 1985), 85–88.

the Japanese announced the official "fifth-generation" project in which Prolog would be used as the kernel language. Prolog is based on the concept of "logic programming", which deals with statements involving objects and their relationships, such as

```
professor(david, peter).
```

In this statement, `professor` is the predicate defining the relationship between the arguments of `david` and `peter`, which indicates that David is the professor of Peter.

Prolog has yet to win widespread commercial acceptance in the United States for two reasons: (1) the difficulty of interfacing with conventional languages such as Fortran and (2) the slowness of Prolog programs in production use. Even though Turbo Prolog claims to have eliminated these problems, it may have compromised other critical Prolog features, such as unification. Available PC Prolog packages are summarized in Table 2-4; many of these packages are European products. Chapter 5 gives details on programming in Prolog. Books for programming Prolog include those cited in references 24 and 25 at the end of this chapter.

**Table 2-4**
***PC Prolog packages***

| Name of Package | Applicable PC | Developer | Telephone |
|---|---|---|---|
| Arity Prolog | IBM | Arity | (617) 371-1243 |
| IF/Prolog | IBM | Interface Computer, W. Germany | 089/984444 |
| LPA Micro-Prolog | IBM | Logic Programming Assoc., UK | 018740350 |
| MPROLOG | all | Logicware | (714) 476-3634 |
| Micro-Prolog | IBM | Programming Logic Systems | (203) 877-7988 |
| PC-Prolog | IBM | SuInfologics AB, Stockholm, Sweden | |
| PROLOG-1 & -2 | IBM | Expert Systems Int'l | (215) 337-2300 |
| PROLOG V | IBM | Chalcedony Software | (619) 483-8513 |
| Prolog-86 | IBM | Solution Systems | (617) 337-6963 |
| Turbo Prolog | IBM | Borland Int'l | (408) 438-8400 |

## Smalltalk

Smalltalk is an object-oriented programming language. An object-oriented programming language often has several of the following five features: information hiding, data abstraction, dynamic binding, class inheritance, and automatic storage management, (for example, garbage collection). Smalltalk possesses all of these features.

The main vocabulary of Smalltalk has five words: object, message, class, instance, and method. These five words present the concepts of Smalltalk: they are defined as follows:

*Object* A basic element of Smalltalk, represented by private memory and operation instructions

*Message* A request for an object to accomplish its operations

*Class* A description of a set of similar objects

*Instance* One member object in a class

*Method* A description of how to perform an object's operation

Smalltalk is different from traditional procedural languages. In Smalltalk, an object carries its own operation instance, and messages represent the interaction between components by requesting them to perform operations on themselves. For example

- `beta sin`
  Explanation — a message requesting the object name `beta` to compute the sine of itself.
- `list addLast: newComponent`
  Explanation — a message requesting the object, a linear data structure named `list`, to add the object named `newComponent` as the last element of itself.

A Smalltalk program (*implementation description*) consists of three parts: a class name, a declaration of the variables available to the instances, and the methods used by instances to respond to messages. Messages are grouped together in the form of message patterns, which in turn are commented by a protocol description. The comment describes what will happen, not how the operation will be performed. Further discussion on how to program in Smalltalk is provided in Chapter 6 and references 26, 27, and 28 at the end of this chapter.

Smalltalk has several programming advantages, including the ability to add new classes of objects without modifying existing code due to dynamic binding capability, and the ability to reuse original codes that perform a particular task to reduce the number of lines of repeated code. Smalltalk has been implemented for the IBM PC/AT (Smalltalk-80) by Softsmarts, Inc. of Woodside, CA, at a cost of $995 per copy, and for the IBM PC (Smalltalk/V) by Digitalk, Inc. of Los Angeles, at a cost of $99 per copy.

# Expert System Shells/Tools

Most of the shells/tools available in the market lack the sophistication and capability needed to develop a sophisticated expert system. These tools can be classified according to two criteria: sophistication and knowledge acquisition requirement. A list of the majority of PC tools is presented in Appendix D. A discussion of tools according to these two criteria follows.

## Sophistication of Tools

Tools for PCs normally cannot be as sophisticated as tools for LISP workstations; however, sophistication varies among PC tools. Based on tool complexity, PC tools can be classified as simple rule-based, structured rule-based, logic-based hybrid, frame-based hybrid, and object-oriented hybrid.

*Simple rule-based tools* use IF-THEN production rules for knowledge that can be expressed by 50 to 500 rules in an expert system. These tools are adequate for instructional problems. Examples include Insight-1, -2 [30], KES [18], and M.1 [14].

*Structured rule-based tools* use IF-THEN rules subdivided into groups that can be structured in hierarchy. Different groups of rules can be examined without going through every rule each time the system is called upon. These systems are more suitable for complex problems. A good example is Personal Consultant [15].

*Logic-based hybrid tools* use logical analysis (predicate calculus) to represent knowledge and can be combined with simple rule-based or induction features to help input knowledge in expert systems. The logic-based method uses predicate logic to control the analysis of declarative clauses in the form *consequent: antecedent-1, antecedent-2, . . . antecedent-n,* or where both consequent and antecedents are predicates. The antecedents are predicates that can be tested for their true value. The consequent can only be true if all antecedents can be proved true. Logic-based hybrid tools are more widely used in Europe, where Prolog is employed, than in the United States, where LISP is popular. They are powerful with complex problems. ES/P Advisor [31] is an example of a logic-based hybrid tool in which simple rule-based and logic-based features are combined.

*Frame-based hybrid tools* use frames as well as rules to represent knowledge. These tools are useful for complex problem areas where the form and content of the data are important in problem solving—for example, interpreting visual scenes, understanding speech, or representing a variety of information in a single set of data structures. These tools tend to use both backward and forward chaining control schemes. Few tools have been developed yet.

*Object-oriented hybrid tools* represent the problem elements as objects that can contain facts, IF-THEN rules, or pointers to other objects. The tools facilitate the development of expert systems that incorporate complex, graphical user interfaces. If these tools also combine induction features, they can be very powerful for experts/specialists to use in developing intelligent job aids. This type of tool is not yet fully developed.

## Knowledge Acquisition Requirement

Knowledge acquisition requirement can also be used to further classify PC tools for expert system development into three categories: induction, induction hybrid, and noninduction tools.

*Induction tools* take examples from the user, convert them into rules, and then apply specific algorithms to the rule to determine the order the system follows in inferencing. These systems are user-friendly but weak and inflexible in performance. They are useful only for very simple tasks. Examples include Expert Ease [32] and TIMM [33]. Induction tools can be used to test rules extracted by knowledge engineers, even though rules induced from examples often are not useful in a structured knowledge base because these tools can extract only simple rules. These tools can be used as "test stones" in identifying shortcuts and appropriate knowledge areas for software engineers to undertake in knowledge acquisition.

*Induction hybrid tools* use the induction method to obtain rules. They are combined with frame-based or object-oriented methods to assist in putting knowledge into expert systems. These tools can be very powerful in solving real-time complex problems. I know of no example tools on the market yet.

*Noninduction tools* include most PC tools available on the market that do not use induction methods to extract rules. These tools include all those discussed previously that are not inductive, such as Personal Consultant and M.1.

## *Software Available for Serious Programmers*

Most AI languages and shells/tools available for the IBM PC environment are insufficient for serious programmers due to the inaccessibility of RAM memory larger than 640K that is addressable by MS-DOS. Exceptions include 286-Developer (a LISP package developed by Gold Hill Common LISP), Smalltalk/V, and Smalltalk-80.

# Summary

- Personal computers are most accessible to casual programmers for developing toy expert systems.
- The IBM PC/AT and its clones may offer sufficient capacity to allow a serious software engineer to enter expert system development if appropriately configured.
- The three major AI languages are LISP, Prolog, and Smalltalk.
- Shells/tools, mostly useful for developing toy expert systems, can be classified as simple rule-based, structured rule-based, induction, logic-based hybrid, frame-based hybrid, and object-oriented hybrid.
- The few language packages available for serious programmers to develop sophisticated expert systems are 286-Developer, Smalltalk/V, and Smalltalk-80.

# References

[1] John K. Foderaro, *The FRANZ LISP Manual* (University of California, Berkeley, CA, 1979).

[2] M. L. Griss and B. Morrison, “The Portable Standard LISP Users Manual” (Utah Symbolic Computation Group Technical Report TR-10, University of Utah, Department of Computer Science, Salt Lake City, 1981).

Book Mark

## *HOWARD W. SAMS & COMPANY*

*Excellence In Publishing*

DEAR VALUED CUSTOMER:

Howard W. Sams & Company is dedicated to bringing you timely and authoritative books for your personal and professional library. Our goal is to provide you with excellent technical books written by the most qualified authors. You can assist us in this endeavor by checking the box next to your particular areas of interest.

We appreciate your comments and will use the information to provide you with a more comprehensive selection of titles.

Thank you,

Vice President, Book Publishing
Howard W. Sams & Company

SUBJECT AREAS:

Computer Titles:
- ☐ Apple/Macintosh
- ☐ Commodore
- ☐ IBM & Compatibles
- ☐ Business Applications
- ☐ Communications
- ☐ Operating Systems
- ☐ Programming Languages

Electronics Titles:
- ☐ Amateur Radio
- ☐ Audio
- ☐ Basic Electronics
- ☐ Electronic Design
- ☐ Electronic Projects
- ☐ Satellites
- ☐ Troubleshooting & Repair

Other interests or comments:

______________________________________________

______________________________________________

Name ______________________________________

Title ______________________________________

Company ____________________________________

Address ____________________________________

City _______________________________________

State/Zip ___________________________________

Daytime Telephone No. _______________________

*A Division of Macmillan, Inc.*
*4300 West 62nd Street*
*Indianapolis, Indiana 46268 USA*

22566

Please send additional information on the following products:

_____ Baldur IQ 100: The Intelligent Data Communications Shell
_____ Expert Knowledge Organizer
_____ Blackjack Assistant
    _____ in M.1
    _____ in Personal Consultant
_____ Heavy-Vehicle Configurer
_____ Hardware/Software Configuration Kit for PC Expert System Development (to convert your PC into an AI workstation)

Name ____________________________________________
Address __________________________________________
City ______________________________ State _______ Zip _______
Telephone ________________________________

Or call 415/732-9715 (FAX: 415/732-9716) for more information. 22566

**FOR MORE INFORMATION**
about products described in this book, use this handy tear-out card

fold and tape or staple

STAMP

Baldur Systems Corporation
℅ Howard W. Sams & Company
4300 West 62nd Street
Indianapolis, IN 46268 USA

[3] J. Marti, A. C. Hearn, M. L. Griss, and C. Griss, "Standard LISP Report," *SIGPLAN Notices* 14, no. 10 (October 1979), 48-68.

[4] James Meehan, *New UCI LISP Manual* (Lawrence Erlbaum Associates, Hillsdale, NJ, 1970).

[5] David Moon, *MacLISP Reference Manual*, Rev. 0 (MIT Project MAC, Cambridge, MA, April 1974).

[6] David Moon, Richard Stallman, and Daniel Weinreb, *LISP Machine Manual*, 5th ed. (MIT Artificial Intelligence Lab, Cambridge, MA, January 1983).

[7] Kent M. Pitman, *The Revised MacLISP Manual*, MIT/LCR/TR 295 (MIT Lab for Computer Science, Cambridge, MA, May 1983).

[8] Guy L. Steele, Jr., *Common LISP Reference Manual* (Spice Project Internal Report, Carnegie-Mellon University, Digital Press, Pittsburgh, 1982).

[9] Guy L. Steele, Jr. and Gerald Jay Sussman, "The Revised Report on SCHEME: A Dialect of LISP" (AI Memo 452, MIT Artificial Intelligence Lab, Cambridge, MA, January 1978).

[10] Warren Teitelman, *INTERLISP Reference Manual* (Xerox Palo Alto Research Center, Palo Alto, CA, and Bolt, Beranek, and Newman, Cambridge, MA, 1974, rev. 1978).

[11] Jaak Urmi, *INTERLISP/370 Reference Manual* (Linkoeping University, Department of Mathematics, Linkoeping, Sweden, 1976).

[12] Daniel Weinreb and David Moon, *LISP Machine Manual*, 3rd ed. (MIT Artificial Intelligence Lab, Cambridge, MA, 1971).

[13] Jon L. White, "NIL: A Perspective," *Proceedings of the 1979 MACSYMA Users' Conference* (MIT Lab for Computer Science, Cambridge, MA, June 1979).

[14] Teknowledge, *M.1 Product Description* (Palo Alto, CA, 1984).

[15] "Artificial Intelligence Publications, the Personal Consultant," *The AI Report*, vol. 1, no. 12 (1984).

[16] N. Aiello, C. Bock, H. P. Nii, and W. C. White, "Joy of AGEing: an Introduction to the AGE-1 System" (Report HPP-81-23, Computer Science Department, Stanford University, 1981).

[17] J. C. Kunz, T. P. Kehler, and M. D. Williams, "Applications development using a hybrid AI development system," *The AI Magazine*, vol. 5, no. 3 (Fall 1984).

[18] Software Architecture and Engineering, Inc., "Knowledge engineering systems" (Artificial Intelligence Center, Arlington, VA, November 1983).

[19] Carnegie Group, Inc., "Knowledge Craft, an Environment for Developing Knowledge-Based Systems" (Pittsburgh, 1985).

[20] D. Michie, S. Muggleton, C. Reise, and S. Zubrick, "RULEMASTER: a second-generation knowledge-engineering facility," *Proceedings of the*

*First Conference on Artificial Intelligence Applications* (IEEE Computer Society, December 1984).

[21] Donald A. Waterman, *A Guide to Expert Systems* (Reading, MA: Addison-Wesley, 1986).

[22] P. H. Winston and B. K. P. Horn, *LISP*, 2nd ed. (Reading, MA: Addison-Wesley, 1984).

[23] D. Touretzky, *LISP, a Gentle Introduction to Symbolic Computation* (New York: Harper & Row, 1984).

[24] W. Clocksin and C. Mellish, *Programming in Prolog* (New York: Springer-Verlag, 1981).

[25] J. Ennals, *Beginning Micro-Prolog*, 2nd rev. ed. (New York: Harper & Row, 1984).

[26] T. Kaehler and D. Patterson, *Taste of Smalltalk* (New York: W. W. Norton & Co., 1986).

[27] A. Goldberg and D. Robson, *Smalltalk-80: The Language and Its Implementation* (Reading, MA: Addison-Wesley, 1983).

[28] A. Goldberg, *Smalltalk-80: The Interactive Programming Environment* (Reading, MA: Addison-Wesley, 1984).

[29] Teknowledge, *S.1 Product Description* (Palo Alto, CA, 1984).

[30] Level Five Research, Inc., *Insight 1 and 2 Product Description* (Melbourne Beach, FL, 1985).

[31] Expert Systems International, *ES/P Advisor Product Description* (King of Prussia, PA, 1985).

[32] Human Edge Software, Inc. *Expert-Ease Product Description* (Palo Alto, CA, 1985).

[33] R. E. Parker and S. J. Kiselewich, "The Modeling of Human Cognitive Decision Processes in the Intelligent Machine Model (TIMM)" (Report, Artificial Intelligence Laboratory, General Research Corporation, Santa Barbara, CA, 1984).

# 3

# Distinctive Expert System Programming

The most distinctive method of expert system programming is rapid production of expert system prototypes, in contrast to the conventional "waterfall" or structured programming approach. Rapid production of expert system prototypes is also called "rapid prototyping." This is defined as the heuristic approach to developing an expert system because a rudimentary system is rapidly built to capture an initial set of user needs with the intent of iterative expansion and refinement of the system. The primitive system is immediately put to use by the user and is then gradually improved as the user and the developer establish a mutual understanding of the problem. The rapid prototyping approach is based on the belief that the risk of expert system projects can best be minimized by gradual learning and incremental improvement. Incomplete understanding of the problem means that development of an expert system is incremental, paralleling increases in understanding of the problem.

The use of rapid prototyping brings together the developer and the intended user to define the requirements and design specifications for the full-scale expert system. This approach significantly reduces the risk of misidentifying the problem, experts, or problem-solving methods.

## Development Approaches

The main focus of rapid prototyping is the intended user. The internal strategy for developing a rapid prototype centers around gaining the user's cooperation and perfecting the prototype to meet the user's needs. The six elements in the strategy are (1) involving the user early, (2) identifying functional areas for building the prototype, (3) establishing requirements for the prototype, (4) obtaining the first cut quickly, testing it, and iterating improvements between the intended user and the developer, (5) stressing that the purpose of the prototype is not to replace human experts/specialists, and (6) maintaining a small prototyping team. Each strategy is discussed below.

## Getting the User Involved Early

Because application areas for expert systems are usually ill defined, the only effective way to build the prototype is to involve the user in discussions of the functional areas of daily operations that concern him/her most, with respect to cost and time required. The flowchart in Figure 3-1 illustrates this process. Meetings between the intended user and the developer are arranged to examine the operations. Operational documents and textbooks, if available, are provided to assist the developer in understanding the user's requirements. The underlying belief is that the intended user understands the operations and his/her knowledge is to be extracted. In many cases, the intended user has twenty to thirty years experience in the operations and may be the only source of information for the developer. This user is generally irreplaceable for operations that rely on aged but still cost-effective equipment. A case in point is the use of long-durable battleships in military operations.

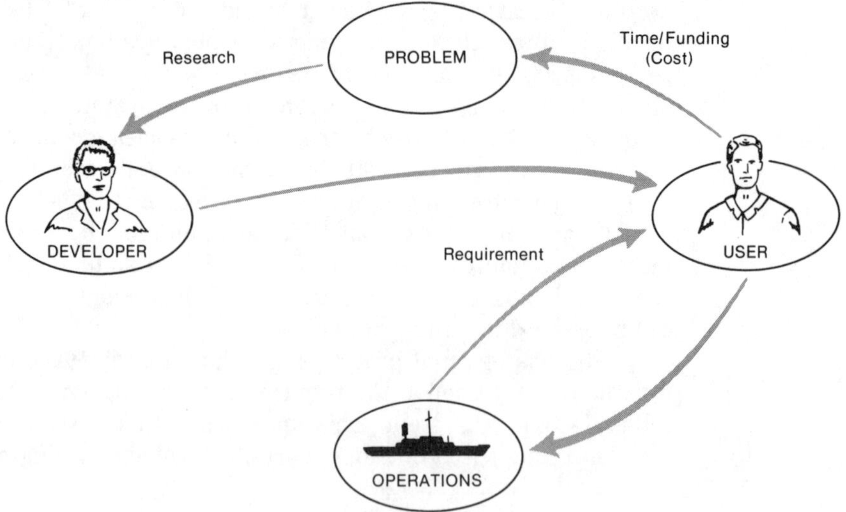


**Figure 3-1**
***Getting the user involved in developing a prototype***

## Identifying Functional Areas for Building Prototypes

Identifying functional areas for building prototypes is an important strategy because the selection of an "appropriate" application ensures a good likelihood of success in implementation. The intended user is consulted early to identify the areas where he/she needs help most. A prototype of the expert system is then built to assist the user in these functional routines, thus freeing him/her to undertake creative work.

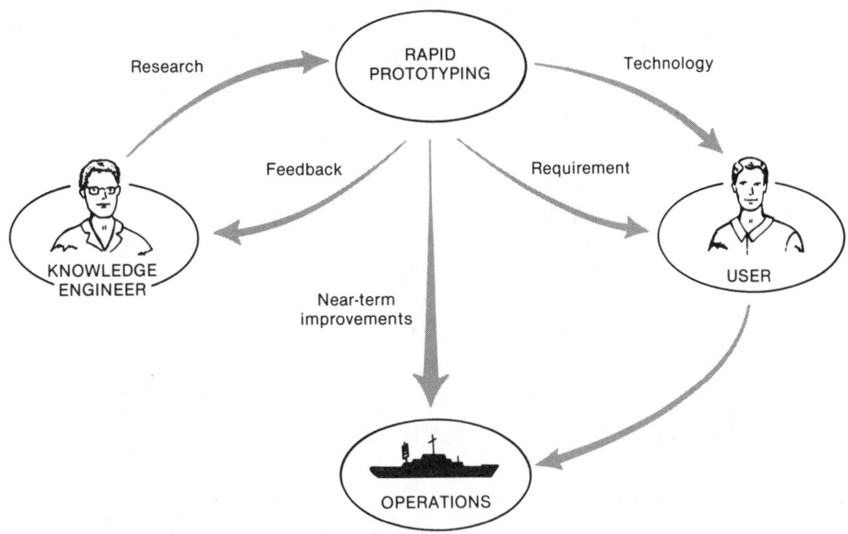


**Figure 3-2**
***The strategic process in building rapid prototypes***

Figure 3-2 demonstrates the process in a military application, where large expert systems have proliferated. When approached by the developer for an expert system, the potential user identifies the functional routines that can be replaced by expert systems. Some sophisticated methods such as Delphi techniques [1] may be needed to reach a consensus of functional areas that are most cost effective for expert systems. As shown in Figure 3-1, either cost or time saved can be used as the criterion for judging cost effectiveness.

## *Establishing Requirements for Rapid Prototypes*

Establishing the requirements for a rapid prototype to perform routines in the functional areas identified by the user is the third element in the internal strategy. In this step, the user and the developer establish the "blueprint" of the requirements that must be satisfied for the prototype to perform properly. Depending on the application, requirements may include physical characteristics (e.g., speed, precision, accuracy, and performance), appearance (e.g., dimension and color), and user interface (e.g., natural languages, graphics, and voice recognition). Iteration may be needed to refine requirements between the user and the developer.

## *Obtaining and Testing the First Cut and Iterating Improvements*

The previous three steps may raise the intended user's expectations to a certain level. In this step the expectation is partially fulfilled by quickly (within three months) providing the user with a first-cut prototype for testing. Functionally, the first cut does not have to be complete, but it must have an effective, user friendly interface with graphic and semi-natural language commands to ensure that the user will not become discouraged immediately. The user in most cases will not be computer literate. As shown in the center of Figure 3-2, the rapid prototype is built quickly, presented to the user for testing in actual operations, and then subjected to iterations of near-term improvements by the user and the developer. Rapid prototyping serves as a formal approach to providing the user with a useful step-by-step incremental development.

## *Stressing the Purpose of Prototypes*

In gaining the support of the intended user, it is crucial to stress that the purpose of the prototype is not to replace him or her. In most cases, it is true that expert systems take over only the functional routines of human experts, rather than replacing the human expert per se. Human experts often have more than twenty years of on-the-job experience, and have established job security. Initially, they are suspicious concerning the motive for developing prototypes. If their job security is assured, however, their cooperation and enthusiasm can be gained quickly. This crucial step in the internal strategy can easily be ignored, resulting in failure of the prototyping project due to a lack of cooperation by human experts.

## *Maintaining a Small Prototyping Team*

Development of rapid prototypes by large groups is difficult. A prototyping team should be composed of no more than three or four individuals, to avoid the need for elaborate project management such as formal documentation, checkpoints, and reviews. A large team impedes speed, unity of objective, unity of approach, good communications, and low overhead in a rapid prototyping environment, where speed, communication, and cost are essential to success.

# Design Rules

The five principles in designing rapid prototypes are modularity, object-oriented programming, a simple inference engine, redundancy of knowledge, and good man-machine interface. These five design principles are highlighted below.

## Modularity

Modularity refers to building the components in the prototypes as modules that can be reused over and over. These modules consist of "black boxes" that have input/output characteristics and can be recombined for use in other prototypes. Modules are portable. If the approach of a prototype is unsatisfactory, its modules of knowledge can be transferred to a new prototype. Modularity may also imply simple, consistent knowledge representation.

## Object-Oriented Programming

In object-oriented programming, the entities in a program are viewed as objects that communicate with each other via messages. Each object has distinct properties and rules/procedures associated with it. When a message arrives at an object, attachments (properties and rules/procedures) to the object process the message and carry out its effects. Object-oriented programming can thus be highly modular, can perform local actions such as display or self-modification, and can both receive information from and return information to the other objects. The purpose of object-oriented programming is also reusability because objects representing knowledge can be reused over and over either in the same prototype or in other prototypes. Object-oriented programming also provides a simple means for unifying the major knowledge representation methodologies (such as rules, frames, or graphic images) and prevents the developer from writing "spaghetti" code in which all subroutines are intertwined.

## Simple Inference Engine

In knowledge lies the power; therefore, inference is not critical in prototypes. A simple inference engine is helpful in two ways. First, explanations are easier to produce because they are currently generated by replaying the actions taken in the system. Keeping those actions simple ensures that less work is needed to generate comprehensive explanations that the user can understand. Second, knowledge acquisition is simpler because less effort is needed to determine the exact knowledge to be added to improve system performance. The work of building prototypes becomes less complicated and errors can be more easily traced when the inference engine is simple.

## Redundancy of Knowledge

Redundancy of knowledge, the fourth principle, is a convenient remedy for incomplete and inexact knowledge, because human experts themselves do not always know exactly what it is they comprehend most thoroughly in their areas of expertise. To build redundancy of knowledge into prototypes, the developer needs to obtain multiple, overlapping sources of knowledge with different areas of strength and weakness. Proper use of multiple sources of knowledge can enrich the knowledge representation in the knowledge base.

### *Good Man-Machine Interface*

The last design principle—good man-machine interface—is also the most important principle for developing rapid prototypes. Without it, prototypes are not properly used and tested, and are eventually forgotten due to difficulty of use. Good man-machine interface includes effective display, data input/output, and easy-to-use functions. These elements can easily be ignored by developers who are so involved in computers that they forget the user may be computer-illiterate. Good man-machine interface offers the only assurance that the prototype developed will be accepted by the user.

## Summary

- Rapid prototyping is a heuristic approach to developing an expert system. A rudimentary system is rapidly built to capture an initial set of user needs with the intent of iterative expansion. This approach reduces the risk of expert system projects. The four aspects of rapid prototyping are internal strategy, design principles, step-by-step method and selection of experts, and acquisition of knowledge.
- The main focus of rapid prototyping is the user. The internal strategy for developing a rapid prototype centers around gaining the user's cooperation and perfecting the prototype to meet the user's needs. This includes involving the user early, identifying functional areas for building the prototype, establishing requirements for the prototype, obtaining the first cut quickly, testing it, and iterating improvements.
- The five rules for designing rapid prototypes are modularity, object-oriented programming, a simple inference engine, redundancy of knowledge, and good man-machine interface.

## References

[1] Joseph P. Martino, *Technological Forecasting for Decision Making* (New York: American Elsevier, 1983).

SECTION

# 2

# Basic Language Vocabulary

Section 2 presents the basic language vocabulary for the three AI/expert system languages: LISP, Prolog, and Smalltalk. The vocabulary is based on the PC implementation of these languages, which is considered to be most cost effective for personal computer programmers. Commands of selected implementations of these languages are presented in Appendixes A, B, and C respectively.

# 4

# LISP Vocabulary

The previous chapters have discussed the definition, available software and hardware, and rules for developing expert systems. Chapters 4 through 6 present the basic vocabulary for the three AI/expert system programming languages. Chapter 4 examines LISP, Chapter 5 describes Prolog, and Chapter 6 discusses Smalltalk.

A variety of LISP dialects exists. This chapter is based on Common LISP as described in the definitive book entitled *Common LISP: Reference Manual*, by Guy L. Steele, Jr. [1] and as implemented by Gold Hill Computers [2]. This implementation of Commmon LISP is referred to as GCLISP in the text. The frequently used commands (functions, macros, and variables) are listed in Appendix A.

This chapter covers the following major topics in LISP:

- Becoming acquainted with LISP
- Program structure
- Arithmetic operations and predicates
- List operations
- Evaluation
- User-defined functions
- Conditional actions
- Recursion
- Iteration and binding
- Input/output
- Macros
- Global variables and named constants
- Creating record structures

- Message passing
- File system interface

These topics are discussed with examples for illustration.

# Becoming Acquainted with LISP

Programming languages in general have their own idiosyncrasies. The LISP idiosyncrasy is embracing parentheses for every statement in a program; nonmatching parentheses are often the sources of errors in a long program. In the examples that follow, statements beginning with an asterisk (*) are LISP expressions; statements without an asterisk are the computer's responses:

```
* (sqrt 25);this is a comment for the square root of 25
5
* 9
9
* ()
nil
(expt 5 2
```

Note that at least one blank is used to separate elements in a statement, and comments begin with a semicolon. Program accuracy is not affected by the use of upper or lower case, or the number of spaces between parentheses or between elements. The last expression does not return anything until the right parenthesis is supplied. An error may occur if anything but a matching parenthesis is input.

In LISP, everything is accomplished by executing functions. All programs receive zero or more arguments and return exactly one value. For example:

```
* (- 4.98  7.38)
2.40
* (abs -9.50)
9.50
```

In these examples, the function - (minus) requires two arguments, but the function `abs` requires only one argument. Functions can be defined either internally in the package by the developer (for example, `plus(+)`) or externally by the programmer.

Programs and data use the same symbolic expressions (also called *s-expressions*, or simply stated as expressions), which consist of *atoms* and *lists*. Indivisible characters such as 9, 5, 3.1416 are called *numeric atoms*. Numeric atoms include both integers and floating point numbers. Symbols such as +, sum, total, verb, and dog are called *symbolic atoms*. A *list* is composed of a left parenthesis, followed by zero or more atoms or lists, then a right parenthesis.

Everything in a LISP expression is evaluated immediately after the right parenthesis is typed unless the evaluation is blocked with a quote as shown in the third example following.

```
*(expt 5 2)
25
*(quote (I love you.))
I love you.
*(list 'U'S'A)
(USA)
```

The three rules in evaluating expressions are as follows:

1. Numbers evaluate to themselves, and nil ( ) evaluates to nil.

   ```
   * 120
   120
   * ()
   nil
   ```

2. Symbols evaluate to the last value assigned to them.

   ```
   * L
   Error
   ```

   `Error` is shown above because no value was previously assigned to `L`. You can assign a value to L by using `setq`.

   ```
   *(setq L 'a)
   ```

   The single quote (') is similar to a double quote, which indicates that atoms or lists following the symbol require no evaluation when `L` is reevaluated:

   ```
   * L
   A
   ```

3. Lists are evaluated by considering the first element as a function and the remaining elements as arguments for that function.

   ```
   *(min 7 4 9 5 7)
   4
   ```

   `Min` means the minimum of the arguments: 7, 4, 9, 5, 7.

# Program Structure

LISP programs consist of forms and functions. A *form* is an object which may legally be evaluated—that is, an expression that, when evaluated, returns a value. *Functions* are invoked by applying them to arguments; a function also returns a value.

Forms are divided into the following five categories:

| | |
|---|---|
| *Self-evaluating form* | Includes all numbers, characters, strings, and bit vectors. When evaluated, it is simply returned. |
| *Variable* | Represented by a symbol. Includes local (lexical or static) and global (special or dynamic) variables. |
| *Special form* | Represented by a list whose first element is a special symbol reserved by Common LISP, as shown in the box below. |
| *Macro call* | Represented by a list whose first element is a symbol that is not the name of a special form and that is defined by a *macro*. |
| *Function call* | Represented by a nonempty list whose first element is neither the name of a special form nor the name of a macro. |

**Names of All Common LISP Special Forms**

| | | |
|---|---|---|
| block | if | progv |
| catch | labels | quote |
| compiler-let | let | return-from |
| declare | let* | setq |
| eval-when | macrolet | tagbody |
| flet | multiple-value-call | the |
| function | multiple-value-prog1 | throw |
| go | progn | unwind-protect |

G. Steele, et al. *Common LISP References Manual* (Digital Press, 1984), 57.

Functions include named functions and lambda-expressions. A *named function* begins with a special form of defun (from the boxed List of Common LISP Special Forms), while a *lambda-expression* is an unnamed function whose first element is the symbol **lambda.**

Like most other computer languages, declared global variables need to appear at top level (beginning of a program) in a function, lambda, or macro.

We will discuss these terms as well as the other Common LISP special forms in the boxed list, in the perspective on expert system applications.

# Arithmetic Operations and Predicates

We commence the introduction of LISP programming with numbers to allow the conventional programmer to move into the LISP world. Note, however, that mathematical calculations are not the principal use of the language. The strength of LISP is in symbolic manipulation.

Numbers in Common LISP can be categorized as integers, ratios of two integers, floating point numbers, and complex numbers. The current version of GCLISP does not support complex numbers. Floating point numbers can be further divided into short, single, double, and long float. The minimum precision for these floats is short (13 bits), single (24 bits), double (50 bits), and long (50 bits). Actual precision varies among implementations. The basic arithmetic operations are listed in Table 4-1.

## *Arithmetic Predicates*

`Nil` and `t` are constants in Common LISP. `Nil` represents the logical false value ("F" in the following expressions) and also the empty list. The value of `t` is always true ("T" in the following expressions). Arithmetic predicates are listed in Table 4-2.

# List Operations

The list is the most frequently used data type in LISP. Basic list functions include `list`, `append`, `cons`, `display`, `member`, `car`, `cdr`, `set`, `setq`, `length`, `reverse`, `subst`, and `last`. Because they are new to the programmer, these and related functions are described in greater detail in the sections that follow.

## *Assign Values*

Three functions—`setq`, `psetq` and `set`—perform assignment in slightly different ways, although they are all used to alter the value of a variable.

`Setq` causes the value of the second argument to become that of the first argument, which can only be a symbol.

```
* (setq x (+2 3))
5
* (setq Hometown '(San Francisco))
(San Francisco)
* (setq)
nil
```

`Setq` can assign an unlimited even number of arguments sequentially; for example:

```
* (setq x (-9 4) y x)
5
```

in which `x` is set to 5, `y` is set to x,5, and `setq` returns 5.

**Table 4-1**
***Arithmetic operations***

| Function | Symbol | Arguments | Description | Example | Evaluation |
|---|---|---|---|---|---|
| abs | abs | 1 | Absolute value | (abs-5) | 5 |
| Add | + | n | Add numbers | (+5 4) | 9 |
| add1 | 1+ | 1 | Add one | (1+8) | 9 |
| atan | atan | 1 or 2 | Arc tangent of | (atan 2.5) | |
| ceiling | ceiling | 1 | Least integer not less than first | (ceiling 3.5) | 4 |
| cos | cos | 1 | Cosine of radians | (cos2.5) | |
| decf | decf | 2 | Subtract value of second from first; default for second is 1 | (decf m) if m=0 | −1 |
| difference | - | | Subtract numbers from first | (- 5 3 1) | 1 |
| exp | exp | 1 | Exponent on e | (exp 3) | 20.0855 |
| expt | expt | 2 | Exponent on first | (expt 3 2) | 9 |
| float | float | 1 or 2 | Convert first to float of same type as second | (float 6 3.0) | 6.0 |
| floor | floor | 1 | Greatest integer <= first | (floor 3.5) | 3 |
| incf | incf | 2 | Add value of second to first; default for second is 1 | (incf m-3) if m=0 | −2 |
| log | log | 1 or 2 | A logarithm of first on second | (log 50 10) | 1.699 |
| quotient | / | 2 or n | Divide first by second then third . . . | (/ 4 5 2) | .4 |
| rem | mod | 2 | Smallest integer remainder | (mod 9 4) | 1 |
| round | round | 1 | Round number | (round 9.8) | 10 |
| signum | signum | 1 | Sign of number: if negative, −1 if zero, 0 if positive, 1 | (signum -2) | −1 |
| sin | sin | 1 | Sine of radians | (sin 2.5) | |
| sqrt | sqrt | 1 | Square root | (sqrt 9) | 3 |
| sub1 | 1- | 1 | Subtract one | (1- 8) | 7 |
| tan | tan | 1 | Tangent of radians | (tan 2.5) | |
| times | * | n | Multiply | (* 3 2 4) | 24 |
| truncate | truncate | 2 | Truncate first toward second | (truncate 9 4) | 2 |

**Table 4-2**
***Arithmetic predicates***

| Function | Symbol | Arguments | Description | Example | Evaluation |
|---|---|---|---|---|---|
| evenp | `evenp` | 1 | True if even integer | `(even 8)` | T |
| equal | `=` | n | True if arguments are all same | `(= 2 2 2)` | T |
| greater than | `>` | n | True if arguments are monotonically decreasing | `(> 7 6 5)` | T |
| less than | `<` | n | True if arguments are monotonically increasing | `(< 2 3 4)` | T |
| max | `max` | n | Maximum argument | `(max 2 3 4)` | 4 |
| min | `min` | n | Minimum argument | `(min 2 3 4)` | 3 |
| minusp | `minusp` | 1 | True if negative | `(minusp -5)` | T |
| not equal | `/=` | n | True if arguments are all different | `(/= 2 3 4)` | T |
| oddp | `oddp` | 1 | True if odd integer | `(oddp 7)` | T |
| plusp | `plusp` | 1 | True if number is positive | `(plusp 5)` | T |
| zerop | `zerop` | 1 | True if number zero | `(zerop 5)` | F |

*`Psetq`* is similar to `setq`, except that assignment happens in parallel. The variables are set to the resulting values at the same time.

```
*(setq x 5)
5
*(setq y 7)
7
*(psetq x y y x)
*x
7
*y
5
```

Here the values of x and y are exchanged by executing `psetq`.

*`Set`* is similar to `setq`; however, since the former evaluates the first argument and works with dynamic (global) variables but not locally bound variables, a quote is needed on the first argument. Note that `setq` does not require the quote.

```
* (set 'x 7)    ;; if x has not been assigned by setq
7
```

## *Take Lists Apart*

`Car` and `cdr` are the most distinctive concepts for the conventional programmer. These functions can be combined to create new functions.

*Car* returns the value of the first element of a list.

```
*(car '( x y z))
x
*(car '(( USA Washington-DC) China))
(USA Washington-DC)
```

*Cdr* is complementary to `car`. It returns the rest of a list, which always contains all but the first element of the original list.

```
*(cdr '(x y z))
(y z)
```

Occasionally, several `car` and `cdr` functions are needed to "dig out" from deep within a nested expression; for example:

```
*(car(car(cdr '((plus 7 8) (x y) 1))))
x
```

A convenient means has been devised to abbreviate the combination of these `cars` or `cdrs`. An 'a' is used to represent a `car` and a 'd' is used to represent a `cdr`. For the foregoing example, the abbreviated name is `caadr`.

*Second* returns the second element of a list; it is equivalent to `cadr`.

```
*(second '(a b c d ))
b
```

## *Construct and Display Lists*

`List`, `append`, and `cons` are used to assemble lists, while `car` and `cdr` take lists apart.

*List* is a function that puts together elements of all lists called upon.

```
*(setq x '(p q))
(p q)
*(list x x x)
((p q) (p q)
*(list 'U 'S 'A)
(U S A)
```

Note that parentheses around p and q are not removed. To remove them, *append* is used to run the elements of its arguments together.

```
*(append x x x)
(p q p q p q)
```

If for some reason, the elements in the first x need to be kept intact, then *cons* is used to insert a new first element into a list:

```
*(cons x x x)
((p q) p q p q)
```

An inverse relationship can be drawn between cons and the pair, car and cdr:

```
*(cons (car x) (cdr x))
x
```

Note that the effect of (cons 'p () ) is the same as (list 'p).

*To display a list* which has been assigned, the name of the list is typed:

```
* x
(p q)
```

## *Reorganize Lists*

Functions to reorganize a list and its elements include member, union, intersection, setdifference, length, last, nth, remove, reverse, and subst.

*Member* determines whether an item is a member of a list. If the item is found in the list, then the sublist beginning with that item is returned; otherwise, nil is returned.

```
* (member Dave '(Peter Lin Dave Linda))
(Dave Linda)
```

*Union* takes the union of two sets in the list and returns a list of items that appear in either set.

```
*(union '(Peter Lin Dave Linda) '(Dave Lisa Eileen Emily))
(Peter Lin Dave Linda Lisa Eileen Emily)
```

*Intersection* takes the intersection of two sets and returns a list of only those items that appear in both sets.

```
*(intersection '(Peter Lin Dave Linda) '(Dave Lisa Eileen
     Emily))
(Dave)
```

*Setdifference* subtracts elements of the second set that are common to both sets from those of the first set.

```
*(setdifference '(Peter Lin Dave Linda) '(Dave Lisa Eileen
     Emily))
(Peter Lin Linda)
```

*Length* counts the number of top-level elements in a list.

```
*(length '(p q))
2
*(length '((p q) (p q) (p q)))
3
```

*Last* returns a list that contains only the last element of the original list.

```
*(last '(Peter Lin Dave Linda))
(Linda)
```

*Nth* takes the `car` of the `nth cdr` of a list. The first element of the list is `nth` 0; the second element is `nth` 1; and so on.

```
*(nth 1 '(p q r))
q
```

*Remove* returns a copy of a list with all top-level elements except those to be excluded.

```
*(remove 'p '(p q r p s))
(q r s)
```

*Reverse* returns the reversal of a list. It works only on lists and does not change the value of any variables.

```
*(setq love '(I love you))
(I love you)
*(reverse love)
(you love I)
*love
(I love you)
```

*Subst* substitutes one symbol for another wherever it appears in a list. It takes three arguments as in "substitute a for b in c."

```
*(subst 'like 'love '(I love you))
(I like you)
```

## Predicates

The predicates atom, listp, null, numberp, eq, eql, equal, and, or, and not are functions for use in decision making. They respond to queries with *true* or *false*. True is represented in LISP by t; false is represented in LISP by nil.

*Atom* and *listp* are used to test the contents of a list. **Atom** tests to determine whether its argument is an atom, while listp tests to determine whether its argument is a list.

```
*(atom 'expert)
t
*(listp '(expert system))
t
*(listp 'expert)
nil
```

*Null* tests to determine whether its argument is empty.

```
*(null 'AI)
nil
```

Eq, eql, and equal test for sameness between two lists. *Eq* tests to determine whether two LISP objects are in the same storage location.

```
*(setq p 'x)
x
*(setq q 'x)
x
*(eq p q)
nil
*(eq p (car (list p q)))
t
*(eq (float 3) (float 3))
nil
```

*Eql* is similar to eq, except it returns true only if its two arguments are eq or are numbers with the same type and value.

```
*(eql (float 3) (float 3))
t
```

*Equal* tests whether two expressions look alike, that is, whether they are printed the same way.

```
*(equal 5 (- 7 2))
t
```

*And*, *or*, and *not* are logical operators. Not returns true only if its argument is nil. And returns true only if all arguments are non-nil. Or returns true only if any one argument is non-nil.

```
*(not nil)
t
*(and t t nil nil)
nil
*(or nil nil t t t)
t
```

In evaluation, and and or are slightly different from the standard logical operators. Both evaluate their arguments from left to right. If a nil is encountered by and, or something other than nil is encountered by or, it is returned. Any remaining arguments are not evaluated. Otherwise, the value of the last argument is returned. For example:

```
*(setq family '(David Lisa Eileen Emily))
(David Lisa Eileen Emily)
*(and ( member 'Lisa family) (member 'Eileen family))
(Eileen Emily)
*(or (member 'Lisa family) (member 'Tam family))
(Lisa Eileen Emily)
```

# Evaluation and User-Defined Functions

So far, the expressions you have typed have been evaluated by an interpreter immediately, and the functions you have used were written by someone else. This section examines five new functions that extend the convenience of the language. The first three can be used to evaluate and the other two to write your own functions.

## *Functions That Evaluate*

Eval performs evaluation on lists; apply and mapcar perform evaluation on functions.

*Eval* causes another evaluation beyond the one performed by the interpreter; each use of eval gives one more level of evaluation.

```
*(setq x 'y)
y
*(setq y 'z)
```

```
z
*x
y
*y
z
*(eval x)
z
*(eval (eval '''''Dave))
''Dave
*(eval (eval (eval '''''Dave)))
'Dave
```

*Apply* takes a function name and its parameters, and evokes that function with the parameters. The parameters are not evaluated first.

```
*(apply #'cons '(because (I love you)))
(because I love you)
```

Note that the symbol **#'** is required to tell LISP that it should expect a function name. This practice is similar to use of the symbol **'** as a quote preceding the string of letters in an expression.

*Mapcar* (sometimes called `apply-to-all`) applies a function to each element of the list and returns a list of resultant elements. For example, the following statement adds the elements of two equal length lists:

```
*(mapcar #'+ '(1 5 10 20 25) '(1 2 3 4 5))
(2 7 13 24 30)
```

# *Functions That Write Other Functions*

`Defun` and `lambda` are two functions that allow you to write your own functions. `Defun` defines named procedures and `lambda` defines anonymous procedures.

*Defun* has the following syntax format:

**(defun procedure name (parameter1, parameter2, . . . )*
*(things to be processed in this function)*
⋮
*)*

All parameters must appear in the main body of the function. A pair of parentheses may be used instead of a parameter. For example, a very useful function in rapid production of an expert system to indicate a component that is not implemented yet can be defined as follows:

```
*(defun not-implemented-yet ()
 (print 'This function is not implemented yet.)  ;print a
     message
 )
```

Defun can consist of any number of expressions, with the last expression determining the procedure's value.

*Lambda* is used to define a function that will not be called upon often (maybe once in its lifetime). The only difference between lambda and defun is that lambda does not have a procedure name. Lambda is particularly powerful for interfacing procedures to parameters when applying functions to more than one element in a list. For example, if you wish to convert a list of miles to kilometers, you might attempt it with a statement such as this:

```
*(mapcar #'* '(1.6) (5 10 15 20 25))
(8)
```

Two problems cause the statement to be returned with a value (8):

1. The conversion factor list (1.6) has only one element.
2. The *times* operator (*) needs two arguments.

A lambda function easily solves these problems:

```
*(mapcar #'(lambda (x)
(* x 1.6))
'(5 10 15 20 25)
)
(8 16 24 32 40)
```

# Conditional Actions

As in other programming languages, the *cond* structure is used with logical conditions to control the flow of a program. The general form of a cond expression is as follows:

**(cond (test1 result1)*
  *(test 2 result2)*
   ⋮
 *)*

Each list is a cond clause. It is good practice to use a t in the last cond clause to show what is done if none of the conditions of previous clauses are true as shown in the following example. Cond expressions can be used to facilitate defun. For example, the following function member is enhanced by the use of cond:

```
*(defun member (element list)
   (cond ((null list) 'nil)
         ((eql element (car list)) list)
         (t (member element (car list))))
         )
```

*If* takes three arguments, as in the conventional IF-THEN-ELSE format: a condition (test), a true part (then), and a false part (else). In LISP, it is equivalent to cond as shown below:

```
(if test then else) = (cond (test then) (t else))
```

If first evaluates the test. If the result is not nil, the expression then is selected; otherwise, the expression else is selected. The expression selected is then evaluated and if returns the evaluation of the selected form. The else expression may be omitted; in this case, if the value of test is nil, then nothing is done and nil is returned. For example, the function made-even makes an odd number even by adding one to it, using if for conditional action.

```
*(Defun make-even (y)
        (if (oddp y)  (add1 y) y)
        )
```

*Ifn* is a derivative of if that is available from GCLISP only. Ifn evaluates the then clause or the else clause, depending on the value of (*not* test). Use the above example to illustrate the difference:

```
*(Defun make-odd (y)
(ifn (oddp y) (add1 y) y)
 )
```

Instead of making an odd number even, changing if to ifn makes an even number odd.

*When* performs a similar function to cond or if. It has the following general format:

**(when (test) (action1) (action2) . . . )*

If the result of evaluating *test* is non-nil, then *action 1, action 2, . . .* is evaluated, and the result of the last action is returned. Otherwise, the actions are not evaluated and nil is returned. Examples:

```
*(when (not (zerop 3)) (list ' (This is a non-zero number)))
(This is a non-zero number)
```

```
*(when (zerop 3) (list '(This is a non-zerop number)))
 nil
```

*Unless* is similar to when except that the actions are evaluated and the results of the last action are returned only when the result of the evaluating test is nil. Otherwise the actions are not evaluated and nil is returned. The general format of unless is as follows:

**(unless (test) (action1) (action2) . . . )*

Two examples are as follows:

```
*(Unless (zerop 3) (List '(This is a non-zero number.)))
(This is a non-zerop number.)
*(Unless (zerop 0) (List '(This is a non-zero number.)))
nil
```

*And* can serve as a logical operator and as a conditional control structure. If any form evaluates to nil, the value nil is immediately returned without evaluating the remaining forms. The general format for and as a control structure is as follows:

*(and (test) (action1, action2, . . . ))*

One example is:

```
*(and (not (zerop 3)) (List '(This is a non-zero number.)))
(This is a non-zerop number.)
```

*Case* is a conditional function that executes one of its clauses by matching a value (a key) to a set of constants. The key must be one of the following: symbol, integer, or characters. Duplicate keys are not allowed. The general format of case is as follows:

**(case key*
*(keylist1 consequent 1-1 . . . )*
*(keylist2 consequent 2-1 . . . )*
    ⋮
*)*

Case evaluates the key first and then evaluates each clause in turn, with the exception that a t or otherwise in the key list is evaluated last. If the key matches (is eql to) one of the objects in a key list, the consequents are evaluated and the value of the last consequent is returned. A clause containing no consequents other than the key list is returned with a nil. For example,

```
*(defun odd-even (x)
(case  x  ((1 3 5 7 9) 'odd)
(( 2 4 6 8 10) 'even)
(otherwise '>10)
 ))
```

# Recursion

Recursion in LISP is similar to that in other programming languages such as C. A function is recursive if it calls itself. A recursive function is written to reduce a given problem to a part and remainder, solve the part, and pass the remainder to a copy of the function. The three basic rules in recursive programs are

1. Find out the initial (base) step.
2. Identify the next step, perform an action, and determine the remainder (the remainder should be smaller).
3. Know the last step (with an end test).

For example, a function for the factorial of n (`n!`) is defined as follows:

```
*(defun factorial (n)
(cond ((zerop n) 1); last step
(t (times n (factorial (sub1 n)))); first & next step
))
```

This program can be translated as follows:

1. Define function factorial (n).
2. If n is zero, then the factorial of n is 1.
3. If n is not zero, then the factorial of n is equal to n $\times$ factorial (n$-$1).

The program (factorial) is recursive on itself by subtracting 1 from n each time n is greater than 1. The three basic rules are applied as follows:

1. The initial step is n = n.
2. The next (iterative) step is n = n$-$1 and the action is n $\times$ (n$-$1).
3. The stop point is n = 0.

# Iteration and Binding

`Prog` (for "program") and `do` are the two LISP functions that allow you to repeat a sequence. `Prog`, `do` and `let` allow you to bind local variables. `Prog` is most familiar to the conventional programmer; `let` and `do` are powerful function-facilitating iterations in LISP that can reduce the abuse of prog. Value allows you to control the return of multiple values. These and related functions are described in the sections that follow.

## *Prog, Prog1, Prog2, Progn*

Prog enables you write LISP programs that are similar to the traditional program, with statements and branches in familiar terms such as go, loop, and return. The general form of prog is as follows:

```
*(prog (local variable 1,variable 2, . . . );Bind local variables to zero
(Setq . . . )       ;initialize variable
(Setq . . . )       ;initialize variable
Loop                ;start loop
(expression 1)      ;actions
(expression 2)      ;repeat
  :
(Go Loop )          ;go to "Loop"
(Return variable-name) ;return the value of the variable
```

In a prog program, the first line lists the local parameters that are to be bound to nil when the program is called and to become unbound when it returns. Setq is used to initialize these variables. The remaining expressions in the program are evaluated sequentially. The values of these expressions are not returned after evaluation. If an expression is a symbol, it is not evaluated. The symbol is referred to as a *tag* and is used with a go expression at some point in the program to perform iteration.

After the last expression of the program has been evaluated, nil is returned. When a return expression is encountered, prog is terminated immediately and returns the value of the argument in the return expression. Return works only inside prog, but it need not always appear at the end of a program.

Prog allows you to write iterative loops to perform many tasks that might be performed more efficiently by other functions, such as recursive functions. It is therefore important not to abuse prog. Prog expressions, if they must be used, should contain only a single tag and a single go, forming a single loop. Iterative solutions are better performed by do, which is discussed in the next section.

The three functions *prog1*, *prog2*, and *progn* resemble prog semantically. They are used to evaluate a series of expressions sequentially and return the value of one of the expressions. Prog1 returns the value of the first expression; prog2 returns the value of the second expression, and progn returns the value of the third expression. Examples are:

```
*(prog1  (setq p 'a)
         (setq q 'b)
         (setq r 'c)
```

```
        )
        A

*(progn (setq p 'a)
        (setq q'b)
        (setq r'c)
        )
        C
```

# *Do, Do**

`Do` provides flexible variable binding and convenience for explicit iterations such as `prog`. `Do` supports a built-in loop that cycles through the expressions in its body until it is told to stop.

The general form of `do` is as follows:

**(do ((parameter-1 initial-value-1 update-expression-1)*
*(parameter-2 initial-value-2 update-expression-2)*
*. . . )*
*(condition action-1 action-2...)*
*(expression 1)*
⋮
*(expression n)*
*)*

An example of a simple `do` expression is given below:

```
*;count and print from 5 to 55 by 10
*(do i 5 (+ i 10)
(zerop (- 55 i))
(print i)          ;print i
(terpri)           ;print a new line
 )
```

`Do*` is exactly like `do` except that `do*` performs serial (sequential) rather than parallel value assignments. It is as if `psetq` were replaced by `setq` in the previous section. Sequential assignment of values is useful in knowledge representation, especially in a frame or unit.

`Do*` is particularly useful when certain variables in the initial assignment depend on other variables that have been previously assigned.

```
*(Defun do*-test (i j)
(do*
    ((bag1 i (sub1 bag1)
    (bag2 j (sub1 bag2))
    (payoff (sqrt (+(expt i 2) (expt j 2))) (+ payoff (sqrt
    (+(expt bag1 2)(expt bag2 2)))))
```

```
(counter (sub1 bag2) (sub1 bag1))))
 ((zerop counter) payoff)
  ))
```

The above example shows that because `do*` performs sequential assignment of values, there is no unbound variable in the `payoff` expression. If `do` were used, then unbound variables `bag1` and `bag2` would be found in this expression.

## *Binding Variables: Let and Let**

`Let` empowers you to declare local variables and assign their initial values. `Let` does not accept tags, `go`, or `return` and is not an iteration function. The general form of a `let` expression is as follows:

**(let ((variable-1 value-1) (variable-2 value-2) . . . )*
*(expression-1)*
*(expression-2)*
⋮
*)*

`Let` sets each local variable to its initial value, then evaluates the expression in the program. The value of the last expression is returned. For example:

```
*(let ((Class 'A) (Rule 'B) (Unit 'C))
(List Class Rule Unit)
   )
(A B C)
```

`Let` is useful in reducing repeated computations within a function. If an expression needs to be evaluated more than once in a program and `setq` is not desirable because it assigns a global variable, either `prog` or `let` can be employed to assign a local variable. Since `prog` is often abused, `let` is used to illustrate in the example below. The following function may be called to obtain the first and last element of a list:

```
*(defun first-and-last-element (x)
     (append ( car (last (reverse x)))
     (car (reverse x))
   )
```

This function can be enhanced by using `let`:

```
*(defund  first-and-last-element (x)
    (let  (y (reverse x)))
    (append (car (last (y))))
```

```
    (car (y))
    )
```

*Let** is slightly different from `let`. While `let` assigns initial values in parallel, `let*` allows you to assign initial values sequentially. The following two expressions demonstrate the difference:

```
*(Let (a (b (con (1 a))) (c (cons (2 b)))
 (values a b c ))); the term "values" is discussed below.
Error
unbound variable a

*(let* (a (b (con (3 a))) (c (cons (5 b)))
       (values a b c )))
nil
(3)
(5 3)
```

In the foregoing examples, when `let` is used, the variables are assigned in parallel; thus `con(1 a)` has an unbound variable `a`. However, when `let*` is used, because the variables are assigned sequentially, `a` is assigned `nil`; therefore, there is no error in the expression.

## *Values*

Heretofore all LISP expressions have returned exactly one value. *Values* is used to produce multiple values. It takes and returns any number of arguments. If the last expression in the body of a function contains `values` with five arguments specified, then a call to that function returns five values. In the previous `let` example, `values` returned three values—`nil`, `(3)`, and `(5 3)`. If `values` is not used to explicitly return three values, then the first value is normally given to the caller and all other values are discarded.

# Input/Output

Input/Output (I/O) is one of the areas of great disagreement among LISP implementations and no absolute standards exist. Messages can be printed in LISP by placing a sequence of characters (a *character string*) in quotation marks, as shown in the following example,

```
*"Good morning, this is an expert system."
"Good morning, this is an expert system."
```

Like numbers, strings evaluate to themselves.

*Print* evaluates its arguments and prints the result preceded by a new line and followed by a space. Its general format is as follows:

*(print object & optional output-stream)

The second argument, output-stream, is optional, as indicated by &optional, and its default value is that of the variable *standard-output*. Print returns the object. For example:

```
*;count and print 1 to 20 by 5
*(do i 1 (+ i 5)
(zerop (- 55 i))
(print i )
(terpri )
 )
```

*Princ* is similar to print except that it is not preceded by a new line and is not followed by a space. A symbol is printed as the characters of its name and a string is printed without enclosing double quotes to make printing look more pleasing. Princ returns the object.

*Prin1* is the machine version of print. It is intended to be accepted by the function read. Prin1 does not start with a new line nor does it finish with a space. Escape characters are used as appropriate for read. It returns the object.

*Pprint* is just like print except that the subsequent space is omitted and the object is formatted for user readability. It returns no values.

*Terpi* is a function that starts a new line, as shown in the example for print.

*Format* is useful for producing a formatted document. Its general form is as follows:

*(Format destination control-string other-arguments)

The characters of the control string and other arguments are output by format to their destination, according to directions that are followed by a tilde ( ~ ). For example:

```
*(Setq p "you")
*(Format nil "We need  ~ A !" p)
"We need you!"
```

In this example, the destination is nil, so that format creates a string to contain its output and returns that string. The control string is "We need A !", in which A is a directive indicating that the argument (p), to be printed between "we need and !", is a LISP object and will be printed without a new line and space, as in the case of princ. The resulting output is " We need you ! "

The destination in a `format` expression must be either `nil`, `t`, or a string. If the destination is `t`, the output is sent to the stream of the variable `*standard-output*`, and `format` returns `nil`. If the destination is a string, the output characters are added to the end of the string and `format` returns `nil`.

A `format` directive includes a tilde character (~), an optional colon (:), "at" sign (@) modifiers, and a single character that specifies the type of directive, as shown in Table 4-3.

**Table 4-3**
***Characters used in a format directive***

| Character | Means | Explanation |
|---|---|---|
| A | Ascii | Argument (arg) is printed as if by `princ`. |
| S | S-expression | Arg is printed as if by `prin1`. |
| D | Decimal | Arg (which must be an integer) is printed in decimal radix with no trailing decimal point. |
| B | Binary | Arg (which must be an integer) is printed in binary radix. |
| O | Octal | Arg (which must be an integer) is printed in octal radix. |
| X | Hexadecimal | Arg (which must be an integer) is printed in hexadecimal radix. |
| C | Character | Arg (which must be a character) is printed. |
| % | Newline | A #newline character is printed. |
| & | Freshline | Identical to newline. |
| ~ | Tilde | A tilde character is printed. |
| | <newline> | The newline character and any following white space is ignored. With a colon (:), only the newline is ignored. With an @ sign, only the white space following the newline is ignored. |
| : | [false~;true~] | IF-THEN expression. If arg is `nil`, false is processed as a format control string; otherwise, true is processed. |
| @ | [true~] test | If arg is not `nil`, then arg is not consumed (i.e., it remains the next arg to be processed) and true is processed as a format control string; otherwise, arg is consumed and true is ignored. |

Many of these directives are infrequently used, particularly by the beginner. Some more examples:

```
*(Setq *monitor-stream* "xyz data base")
*(Format *Monitor-stream* " Environment ~A Not saved."env )
;example of format with control string
*(Format nil " ~& System loaded"); & indicates printing
     a new line
```

The **backquote** character provides an easy way to create an expression that combines fixed and variable portions. The backquote character, ', inserts the contents of the variable into the expression when a comma appears.

```
*(Setq x 5)
*'(x y ,x ,(+ x z))
(x y 5 7)
```

The backquote before the parenthesis indicates that the expression is a template. When a comma occurs, the form following the comma is evaluated and its result replaces the original object after the comma.

If a comma is followed by an "at" sign (@), then the form subsequent to @ is evaluated to obtain a list. The elements of the list are substituted into the expression without the usual embracing parentheses, as shown in the following example:

```
*(Setq p (x y z))
*'(p , p ,@p,(cdr p),@(cdr p))
(p (x y z) x y z (y z) y z)
```

A backquote can be used to help `print` arrange a hodgepodge of atoms and lists into a convenient and efficient format. For example:

```
*(print (p "=", @p)
p = xyz
```

*Read* is a function that reads one LISP object from the terminal and returns that object as its value. `Read` causes the computer to wait for the user to type a response.

```
*(read) Hi
Hi
```

Because `read` prints nothing to warn the user that the computer is waiting for him/her to prompt an answer, it is usually preceded by a `print` expression, which tells the user what kind of response is expected.

# Macros and Other Programming Conveniences

Macros allow you to define arbitrary functions before evaluation or compilation. Unlike other computing languages, macros in LISP are performed at the expression level, not at the character string level. Thus using a macro does not introduce inefficiencies in a compiled program. Macros are not functions and cannot be used as arguments to such functions as `apply`. Macros are defined using the same general format as an ordinary procedure:

```
*(defmacro macro-name (parameter-1 parameter-2 . . . )
  (expression-1  . . . )
  (expression-2  . . . )
   :
  )
```

A macro does not evaluate its arguments; it returns an expression that is evaluated. The variables in a macro's argument are bound to the entire macro program. A macro, when combined with a backquote, becomes a powerful programming technique. For example, you can define `macro-when` as follows:

```
*(defmacro macro-when (test &rest argument); &rest is
     discussed below
        "(cond (,test ,@argument ))
     )
```

## *Lambda List Keywords*

The keyword *&rest* in the previous example indicates that `argument` is optional. A similar keyword is *&optional*. These keywords are discussed below.

Both `&optional` and `&rest` provide the option to supply arguments only when they are needed. The `&` of `&optional` and `&rest` tells the computer that these keywords are not parameters but parameter separators, and that the optional parameters are set to `nil` if there is no matching argument. For example, the `output-stream` in `princ` is optional:

```
*(Princ object &optional output-stream)
```

If `output-stream` is not specified, `*standard-output*`, a global variable, is assumed. The LISP printer writes to the output stream that is assigned to this variable.

If the number of optional parameters is known, then `&optional` suffices. The number of optional parameters can be one or more. However, if you do not know the number of optional parameters, you can use `&rest` to signal a single optional parameter that represents more arguments than the required and optional parameters. The `macro-when` definition given above can be used as an example because it contains `&rest` in the argument—any number of arguments are permitted.

```
*(macro-when (t (value 7 8 9)))
7 8 9
```

```
*(Setq x 3)
*(macro-when ((zerop X) (Format nil "X is equal to ~ D."
x))
(Format nil "X is equal to zero."))
```

# Declaring Global Variables and Name Constants

As discussed in the previous section, `set` evaluates its argument and works only with global (dynamic) variables. Because all variables in LISP are local (lexical) by default, a declaration of global variables for the argument may be required.

*`Defvar`* is the recommended way to declare the use of a special variable in a program. The general format of `defvar` is

**(defvar variable initial-value "documentation")*

The variable name is customarily inserted with beginning and ending asterisks (*) to signal that it is a global variable. For example:

```
*(defvar *menu-sensitive-items* nil "These are for menus
that enhance user-convenience in using the system")
```

`Initial-value` may not be required. If it is supplied, then `variable` is initialized to the result of evaluating `initial-value`, unless it already has a value. `Defvar` suggests that the value of the variable will be changed by the program during execution, and that the variable name will be returned.

*`Defparameter`* is similar to `defvar` except that `defparameter` requires an `initial-value` to initialize `variable`. `Defparameter` is intended to declare a variable that is normally constant but can be changed even during execution. Such a change, however, is considered a change to the program. `Defparameter` implies that the value of the variable will be changed by the user before program execution. It does not allow the compiler to assume the value for the program being executed. For example,

```
*(defparameter *system-file-list* '(until user-int slot
    toplevel)
"These are the files to be loaded for the expert system
being executed.")
```

In the above statement, the global variable is inserted with beginning and ending asterisks (*).

*`Defconstant`* is similar to `defparameter`, but asserts that the value of the variable will not be changed. Once a name has been declared by

`defconstant` to be constant, any further assignment to that variable results in an error. The general format is the same as `defvar` or `defparameter`. For example,

```
*(defconstant *slot-attributes* '(value documentation type-
restriction inheritance) "Slot attributes that may be
     assigned by the user")
```

*`Declare`* and *`proclaim`* allow you to specify variable bindings in a program. They should be used with caution because many implementations may not support them. Even among implementations that do support them, the effect varies over implementations. `Declare` has no effect on the variable in the current version of GCLISP, which does not support `proclaim`. The general formats for `declare` and `proclaim` are as follows:

**(declare (argument-1 . . . ))*

**(proclaim '(argument-1 . . . ))*

`Declare` affects only executable code such as `lambda` or `defun` programs, while `proclaim` has a global effect. Examples are

```
*(defun declare-example (X))

*(declare (type float X)); "type" is discussed below

*(proclaim '(type float *X*))
```

*`Type`*, used in the above expressions, is a common LISP function that specifies that the variables mentioned take on values only of the given type. Its general format is as follows:

**(type variable-type variable-1 variable-2 . . . )*

# Creating Record Structures

In representing structured knowledge, *`defstruct`* is a powerful mechanism for data abstraction and representation. It allows the programmer to organize fields and field values neatly. The general format for `defstruct` is

**(defstruct (name option 1 option 2 . . . )*
*document-string*
*slot-description-1*
*slot-description-2*

The name, which must be a symbol, is returned as the value of `defstruct`. Options are not required. If no options are given, the word `defstruct` may be omitted. Options include:

`:conc-name` Specifies an alternate prefix to be used—for example:

```
*(defstruct (slot (:conc-name unit-)))
```

`:include` Includes a new structure definition as an extension of an old structure definition. For example, if an old structure called `student` looks like this:

```
*(defstruct student person grade major sex)
```

and you want to make a new structure to represent a graduate student, including all of the features of `student` plus financial aid, you would proceed as follows:

```
*(defstruct (graduate student (:include
     student) (:conc-name graduate-))
financial-aid)
```

The `:include` option causes `graduate-student` to have the same slots as `student` in addition to the new slot `financial-aid`. `Graduate-student` can be further restricted by other `:include` options such as:

```
*(defstruct (graduate-student (:include
     student (grade 3.8)))
financial-aid)
```

`:print-function` Prints a structure of this type. It requires three optional arguments: the structure to be printed, a stream to print to, and an integer indicating the current depth. For example:

```
*(defstruct (graduate-student (:print-
     function 'print-stext)))
```

`Print-stext` is the stream to print to and, as discussed before, the single quote (`'`) signals to LISP that the subsequent form `print-stext` will not be evaluated.

`:type` Specifies the representation to be used for the structure. It takes one argument, which can be either a vector or a list—for example:

```
*(defstruct (graduate-student (:type list)
     (:include student))
financial-aid)
```

| | |
|---|---|
| | `:type` and `:print-function` cannot appear in the same `defstruct`. |
| `:initial-offset` | Tells `defstruct` to skip over a certain number of slots before it starts allocating the slots in the structure. For example: |

```
*(defstruct (graduate-student (:include
     student) (:initial-offset 2))
financial-aid)
```

The *document string* in a `defstruct` is optional. If it is present, it is attached to the *name* as the document string of the structure. Each *slot description* is in the following format:

**(slot-name default-initial*
*Slot-option-name-1 slot-option-value-1*
*Slot-option-name-2 slot-option-value-2*
*. . . .)*

For example:

```
*(defstruct (slot (:print-function 'print-
     slot))
*(name nil)
*(value nil)
....)
```

In the above example, `name` and `value` are *slot-names*, and `nil` is the *default-initial* for these slots.

After the structure has been defined, instances of the structure can be created by using the *`constructor`* function. `Defstruct` names the `constructor` function with a prefix of `make`. For example, if the structure name is `slot`, the `constructor` function is `make-slot`. The general format for a `constructor` function is as follows:

**(defun name-of-constructor-function*
*(slot-keyword-1 form1*
*slot-keyword-2 form2)*
*. . . .)*

For example, the `constructor` function for `slot` is

```
*(defun make-slot (&rest keys-and-values)
....)
```

# Message Passing (Object-Oriented Programming)

The functions `send` and `funcall` are identical: they enable the user to pass messages as in object-oriented programming. These two functions call a function with its arguments and return the results of this function call. The general format for the message passing is as follows:

**(send message-receiver : message-name message-argument)*
**(funcall message-receiver : message-name message-argument)*

The following example explains:

```
*(send *terminal-io* : set-attribute a)
```

In this example, `send` acts as the message-sending mechanism. `*Terminal-io*` acts as the receiver of the message, which is an output stream to the terminal. `Set-attribute` is the message name (a function to perform a certain task) and `a` is an argument that indicates the output stream is in the *ascii* file format.

# File System Interface

`Load` enables the computer to load the file named by *pathname* into the LISP environment. The general format and an example are as follows:

**(Load pathname &key)*

```
*(Load "D:\\EKO\\BOOT.LSP")
```

`Directory` returns a list of *pathnames*, which match the *pathname* given. The general format and an example are

**(Directory pathname)*

```
*(Directory "D:\\EKO\\*.LSP")
```

`Cd` changes the PC-DOS current disk drive and directory to those specified in the *pathname*. General format and an example follow.

**(cd &optional pathname)*

```
*(cd "C:\\GCLISP2")
```

`Dos` and `exit` allow the computer to leave the LISP environment. Depending on the implementation, `dos` may allow the computer to leave and return to the environment, while `exit` may allow it to leave but not return (the user may have to restart the LISP environment if `exit` is executed).

# Summary

- A variety of LISP dialects exists. This chapter is based on Common LISP.
- In LISP, everything is accomplished by executing functions.
- Programs and data use the same symbolic expressions, which consist of atoms and lists.
- Everything in a LISP expression is evaluated immediately after the right parenthesis is typed, unless the evaluation is blocked with a quote.
- LISP programs consist of forms and functions. Forms include self-evaluating forms (such as numbers and characters), variables, special forms, macro calls, and function calls.
- The strength of LISP is in symbolic manipulation.
- Major topics in LISP include: LISP operation, evaluation, user-defined functions, conditioned actions, recursion, iteration and binding, macros, creating record structures, and message passing.

# References

[1] G. Steele, et al, *Common LISP References Manual* (Digital Press, 1984).

[2] Gold Hill Computers, "Golden Common LISP," various versions (Cambridge, MA, 1986).

# 5

# Prolog Vocabulary

Prolog was chosen by the Japanese as the basis for software to be developed in the Fifth Generation Computer Project in 1981. Until then, Prolog had been a research language developed and expanded in European locations such as Marseilles, France and Edinburgh, Scotland. Although a number of versions of Prolog are available, with certain differences in syntax, the generally accepted standard seems to be the version that appeared in the first definitive textbook on Prolog, entitled *Programming in Prolog* (second edition) by W. F. Clocksin and C. S. Mellish at Edinburgh University, Edinburgh, Scotland [1]. The Prolog-86 package [2] (distributed by Micro-AI of Rheem Valley, CA) implemented the majority of the commands set forth in the definitive textbook. Our discussion in this chapter focuses primarily on the examples executed in Prolog-86. Appendix B lists the commands for Prolog-86 and one other package, Turbo Prolog (distributed by Borland International, Inc. of Scotts Valley, CA).

This chapter covers the following topics: (1) becoming acquainted with Prolog, (2) input/output, (3) modifying the data base, (4) LISP functions in Prolog, and (5) cut-in backtracking.

## Becoming Acquainted with Prolog

Prolog is a programming language that allows you to declare relationships between objects, to accumulate and organize these relationships, and to draw logical deductions from facts in relationships that you supply. Unlike other conventional programming languages, such as C or Pascal, you need not specify step-by-step procedures that the computer must carry out to obtain the desired output.

Prolog programming consists of three steps:

1. Declare facts about objects and their relationships.
2. Define rules which govern objects and their relationships.
3. Ask questions about objects and their relationships.

Step 3 can be placed before Step 2 in many cases. After you declare the facts about objects and their relationships, you can ask questions about them without rules.

## *Declaring and Querying Facts*

To declare a fact such as *David likes Lise* in Prolog, you need to identify the objects and relationships. The objects are *David* and *Lise*, and the relationship is *likes*.

*Example 5-1*

```
likes(david, lise).
```

Note in Example 5-1 that the names of the objects and relationships are in lower-case letters. Prolog distinguishes between upper-case and lower-case letters. Names beginning with a capital letter or underscore (_) are reserved for variables. You can use any sequence surrounded by quotes—for example, `'X'`, `'Apollo'`, `'_add'`. The relationship between the objects (that is, `likes`) appears first and is called the *predicate*. The objects (that is, `david` and `lise`) following the predicate are enclosed in parentheses and are separated by a comma. The order of the objects makes a difference. The statement, `likes (david, lise)`, is different from `likes (lise, david)`. Each expression must be terminated by a period.

A statement such as Example 5-1 in Prolog is referred to as a *clause*. Each clause can be translated into pseudo-English by putting the predicate between the arguments. For example:

*Example 5-2*

```
professor(david, tim).
```

Example 5-2 can be translated into *David is the professor of Tim*. The predicate `professor` stands for the phase *is the professor of*. The names in the example refer to particular objects. Each given name has only one meaning in Prolog. You must carefully differentiate between a name that represents the class of an object and a name that represents an instance of a class. For example, in developing an expert system to identify a particular catfish that is active in the pond, two facts are used:

A catfish resembles an eel.
The catfish is extremely active.

You need to give the two "catfish" different names to distinguish them, as shown in Example 5-3 below.

*Example 5-3*

```
resembles(catfish, eel).
active(catfish1).
```

As in other programming, the names you use to represent a predicate or arguments do not affect the accuracy of a Prolog program as long as they begin with a lower-case letter. However, names of objects should be meaningful for the purpose of later program review or review by someone else.

Examples 5-2 and 5-3 translate relationships about a particular set of objects that constitute a real-world problem into Prolog clauses. The collection of all facts (relationships) that have been input is called a *data base* in Prolog. Once the facts have been stored in the data base, you can query the data base about the objects and their relationship. For example, the data base established in Example 5-1 can be queried as follows:

*Example 5-4*

```
?- likes(david, lise).
```

or

```
likes(david, lise)?
```

Prolog answers questions by searching through the data base for a clause that matches the question. The question matches a fact in the data base if the predicate (e.g., `likes`) of the question (Example 5-4) matches the predicate of a fact in the data base (Example 5-1) and if each argument of the question matches the corresponding argument in the fact. The question of Example 5-4 matches the fact of Example 5-1 because the predicate as well as the two arguments are the same. The answer to the question in Example 5-4 is *yes*. However, if the order of the argument changes, for example:

```
likes(lise, david)?
```

Prolog answers

```
no
```

The above answer indicates that, as far as the computer "knows," the data base does not contain a fact which matches the above question. The fact `likes(david, lise)` is different from the fact `likes(lise, david)`.

## Constants and Variables

In the previous section, only constants have been used. A *constant* is a name which stands for a specific object (such as `david` or `lise`) or a relationship between objects (such as `likes`). The two types of constants are *integers* and *atoms*.

An *integer* is a positive or negative whole number within a range such as −32,765 and 32,764, depending on the implementation. Examples of integers are:

−15, 0, 32, 5001

An *atom* is a sequence of letters, numbers, and special characters that denotes the name of a given object or relationship. The name of an atom cannot start with an integer, an upper-case letter, or the underscore (_) character, and it cannot be hyphenated. If an atom starts with one of these characters, it must be enclosed in single quotes. Examples of atoms are

```
abc

chapter_10

david

'This is an atom.'
```

The following are *not* atoms:

```
479
145street
large-number
Vector
_tax
```

A *variable* is any sequence that begins with an upper-case letter or the underscore (_) character. It is a special type of name that can match any object. `X`, `_ten`, `Y`, `Z`, `David`, and `Lise` are all variables. When variables are used in facts, they usually stand for words like "everybody," "every one," and "everything." For example, to add the fact that *Everyone likes Lise*, enter the clause in Example 5-5 below.

*Example 5-5*

```
likes(X, lise).
```

We can ask the question *Does Eileen like Lise?* by typing

```
likes(eileen, lise)?
```

Prolog answers:

```
yes
```

Any atom that replaces `X` in Example 5-5 makes Prolog answer *yes*. For convenience of future use or other programmers' understanding, `X` in Example 5-5 can be given a more meaningful name such as `Her_friend`.

The misuse of variables, as in Example 5-5, can destroy the special relationship between objects in the data base. The assignment of a variable in such an instance can be removed by the command *retract*.

*Example 5-6*

```
retract(likes(X, lise))!
```

The command `retract` in Example 5-6 contains another Prolog expression as its argument, and ends with a ! symbol rather than with a period.

## Structures (Compound Predicates)

Example 5-6 is a *compound predicate*, which is also called a *structure* or a *compound term*. A typical structure takes the following form:

*predicate (argument1, argument2, . . . )*

where *argument1* can be a constant, a variable, or a structure.

*Example 5-7*

```
likes(david, lise).
union(R, Y, Z).
asserta(isa(Animal, mammal, How)).
owns(david, book(X, author(Western))).
```

Structures can contain an *and* or an *or* to further narrow or expand the answer spaces. Prolog provides the comma (,) operator to stand for *and*, and either the semicolon (;) or vertical bar (¦) to denote *or*. Three examples are given below.

*Example 5-8*

```
likes(david, lise), likes (david, eileen)?
```

*Example 5-9*

```
likes(david, lise); likes (david, eileen)?
```

*Example 5-10*

```
likes(david, lise)¦ likes (david, eileen)?
```

Example 5-8 uses an *and* operator. Examples 5-9 and 5-10 both use an *or* operator.

In answering a question containing the *and* operator, such as Example 5-8, Prolog first tries to match the leftmost clause. If this match fails, the answer to the question is *no*. If the first match succeeds, then Prolog attempts to match the next clause after the comma. If the match fails again, the answer is still *no*. Otherwise, Prolog answers *yes* to the conjunctive question.

When attempting to answer questions containing the `or` operator, such as Example 5-9, Prolog first attempts to match the leftmost clause in the disjunctive question against the facts in the data base. If the match succeeds, Prolog answers *yes*. If the question contains a variable, the variable is binding. If the first match does not succeed, Prolog tries to satisfy the next clause. If this match succeeds, it answers *yes*, or returns the binding variable. Otherwise, the answer is *no*.

## *Instantiation and Backtracking*

Build the small data base shown in Example 5-11, to examine instantiation and backtracking.

*Example 5-11*

```
likes(david, lise).
likes(david, eileen).
likes(david, emily).
likes(david, frank).
likes(david, rob).
likes(eileen, lise).
```

Then ask the following question:

*Example 5-12*

```
likes(david, People_David_likes)?
```

The variable `People_David_likes` is said to be *uninstantiated* before Prolog determines that `David likes Lise`. Once a variable stands for a given object—for example, `People_David_likes=lise`—then `People_David_likes` is said to be *instantiated* to `lise`.

Let us examine how the variable is instantiated. Prolog searches through the Example 5-11 data base from the beginning, to locate a clause that matches the question in Example 5-12. Note that the variable `People_David_likes` matches any object. The question `likes (david, People_David_likes)` matches `likes (david lise)` in Example 5-11 because the predicates and the first argument are the same, and the variable matches anything. When Prolog finds a match, it instantiates the variable to the name of the object it first matches. In this case, `People_David_likes` becomes instantiated to `lise`.

Once a match is found, Prolog marks the place in the data base where the match was found. In some implementations, such as Prolog-86, Prolog automatically returns to this mark and attempts to find another match until all matches in the data base have been found. If there are a large number of matches in the data base, a method such as `cut` is needed to prevent unlimited returns. (`Cut` is discussed later.) The process of returning to the mark to attempt to unify the variable with the object is called *backtracking*.

*Example 5-13*

```
like(david, People_liked), likes(eileen, People_liked)?
```

Example 5-13 queries the data base, *Who is the person whom both David and Eileen like?* In this example, the first clause is matched against the data base in Example 5-11, and `People_liked` is instantiated to `lise`. Prolog then attempts to satisfy the second clause, `likes (eileen, People_liked)`. It fails when Prolog tries to match the clause with `likes (david, eileen)`. However, by backtracking, Prolog returns to the data base as many times as required until the clause is matched with the facts in the data base and Prolog instantiates the variable to the given object or no fact remains in the data base. In Example 5-13, `People_liked` in the second clause is instantiated with `lise` after five attempts.

## Adding Comments to the Program

To add comments to the program, check the symbol for comments in each implementation of Prolog. For example, in Prolog-86, the `%` operator is used to write comments as follows:

```
likes(david, lise). % David likes Lise.
```

In the Clocksin and Mellish definitive book [2], a pair of `/* */` symbols is used as follows:

```
likes(david, lise). /* David likes Lise.*/
```

## Adding Rules to the Data Base

The format for adding a rule to the data base is as follows:

*P*:-
*Q*,
*R*,
⋮
*Z*.

where *P* is true if *Q*, *R*, . . . *Z* are true. To satisfy goal *P*, all subgoals of *Q*, *R*, . . . *Z* must be satisfied first. For example, rules to express whether a person is the brother of another person are shown in the example below.

*Example 5-14*

```
brother_of(Person1, Person2):-
parent(X, Person1),
parent(X, Person2),
```

```
sex(Person1, male),
diff(Person1, Person2).

diff(X, Y):- X/=Y.
```

Example 5-14 means `Person1` is the `brother_of` `Person2` if `X` is the `parent` of `Person1` and also of `Person2`, if `Person1` is of `male sex`, and if `Person1` is `different` from `Person2`.

The rules in Example 5-14 can be used to query the relationship of objects in the data base as follows:

*Example 5-15*

```
brother_of(X, david)?
```

## Arithmetic Operations

Arithmetic operations take a back seat in Prolog to the pattern matching discussed above. Prolog includes mostly integers. The *is* operator is used to accomplish the task of the equal sign (=) in many computer languages:

```
X is 10 + 20?
```

is equivalent to

```
X=10+20
```

The sophistication of arithmetic operations depends on each implementation of Prolog. Most implementations include the operators shown in Table 5-1.

## Writing Programs

As discussed before, a Prolog program consists of rules, facts, and queries. Rules usually appear first in a program. The format for each of the three components is summarized below.

Rules *P:- Q,R, . . . ,Z* means:

(a) *P* is true if *Q,R, . . . ,Z* are true.

(b) To satisfy goal *P*, subgoals *Q,R, . . .* , and *Z* must be satisfied.

Facts *P.* means:

(a) *P* is true.

(b) Goal *P* is satisfied.

Queries *P,Q?* or *?_P,Q.* means:

(a) Are $P$ and $Q$ true?
(b) Satisfy goals $P$ and $Q$.

*P;Q?* or *?_P;Q.* means:
(a) Is $P$ or $Q$ true?
(b) Satisfy goal $P$ or $Q$.

**Table 5-1**
***Arithmetic operators used in most Prolog implementations***

| Operators | Meanings | Example | Result |
|---|---|---|---|
| + | Add | 2+3 | 5 |
| - | Subtract | 3-1 | 2 |
| * | Multiply | 3*5 | 15 |
| / | Divide | 7/4 | 4 |
| mod | Integer remainder | 7mod4 | 3 |
| | Power | $2^3$ | 8 |
| = | Equal | 2=2 | True |
| /= | Not equal | 3/=2 | True |
| > | Greater than | 3>5 | False |
| < | Less than | 3<5 | True |
| <= | Less than or equal to | X<=Y | Undetermined |
| >= | Greater than or equal to | X>=Y | Undetermined |

A sample Prolog program to solve the "Tower of Hanoi" game, which is played with three poles and a set of disks with various diameters, is shown in Example 5-16 below.

*Example 5-16*

```
hanoi(I) :- move (I,left,center,right).
move(0,_,_,_) :- !.
move((I,A,B,C) :-
        M is I - 1,
        move(M,A,C,B),
        show(A,B),
        move(M,C,B,A).
show(X,Y) :-
        print('Move the disk on ',X' to 'Y),
        n1.    % n1 indicates a new line on the current
    output stream.
```

The predicate `print` and `!` (the `cut` operator to stop automatic backtracking after the goal is satisfied once) are discussed later.

## *Display All Clauses*

To display all clauses in the current interpreted program, use the predicate `listing`:

```
Listing!
```

This predicate does not list any clauses in Prolog library files such as *prolog.lib*.

# Input/Output

This section discusses saving files, loading files, executing large programs, and input/output of data and characters.

## *Saving and Loading Source Files on Disk*

To save a source file, use `save`. Example 5-17 causes the program (the data base) to be saved under the filename *testfile.pro* on disk A.

*Example 5-17*

```
Save 'a:testfile.pro'!
```

The three ways to load a source file are (1) loading it when you load the Prolog interpreter, (2) using the `load` command, and (3) using the `consult` command.

Load a source file (for example, *testfile.pro*) when the Prolog package is powered up, as shown in Example 5-18:

*Example 5-18*

```
Prolog testfile.pro
```

If you are already in Prolog, you can bring a source file in by typing either of the following commands:

*Example 5-19*

```
load 'testfile.pro'!
```

*Example 5-20*

```
consult('testfile.pro')!
```

The difference between `load` and `consult` is as follows:

- *Load* removes all existing clauses in the current data base before the new file (*testfile.pro*) is brought into the data base.
- *Consult* adds the clauses in the new file into the current data base without removing the existing clauses.

## Running Large Prolog Programs

To avoid an environment stack full error when running a large program, you can increase the size of the variable stack when the Prolog interpreter is loaded.

*Example 5-21*

```
prolog _s1500
```

Note that `_s` is used before the number of desired units of stack size (e.g., 1500).

## Input and Output of Data

To read data from the terminal or a disk file, the predicate `read` is used. For example, to read the next term from the terminal, type

```
read(X)?
```

When the prompt > appears, enter a term such as

```
friends(X,Y).
```

Prolog responds with

```
X=friends(X,Y).
```

To input an atom or a sentence, use single quotes and the predicate `ratom`:

```
ratom(X)?
```

When the prompt appears, type

```
'This is a test'.
```

Prolog answers

```
X='This is a test.'
```

To output data into the terminal, use print:

```
print('This is a test.')!
```

The single quotes are not printed. Each call to print causes the output to be printed on a new line. The predicate, print, can be combined with '\n' and '\t' to produce a new line and tab respectively. The character '\t' inserts four spaces into the print line.

The predicate prin eliminates the newline character.

*Example 5-22*

```
prin('This is line one.'), prin('This is line two.')!
```

Example 5-22 results in

```
This is line one.This is line two.
```

## *Input and Output of Character*

To read a single character (such as a) from the terminal or a disk file, type

```
getc(X)?a
```

Prolog answers

```
X=a
```

Note that a is typed together with the predicate on the same line, before the ⟨Return⟩ key is hit, to avoid errors.

To output a single character (for example, c) use the predicate putc:

```
putc(c)!
```

# Modifying the Data Base

This section discusses predicates that can be used to modify an existing data base. The predicates assert, asserta, and assertz add new clauses to the data base. Retract and retractall remove clauses from the data base.

## *Adding Clauses*

The predicate *asserta* adds new clauses at the beginning of the data base, while *assert* and *assertz* add new clauses at the end of the data base.

*Example 5-23*

```
asserta(likes(lise,emily))!
assert(likes(lise,eileen))!
assertz(likes(eileen,david))!
```

Prolog adds these facts into the data base accordingly.

## *Removing Clauses*

The predicate *retract* removes the first clause in the data base, whereas *retractall* removes all clauses that match the clause in question. For example,

```
retract(likes(X,Y))!
```

only removes the first clause from the data base in Example 5-11, which is `likes(david,lise)`. However, the expression

```
retractall(likes(X,Y))!
```

removes all clauses in the data base that are in the form of `likes(X,Y)`. When you type

```
likes(david,emily)?
```

the response from Prolog is

```
no
```

# Writing LISP Functions in Prolog

Prolog can be used to write LISP functions for processing lists. A list is either an atom that represents an empty list ([]) or a structure with two arguments—a head and a tail—enclosed in a pair of brackets. The *head* of a list is its first element and the *tail* is all remaining elements in the list.

*Example 5-24*

```
friends([a,b,c,d,e])
```

To find the head and tail of the list in Example 5-24, type

```
friends([H¦T])?
```

or

```
friends([H, ..T])?
```

Prolog answers

```
H=a
T=[b,c,d,e]
```

LISP functions, such as `car`, `append`, and `member` can be built using a recursive procedure. Using `member` as an example to describe the procedure, the rules to define `member` are as follows:

- *A* is a member of list *P* if *A* is the first element of *P*.
- If *A* is not the first element of list *P*, then *A* is a member of *P* only if *A* is a member of the tail of the list *P*.

These two rules can be implemented as follows:

*Example 5-25*

```
member(A,[A¦_]).
member(A,[_¦Y]):- member(A,Y).
```

The definition can then be tested by typing

```
member(x,[x,y,z])?
```

Prolog answers

```
yes
```

because `x` is a member of the list `[a,b,c]`.

List and set processing predicates often defined for frequent use in Prolog include: `car`, `cdr`, `last`, `nextto`, `cons`, `append`, `list`, `reverse`, `efface`, `delete`, `subst`, `sublist`, `mapcar`, `member`, `subset`, `disjoint`, `intersection`, and `union`.

# Cut Operator in Backtracking

The *cut* operator is one of the most important operators in Prolog for controlling the effects of automatic backtracking. It is represented by the `!` character. The cut operator allows you to tell Prolog which previous choice it need not consider again when Prolog automatically backtracks. This operator enables programs to run faster and use less memory, and prevents programs from generating large or infinite numbers of solutions. For example, if you type

```
member(X,[a,b,c,d,e])?
```

some implementations of Prolog may return all answers as follows:

```
X=a
```

```
X=b
X=c
X=d
X=e
```

The cut operator can be written into the `member` procedure, which is defined in Example 5-25, to reduce the number of solutions as follows:

*Example 5-26*

```
member(X,[X|_]) :- !.
member(X,[_|Y]) :- member(X,Y).
```

Now, if you type

```
member(X,[a,b,c,d,e])?
```

Prolog answers

```
X=a
```

When the first clause in Example 5-26 is satisfied, the cut is marked. Consequently, when Prolog attempts to backtrack, it stops at the cut mark and the second clause in Example 5-26 is never executed more than once.

# Summary

- Prolog is a programming language that allows the user to declare relationships between objects and draw logical deductions from facts in these relationships.
- Prolog programming consists of three steps: (1) declare relationships between objects, (2) define rules governing objects and their relationships, and (3) query objects and their relationships.
- Constants and variables are used in Prolog. Constants include integers and atoms.
- Instantiation and backtracking are two primary Prolog functions.
- Prolog can be used to write LISP functions for processing lists.
- The cut operator is one of the most important operations in Prolog.

# References

[1] W. Clocksin and C. Mellish, *Programming in Prolog* (New York: Springer-Verlag, 1981).

[2] Micro-AI, *Prolog-86 User's Guide and Reference Manual* (Rheem Valley, CA, 1985).

# 6

# Smalltalk Vocabulary

Smalltalk is an object-oriented language environment. As with Prolog, because no standard of the language has emerged yet, the text in this chapter is written based on the implementation of Smalltalk/V. Structurally, Smalltalk/V is similar to other implementations, such as Smalltalk-80. Smalltalk/V is an interactive environment in which a mouse is more convenient than the keyboard for executing expressions or creating and maintaining programs.

As an object-oriented language, Smalltalk allows you to classify all information into a hierarchy of related characteristics. For example, a Ford sedan, Escort, is an instance of Ford sedan class, which is a subclass of Ford cars. As a Ford car, an Escort inherits many common features and differs only in features unique to it, such as design style, price, etc. This type of class information can be handled with ease in Smalltalk. In Smalltalk, problems can be broken down into more comprehensible subproblems. These subproblems can be prototyped rapidly without extensive pre-planning or flowchart analysis.

Smalltalk is different from conventional and other AI programming languages. You must have extensive knowledge of the class and method library to become proficient in and use the full power of this language. Good documentation and well planned development programs are critical to the mastering of Smalltalk. A list of defined classes for Smalltalk/V is compiled in Appendix C for your convenience.

This chapter focuses first on familiarizing you with the Smalltalk/V interactive environment and then on the distinctive features of Smalltalk, such as classes and methods (for building the frame structure to be discussed in Chapter 7), graphics and windows (for building the user interface that is discussed in Chapter 8), debugging (for facilitating general expert system development), and interface to DOS file systems (for convenient interface with the DOS environment).

# Becoming Familiar with the Smalltalk Interactive Environment

The Smalltalk environment consists of *windows*. Windows are operated by the mouse (or the cursor arrows on the keyboard) to highlight various menus that, in turn, activate files, classes, or other elements to execute expressions.

This section introduces the following main features of the Smalltalk environment:

- Window/menu operations
- Text editing
- Smalltalk expressions and their evaluation
- Smalltalk system operations

## *Window/Menu Operations*

To start Smalltalk/V, type `V` after the subdirectory of Smalltalk/V is activated. The start-up screen is a *system transcript window*, which allows other windows to be activated through system commands. Every window in Smalltalk has a *label* and is surrounded by a *border*. The size of the border can be adjusted by the user. The area inside the border is divided into one or more districts called *panes*. The system transcript window has only one pane, as shown in Figure 6-1. Other windows may contain more panes, depending on the need to perform various tasks. These will be discussed when they are needed.

The *cursor* is the pointer on the screen that directs Smalltalk to the action. The shape of the cursor changes depending on the task it performs. Usually it is an arrow. The cursor is commanded through a two-button mouse or the cursor keys on the numeric keypad. The cursor keys can be used to move the cursor more rapidly if the ⟨Shift⟩ key is also held down. The right mouse button is always clicked to pop up a menu, and the left button is always clicked to activate the command issued by the menu. If a keyboard is used, the ⟨Del⟩ key is equivalent to the right mouse button, and the ⟨+⟩ key is equivalent to the left mouse button.

### Menu Operations

In general, three types of menus—*window menu, pane menu* and *system menu*—are available for performing different kinds of tasks, depending on where the cursor is when a menu is popped up. A *window menu*, specific to that window, pops up when the cursor is over the label of a window. A window menu, as shown in Figure 6-2, contains at least three choices.

The most frequently used choice in a window menu is *frame*, which allows the user to adjust the size of the border to meet his/her needs in operating that particular window. When *frame* is selected, Smalltalk responds with a rectangular outline. The size of the border is determined by

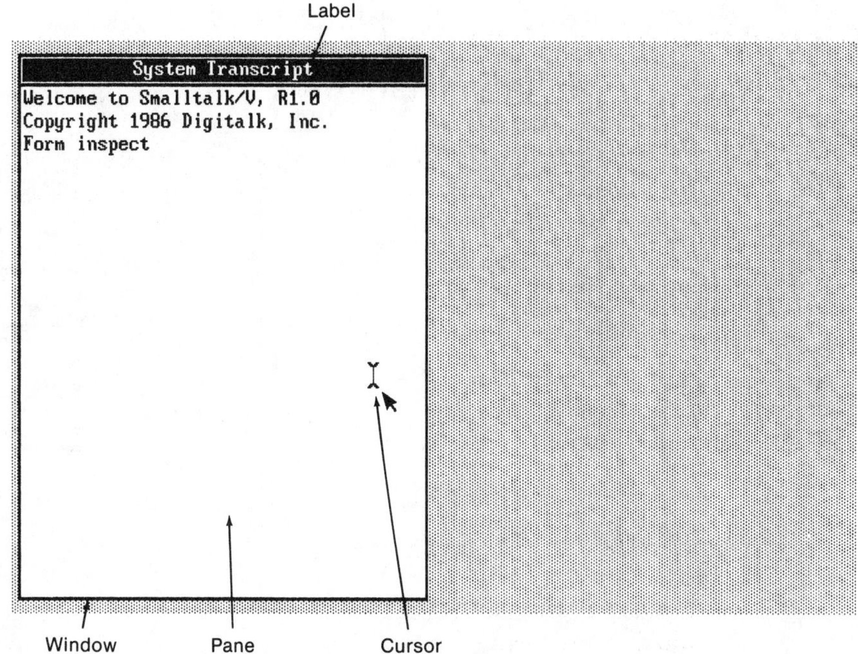


**Figure 6-1**
***The system transcript window and its elements***

two points, the upper left corner and the lower right corner. The cursor is positioned to fix these two points, to move the window to its new location and change its size. The other choices of window menus are:

*Move* — Moves the window to a new location.

*Cycle* — Causes a window to appear underneath other windows and become activated.

*Close* — Causes the window and its contents to be erased.

*Collapse* — Causes the contents of the window to disappear but remain intact, with only the window label visible on the screen.

*Label* — Prompts the user for a new label.

For example, in the system transcript window (Fig. 6-2), the window menu choices are *cycle, frame,* and *move.* Most other windows would have six window menu choices: *label, collapse, cycle, frame, move,* and *close.*

A *pane menu,* specific to that pane, appears when the cursor is over a pane in a window. The pane in the system transcript window is a text pane that allows the user to create, edit, and modify files. The pane menu offers various choices, which are grouped into four types.

1. Systems

   *Install* — Recovers the last chunks of text.

   *Restore* — Restores the screen to original text from the file. It is like `undo` in other computing languages.

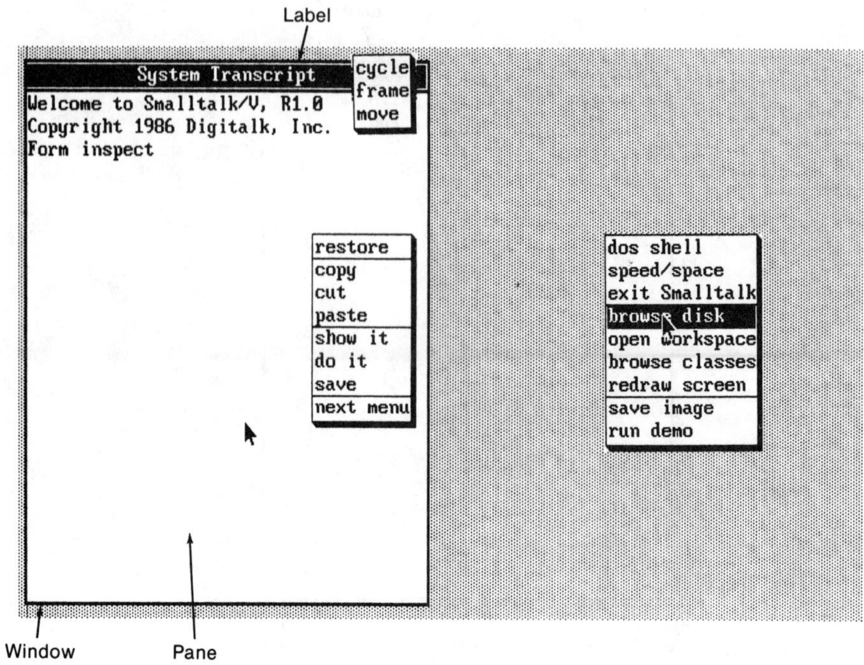


**Figure 6-2**
***Sample window menu***

2. Editing

   The following choices are used for text editing:

   *Copy* Copies the selected text into the edit buffer.

   *Cut* Takes the selected text and puts it in the edit buffer. The selected text is deleted from the original pane.

   *Paste* Inserts the text in the edit buffer into the selected pane.

3. Evaluation

   The following choices are for expression evaluation:

   *Show it* Shows the expression and inserts a character representation of the expression value in the pane after the evaluated text.

   *Do it* Evaluates the expression and discards the expression value.

   *Save* Evaluates the expression and stores the expression value in the temporary buffer.

   *Save as* Writes the directory information on a file.

4. Miscellaneous

   *Next menu* Goes to the next-layer menu that displays choices of *search, print,* etc.

The *system menu* pops up when the cursor is outside every window and the right mouse button is pressed. The alternative system menu choices are

| | |
|---|---|
| *DOS shell* | Causes another menu to appear with several choices of DOS commands. |
| *Space/speed* | May not cause any effect, depending on the system. |
| *Exit Smalltalk* | Leaves the Smalltalk environment and causes another menu to appear. |
| *Brouse disk* | Opens a *directory browser window* and browses the files on the disk. |
| *Open workspace* | Opens a workspace window. |
| *Browse classes* | Opens a *class hierarchy browser window* and browses the classes available. |
| *Redraw screen* | Reinitializes the screen. |
| *Save image* | Saves the entire environment that has been changed. |
| *Run demo* | Opens the *demo class window* and runs the methods available for demonstrating graphics. |

## Window Operations

Window operations include opening, activating, deactivating, and closing a window. To open a new window, issue a system menu choice such as *browse disk, browse classes*, or *open workspace*. The area on the screen for the new window (the upper left and lower right corners of the window) must be defined. To activate an existing window, move the cursor over some position of the window and click the left mouse button. To deactivate a window, simply activate or open a different window. To close an existing window, select *close* from the window menu.

# *Text Editing*

Text editing includes inserting, selecting, replacing, deleting, saving, restoring, cutting, copying, pasting, and scrolling.

## Inserting Text

To insert text into a pane, move the cursor over the position inside the text pane where the text is to be inserted, press the left mouse button to activate an I-beam that marks the text insertion point, and type characters. When the ⟨Backspace⟩ key is pressed, the character to the left of the insertion point is deleted. To move the insertion point, place the cursor at the desired position and press the left mouse button. The insertion point jumps to the new position.

### Selecting, Replacing and Deleting Text

To select the text in a pane, activate the window, move the cursor to one end of the text, press and hold the left mouse button, and move (drag) the cursor to the other end of the text. The text selected is highlighted. To replace the text selected, type the new text. To delete the text selected, press the ⟨Backspace⟩ key.

### Saving and Restoring Text

To save a file after it is complete, click the right mouse button when the cursor is in the pane and then select *save*. To restore the original text or undo the edited text, click the right mouse button when the cursor is in the pane and select *restore*.

### Cutting, Copying, and Pasting

To move a piece of text from one text pane to another, click the right mouse button when the cursor is in the source pane. Select *cut* if the text is to be deleted from the source pane; otherwise, select *copy*. Move the cursor to the new window, activate the window, and click the right mouse button when the cursor is in the target pane. Select *paste* to move the text to the new pane.

### Scrolling

To scroll text, place the cursor at the far right of the text pane if the text is to be scrolled to the left; at the far left of the pane if the text is be scrolled to the right; at the top of the pane if the text is to be scrolled down; or at the bottom of the pane if the text is to be scrolled up. Press the right mouse button and hold it down until the cursor changes to a diamond shape. While holding the right button down, move the cursor outside of the pane in the direction that the text is scrolling.

## *Smalltalk Expressions and Their Evaluation*

Smalltalk expressions are similar to expressions in other computer programming languages. In Smalltalk, you can type the text for an expression in a text pane, select it, evaluate it, and display the result. Simple Smalltalk expressions and evaluation methods are described below. The details of Smalltalk are discussed in a later section of this chapter.

### Basic Smalltalk Expressions

Basic Smalltalk expressions contain objects, messages and methods, and variables. Simple Smalltalk programs are composed of these three elements.

## *Objects*

Objects are the basic building blocks of Smalltalk, analogous to pieces of data in other languages. The three elementary Smalltalk objects are integers, character strings, and arrays, examples of which are shown below.

- Integer—`1050`
- Character string—`$ABC`
- Array—`#('array' 'of' 4 'strings' and 6 'integers')`

A **$** sign is required to indicate that the object is a character string, and a **#** is required to indicate that the object is an array. As shown in the last example, all objects contained inside an object need not be of the same type or size.

## *Messages and Methods*

In Smalltalk, a *message* is sent to an object to evaluate the object itself. Messages perform a task similar to that of function calls in other languages. *Methods* are the internal algorithms which are performed by an object after receiving a message. They represent the internal implementation of an object. A Smalltalk expression contains at least an object and a message as shown below.

*Example 6-1*

```
3 Factorial => 6
```

In Example 6-1, 3 is an object (an integer), `Factorial` is a message that requests 3 to perform a factorial, and = > is a symbol indicating the following element is the result. The internal structure of `Factorial` is a method.

A message consists of three elements, a *receiver object,* a *message selector,* and zero or more *arguments.* In the foregoing example, 3 is the receiver object, `Factorial` is the message selector, and no argument is used. As in functions, the message selector is the function name, the receiver object is the function parameter, and the method is the function definition. A message always returns a single object as its result. More examples are given below.

*Example 6-2*

```
5+7 =>12
```

*Example 6-3*

```
10*3 =>30
```

*Example 6-4*

```
5+4*3 =>27
```

Note that in Example 6-4, the result is 27—not 17—because Smalltalk evaluates an arithmetic expression strictly from left to right.

*Example 6-5*

```
#('what' 'time' 'is' 'it?' ) at: 3   => 'is'
```

In Example 6-5, an array is the receiver object, `at:` is the message selector, `3` is the argument (when an argument is present), and a colon is added after the message. The message requests display of the third element in the array.

*Example 6-6*

```
#(7 8 9), #(10 11 12 13)
    => (7 8 9 10 11 12 13)
```

In Example 6-6, the special character (non-digit and non-letter), comma, is the selector, which concatenates the argument with the receiver object.

*Example 6-7*

```
3 factorial between: 2+1 and: 'Time' size *5
     => True
```

Example 6-7 is a message inside messages. The expression asks whether `3 factorial` is between `2+1` and `'Time' size*5`. It is true that 6 is between 3 and 4*5=20. (`'Time' size` is 4.)

Expressions can be grouped together as a series, which can then be evaluated as a single unit. Each expression except the last expression is separated from the next with a period. If all of the messages in the series are sent to the same receiver, they can be cascaded. The receiver is written only once, and each message (except the last) is terminated with a semicolon instead of a period. For example, the following two series of expressions are equivalent:

*Example 6-8*

```
Series 1
    Pen up.
    Pen go: length.
    Pen down
```

*Example 6-9*

```
Series 2
    Pen
    up;
    go: length;
    down
```

## Variables

Smalltalk variables are containers for objects. The two types of variables used in Smalltalk are temporary variables and global variables. *Temporary variables* are declared after the program is executed, by enclosing them in pairs of vertical bars at the beginning of an expression series. Their names must begin with a lower-case letter as follows:

*Example 6-10*

```
| tempVariable   index value |
```

Temporary variables can be assigned values as follows

*Example 6-11*

```
index := 1.
tempVariable := value at: index.
^value
```

The first line in Example 6-11 assigns an object, `1`, to the temporary variable `index`. Note that the symbol for value assignment is `:=`. The second line in the example assigns the result of a message. A caret (^) symbol is used before the value to be returned as the result of the expression series.

*Global variables* are system-wide objects, which are not automatically disposed of after a program has been executed, and are not confined only to use in an expression. Global variable names always begin with an upper-case letter. When a global variable does not currently exist, a menu pops up automatically to allow the user to decide whether or not to create it. Examples of global variables available in Smalltalk are:

- Disk
- Transcript
- True

As with temporary variables, global variables can be assigned values:

*Example 6-12*

```
Family := 'David Lise Eileen Emily '
```

## *Control Structures and Iterations*

The concept of control structures and iteration in Smalltalk is similar to that of other programming languages. A control structure generally consists of a series of testing expressions and conditional executions. An iteration is composed of an index and looping statements.

***Control Structures***—Certain messages such as `odd`, `=`, `<`, `isVowel`, `isUpperCase`, and `between:` can be used to test whether an expression is true for a control structure. Examples are

```
9 odd =>true
```

```
$t= $T =>false

$C> $D =>true

$c isVowel => false

('Yellow' at:2) isVowel =>true

3/2 between: 0.5 and: 2 => true
```

The object that contains these methods, *Magnitude,* is discussed in the next section. These test expressions can be combined by using logical connectors such as `or:`, `and:`, and `not:`.

*Example 6-14*

```
(x < 3 or: [ x > 5 ])
```

In Example 6-14, a pair of parentheses is required for the whole expression and a pair of brackets is required for a testing expression after the logical connector. The test expression can be nested, as shown below.

*Example 6-15*

```
(X isDigit and: [ X < 3 or: [ X > 5 ]])
```

Example 6-15 tests whether `X` is a digit and whether its value is smaller than 3 or greater than 5. Two messages are required to express a conditional execution following the testing expressions `ifTrue:` and `ifFalse:`.

*Example 6-16*

```
(goalStack isEmpty)
ifTrue: [subgoal := nil]
ifFalse: [subgoal := goalStack].
```

Example 6-16 is a conditional execution expression. It starts from the testing expression, then the `ifTrue:` and `ifFalse:` expression, and ends with a period. The sequence of `ifTrue:` and `ifFalse:` can be reversed.

***Iterations***—Four iteration methods can be selected to send a message to an object to request an iteration service:

- `do:`
- `select:`
- `reject:`
- `collect:`

The format and special features of the four iterators are discussed below.

The *do:* message iterates across its receiver and returns all elements in the range of the arguments. The three variations of the do: format are as follows:

*Example 6-17*

```
i to: j do: [:x¦
 x timesRepeat: [
 .......
..........]]
```

*Example 6-18*

```
i to j by: k do: [:x¦
y := y+x
.......]
```

*Example 6-19*

```
#(i,j,k,l) do: [:x¦
x timesRepeat:[
.......
.......]]
```

In Example 6-17, the temporary variable x increases from i to j by 1 each time, and the expressions that follow are evaluated. This iteration format includes the compound message to: do:, which has two arguments. The receiver object i is the lower limit of the iteration, and the first argument j is the upper limit. The second argument is a block of expressions embraced by a pair of brackets. The to: do: message allows the user to specify his own increment on the receiver. In Example 6-18, the temporary variable x increases from i to j by a k increment.

The third variation of the format (Example 6-19) causes either an array, a string, or a file stream to iterate across itself. In the third example, the elements in the array i, j, k, l are substituted into x for iteration.

The *select:* message gives the user an additional feature, which selects the elements that are evaluated to be true.

*Example 6-20*

```
(#(1,10,12,16,19) select: [:x¦ x odd]
      x := y+x)
```

Example 6-20 indicates that only the odd elements in the array are substituted in the iteration.

The *reject:* iterator works just like select: except that it substitutes all elements of the receiver for which the block of expressions returns false.

*Example 6-21*

```
(#(1,10,12,16,19) reject: [:x¦ x even]
                      x :=y+x)
```

Example 6-21 performs exactly the same task as Example 6-20 even though the message is different.

The `collect:` message works exactly like the third variation of `do:` because the block of expressions returns always true.

*Example 6-22*

```
"Comment: Increase each element in the array by 5"
#(0 5 10 15 ) collect: [:x¦ x+5]
```

### *Writing a Program*

A basic program consists of a comment statement that is embraced by a pair of double quote marks (") as the title of the program, declaration of the temporary variables, and assignment of values and expressions (including control structures).

*Example 6-23*

```
"Explain how the reason originates in a reasoning process"
whyFrom: aMessage with: arguments
¦tempVariable subgoal¦
(goalStack isEmpty)
ifTrue: [subgoal := nil.
    'Because you have told me' asSymbol printOn:
    Transcript. Transcript cr.]
ifFalse: [subgoal := goalStack removeLast.
    'To prove ' asSymbol printOn: Transcript.
    ((subgoal at: 1) at:3) printOn: Transcript. Transcript
    cr].
tempVariable := self perform: aMessage withArguments:
    arguments.
Subgoal isNil ifFalse: [goalStack addLast: subgoal].
^tempVariable!
```

In Example 6-23, the first line is a comment about the title of the program and the second line is the declaration of local variables. Because no assignment is required for the local variables, the first expression—`(goalStack isEmpty)`—appears. The local variables are assigned in the condition statements that follow the first expression.

## Evaluating Expressions

Three commands can be chosen to evaluate expressions: *show it, do it,* and *save.* To evaluate an expression or a short series of expressions, activate the text pane, select the expression or the series of expressions, and select one of the three commands. A long series of expressions is better stored in a file such as *prntst7.st*. The `fileIn` message is used to compose an expression as follows:

*Example 6-24*

```
(file pathName: 'prntst7.st') fileIn
```

The directory browse window is activated, Example 6-24 is selected, and *do it* is chosen to evaluate the expression.

# *Smalltalk System Operations*

Basic system operations include saving the image and exiting the Smalltalk environment.

## Saving the Image

The *image* is the current state of the Smalltalk environment, which is changed constantly when objects (both code and data) are modified or edited. The image is read from the *image* file when the system starts up. If the image is saved when completed, it resumes exactly as it was last modified, the next time the system starts up.

To save an image, pop up the system menu, select *exit Smalltalk*, and then choose *save image* from the submenu that pops up after exit selection.

## Exiting Smalltalk

The *exit* command from the system menu is selected to exit the environment. A submenu with three choices appears. The three choices are

| | |
|---|---|
| *Save image* | Causes the state of the environment, including the location and contents of all windows, to be saved. |
| *Forget image* | Causes all changes made since Smalltalk was started to be forgotten. |
| *Continue* | Returns to the environment as if nothing were selected from the menu. |

These three commands can be used any time during consultation of the environment without loss of continuity.

## Printing the Entire Screen

To dump the entire screen, press the ⟨F2⟩ function key on the keyboard.

# Classes and Their Programming

The concept of classes is one of the most distinctive features of Smalltalk. Together with the other three concepts—objects, messages, and methods—it forms the basis of programming to solve problems. Objects, messages, and methods have been discussed in the previous section. This section focuses on the major classes available in Smalltalk/V and how to program them.

## *Definition of Classes*

Classes describe data structures (objects), algorithms (methods) and external interfaces (messages). Each object is an instance of a certain class. All objects in a class are similar because they share the same structure and respond to the same class messages and methods. The classes themselves are objects that are contained in global variables. Consequently, all classes begin with an upper-case letter.

Classes form a hierarchy that consists of a root class, *Object*, and many subclasses. Subclasses in turn may contain more layers of subclasses. Each class inherits the functionality of its superclasses in the organization. A class builds on its superclasses by adding its own methods and "instance variables" to characterize its behavior. Instance variables are internal variables accessible only to the objects to which they belong. They are similar to fields in a record structure and contain either pointers, words, or bytes. Most object instance variables contain pointers.

Smalltalk provides on the order of 100 classes for selection, modification, and editing, to meet the needs of various applications. The major classes that serve as the basic building blocks for most AI/expert system applications include:

- Magnitude
- Stream (input/output)
- File and Directory (DOS system interface)
- Collection
- Classes for graphics
- Classes for windows

Each of these classes contains more subclasses; the discussion in this chapter focuses on the critical subclasses. A summary of all classes is presented in Appendix C.

Before the details of these critical classes are discussed, we will first concentrate on how to program a class—that is, how to modify its class methods and instance methods to meet the needs of an application.

# *Programming Class Features*

To program class features, pop up the class hierarchy browser window by selecting *browse class* in the system menu. This window allows you to browse through and modify existing methods and class definitions, and to create new ones. The five types of method and class features that can be created are global variables, instance methods, class methods, class variables, and new classes. Each requires a different format and is discussed separately.

## Adding Global Variables

The procedure for adding global variables is as follows:

1. Install the relevant file by evaluating (clicking *do it*) the following expression:

   ```
   (file pathname: 'your filename') fileIn
   ```

2. Activate the *class hierarchy browser window* by clicking *browse classes*.
3. Pop up the class list pane menu and select *update*.
4. Select the target class.
5. Create global variables by assigning global variables to the class and methods. For example, to create a new dog in the subclass *Dog* of the class *Animal*, which has a method of *name*, you need to write the following expressions:

   ```
   "creating a dog, Snoopy"
   Snoopy := Dog new.
   Snoopy name: 'Snoopy'
   ```

   Note that `new` is used to create a new variable, `Snoopy`.
6. Pop up the pane menu and select *save*.

## Modifying and Adding an Instance Method

The procedure for modifying or adding an instance method is

Steps 1 through 4: Same as those used for adding global variables.

Step 5: Select *instance* by clicking the right mouse button when the cursor is over *instance*.

Step 6: Select the appropriate method for modification that shows in the top right pane above *instance*.

Step 7: Modify the code in the text pane or add a new method by changing its name as well as its contents.

Step 8: Evaluate the new code by selecting *save*.

Step 9: The new name, if any, will appear in the top right pane.

## Adding Class Variables

Class variables are global variables that are accessible to all instances of a class. They begin with an upper-case letter. The procedure for adding a class variable to a class is as follows:

Steps 1 through 4: Same as those used for adding global variables.

Step 5: Edit the class definition to include the string of the new class name following the `classVariableNames:` selector.

Step 6: Pop up the pane menu and select *save*.

Step 7: Add the class variable name to related methods to connect it to the class functions.

## Adding a Class Method

The procedure for adding a class method is as follows:

Steps 1 through 4: Same as those used in adding a global variable.

Step 5: Select the pane labeled *class* by clicking the right mouse button.

Step 6: Pop up the method list pane menu and select *new method*.

Step 7: Create the new method by following the template shown in the text pane.

Step 8: Pop up the pane menu and select *save*.

## Adding a Class

The procedure for adding a subclass to a class is as follows:

Steps 1 through 4: Same as those for adding global variables.

Step 5: Pop up the pane menu and select *add subclass*.

Step 6: A prompter appears to ask for the name of the subclass. Enter the name and press the ⟨Return⟩ key.

Step 7: Another menu appears. Select *variable Subclass*.

Step 8: Specify the new class's instance variables by following the template shown in the text pane.

Step 9: Pop up the pane menu and select *save*.

# *Magnitude*

The Magnitude class defines objects that can be compared, measured, ordered, and counted, such as characters, numbers, dates, and times that are frequently used. The hierarchy of the Magnitude class is shown as follows:

Superclass (inherits from): Object

Superclass (inherited by):

- Association
- Character
- Date
- Number
  - Float
  - Fraction
  - Integer
    - LargeNegativeInteger
    - LargePositiveInteger
    - SmallInteger
- Time

Magnitude assumes that its subclasses implement ordering relationship and comparison methods such as `=`, `<=`, `>=`, `<`, `>`, and `=`. Based on these methods, Magnitude provides its subclasses with interval testing (`between:`) and max/min computation.

*Example 6-25*

```
11 between: 20 and: 10 => True
25 max: 30 => 30
25 min: 30 => 30
```

The definition of these classes can be found in Appendix C. The most frequently used subclasses—*Number*, *Character*, *Date* and *Time*—are discussed below.

## Number

The class *Number* implements binary arithmetic operators such as `+`, `-`, `*`, `/`, `quo` (integer quotient), `rem` (integer remainder), `raisedTo` (raised to the power of), and `log`. It also supports other unary arithmetic operators, such as `sqrt`, `exp`, `cos`, `arcSin`, `tan`, `ln`, `floor` (nearest integer less than or equal to), `ceiling`, `reciprocal`, `truncated`, and `rounded`. Number also implements testing methods such as `even`, `odd`, `negative`, `positive` (true if $>=0$), `strictlyPositive` (true if $>0$) and `sign` ($-1$ if negative, 1 if positive, and 0 if zero). Internal testing and max/min methods are inherited from the superclass, Magnitude. All iteration methods are implemented in Number also.

Class Number supports three subclasses: Float (for floating point), Fraction (for rational), and Integer (for integer). Real numbers in the subclass *Float* are represented in an 8-byte IEEE format and are given approximately 18 digits of precision in the value range of $(\pm)$ 4.19 e $-307$ to $(\pm)$ 1.67 e 308. A math co-processor is required to perform arithmetic operations in Float.

Rational numbers are represented by instances of the subclass

*Fraction* and are described by a pair of integers (instance variables numerator and denominator)—for example:

```
5/4
```

In this example, the slash message is sent to the integer receiver, 5, with an integer argument 3 to form a fraction.

Class *Integer* contains integers as its instance. The class is divided into three subclasses—*LargeNegativeInteger*, *LargePositiveInteger*, and *SmallInteger*—for high efficiency in computing speed and memory requirements. For example, small integers are not represented as objects in memory and their values are between −16,384 and 16,383. Large integers, however, can be represented with up to 64K bytes of precision.

## Character

The class *Character* contains the extended ASCII character set from ASCII value 0 to ASCII 255. Characters need not be created and may be referenced by either of the two messages, `asCharacter` or `value:`.

*Example 6-26*

```
65 asCharacter  => $A
Character value: 65 => $A
```

Interval testing and comparison methods are inherited from the class Magnitude.

*Example 6-27*

```
$B <$F =>True
75 asCharacter max: $F => $K
$d between: $A and $E => False
$d asUpperCase => $D
```

## Date and Time

Instances of the class *Date* represent specific dates such as January 3, 1987. Instances of the class *Time* indicate specific times such as 3:00 am. A variety of methods for the classes Date and Time exist. They can be identified by their names, which contain terms such as day, date, month, or time. Testing and comparison methods are inherited from class Magnitude. Examples of simple Date or Time expressions are given below.

*Example 6-28*

```
Date today
Time now
Date newDay: 4 month: #January year: 1987
```

New global variables such as Birthday or Lunchtime can be created for comparison of dates. For example, if *Birthday* is created with the expression:

```
Smalltalk at: #Birthday put: '1 January 1987' asDate
```

then we can make the following comparison:

*Example 6-29*

```
Birthday > Date newDay => false
Birthday  max: Date newDay => 'January 4, 1987'
```

# *Stream (Input/Output)*

The Stream class is used to access file devices and internal objects as sequences of characters, to scan input, and to write edited output. It uses access messages to get or put the next object at the current position. The hierarchy of class Stream is as follows:

Superclass: Object

Subclasses:

- ReadStream
- WriteStream
  - ReadWriteStream
    - FileStream
    - TerminalStream

To create an input stream, as in instances of subclasses ReadStream and WriteStream, the `on:` message with a string as the argument is used. For example, the variable `familyAnimals` is created to accept the stream read from the text pane in Example 6-30 below.

*Example 6-30*

```
familyAnimals := ReadStream on:
        #(Cat Dog Mouse Goldfish).
```

Important messages for screening the input stream include:

| | |
|---|---|
| `fileIn` | Reads and executes Smalltalk source code chunks from the receiver. If a chunk starts with `!` send it the message `fileInFrom: self` (read chunks from a stream until an empty chunk—a single `!` is found). |
| `next: anInteger` | Answers a collection of the next `anInteger` elements of the stream and advances the stream position by an integer. |

| | |
|---|---|
| `skipTo: anObject` | Sets the stream position beyond the next occurrence of `anObject` in the stream. Answers true when there is an occurrence. |
| `atEnd` | Answers true if the receiver is positioned beyond the last object. |

Examples of these messages are shown below.

*Example 6-31*

```
(File pathname: 'chapter7.st') fileIn
familyAnimal isEmpty => false
familyAnimal next:2 => (Cat Dog)
familyAnimal skipTo: #Dog => true
```

The first example is discussed in class File. The remaining three examples are self-explanatory. Important messages for writing streams are

| | |
|---|---|
| `contents` | Answers the collection over which the receiver is streaming. |
| `next put: anObject` | Writes an object to the receiver stream `anInteger` times and answers `anObject`. |
| `cr` | Writes line-terminating characters to the stream. |
| `space` | Writes a space character to the stream. |
| `nextPutAll: aCollection` | Writes the elements of a collection to the stream at once and answers a collection. |

The above messages need to be combined with the message `printOn:` whose argument is a stream to produce a character description of the receiver object on the argument stream. For example, to print a rectangle, the message `printOn:` is sent to the origin and corner points and the message `nextPutAll:` is sent to write the corner point to the stream.

*Example 6-32*

```
origin printOn : aStream.
aStream nextPutAll: 'corner:'
corner printOn: aStream
```

You then need to read and write arrays of objects in a program such as:

*Example 6-33*

```
"Read and Write an arrays of Object"
|input output anArray|
input := ReadStream on: anArray.
output := WriteStream on: Array new.
[input atEnd]
```

```
whileFalse := [output nextPut: input next aMessage].
^output contents
```

In the above example, aMessage represents a message sent to input next. anArray can be an array of objects. If you wish to produce a printed report, you must create a subclass, PrintStream, under class WriteStream, and the following sample expressions can be modified:

```
Printer  := PrintStream new
"print the report on the printer"
x   y..........
..........
Printer
NextPutAll:  X,' ';
NextPutAll: y;
cr]
```

# File and Directory (DOS System Interface)

Classes File and Directory together provide you with a facility for obtaining files stored in a DOS directory. Both classes are subclasses of class Object and have no subclass of their own. The most useful expression often combines messages from the two classes to read a file that contains a Smalltalk program code as follows:

*Example 6-34*

```
(File Pathname: 'c:\Smaltalk\chapter7') fileIn
```

In the example, File is a message from class Directory; pathname: is a message from class File; and fileIn is a message from class Stream as also shown in Example 6-31. The disk name and pathname in the example may not be required if the defaulted values are used.

Other useful methods include:

copy: oldFile to: newFile—Transfers the file named oldFile into the file named newFile.

remove: aString—Removes a file named aString.

close—Closes the file.

create: newPathName—Creates a DOS directory on disk with complete pathname, newPathName.

# Collection

The class Collection is the superclass of all the collection classes. Collections are the basic structures used to store objects in groups in an organized manner. Two kinds of collections have already been discussed: *arrays* and *strings*. Arrays are fixed-size sequences of objects, and strings are fixed-size sequences of characters. The hierarchy of class Collection is as follows:

Superclass: Object

Superclass:

- Bag
- IndexedCollection
  - FixedSizeCollection
  - Array
  - ByteArray
  - Interval
  - String
    - Symbol
  - OrderedCollection
    - SortedCollection
  - Set
    - Dictionary
      - IdentityDictionary

The definition of these classes can be found in Appendix C. Among them, the most frequently used classes are Dictionary, Bag, and Set. The features, attributes, and common protocol of Collection and the special characteristics of the three subclasses are discussed below.

## Features, Attributes, and Common Protocol of Class Collection

Any subclass in class Collection generally provides the following capabilities to the user:

- Searching, adding, removing, accessing, and changing elements of a collection
- Iterating over the elements of a collection

The four attributes that characterize a collection class are

- Order of the elements in a collection
- Flexibility of collection size, fixed or expandable
- Duplicability of collection elements
- Accessibility of a collection by a set of keys

The attributes of the three most frequently used classes are shown in Table 6-1.

**Table 6-1**
***Attributes of frequently used Collection subclasses***

| Class | Ordered | Fixed Size | Element Dup's | Key | Class |
|---|---|---|---|---|---|
| Bag | No | No | Yes | None | Any |
| Set | No | No | No | None | Any |
| Dictionary | No | No | No | Lookup | Any |

A special message—`with:`—can be used to create an instance of any collection class as follows:

```
with: firstObject
with: secondObject
with: thirdObject
with: fourthObject
```

For example, assume you want to create a parts base in which there are two global variables: Engine and Battery. Because arbitrary objects and duplicates may be used in the base class, Bag is more appropriate, so initialize the variable as follows:

*Example 6-35*

```
Engine:= Bag with: #GM
             with: #Toyota
             with: #Ford
             with: #Nissan
Battery:= Bag with: #(Sears JCPenny)
```

Common protocol for manipulating collections includes adding, removing, and testing messages and iteration messages such as `do:` and `select:` to process all elements of a collection. Examples are

```
Engine add: #Mazda =>Mazda
Engine remove: #GM =>GM
Engine size =>4
Engine addAll: Battery  =>(Sears JCPenny)
Engine select: [ :aPart ¦ aPart == #Mazda]
Engine includes: #Mazda =>true
```

## Dictionary

Class Dictionary stores and retrieves objects with an external lookup key. A dictionary can be easily created using Dictionary. For example, you can create a *ClientDictionary* as follows:

*Example 6-36*

```
ClientDictionary := Dictionary new
```

In Example 6-36, `ClientDictionary` is a global variable and `new` is a message indicating it is a new variable. You can perform the following tasks with *ClientDictionary*:

- Add telephone numbers to it, using `at: put:`

  ```
  ClientDictionary
                  at: 'David' put:  '582-0000'
                  at: 'Lise' put:  '583-1111'
  ```

- Retrieve a telephone number, using `at:`

  ```
  ClientDictionary at: 'David' => '582-0000'
  ```

- Check whether a name is in the directory, using `at: ifAbsent`

  ```
  ClientDictionary at: 'Emily' ifAbsent: ['not in the
  Directory']
  ```

- Review all names in the directory, using `inspect`

  ```
  ClientDictionary inspect
  ```

Be sure to follow the above formats precisely with respect to the keys and arguments of the messages.

## Bag and Set

Class *Bag* stores an arbitrary number of objects of any kind, including duplicates. The elements in the bag are not stored with any implied order or sequence. Messages that are used to create, add, retrieve, and test elements in a bag are shown in Example 6-35. These are the common protocols available in class Collection.

Class *Set* like Bag, stores arbitrary objects. However, Set does not store the same object more than once. The common messages available for class Collection are inherited in Set. The special message that is unique to this class is ***asSet***. The message `asSet` can be used to create a set out of the receiver collection object that eliminates duplicates from the collection. For example, to calculate the odd numbers in a string, evaluate the following expression:

```
'1 2 2 3 3 3 3 4 5 5' asSet select: :x¦ x odd]
```

# *Class for Making Graphics*

Smalltalk graphics are generated by bit-mapped operation. A bit map is a linear array of bits. Each bit has a value of 1 or 0, with 1 representing white and 0 representing black. Four classes are involved in bit-mapped graphics:

Point, Rectangle, Form, and BitBlt. Points are used to refer to the position of an individual dot within a bit map. Rectangles are employed to denote areas in which a group of dots can be moved from one place to another. Dots are displayed on a monitor screen as colored pixels and stored internally as a bit map that is contained in a form. Due to the complexity of bit-mapped operation, class BitBlt is needed to handle moves of blocks of bits.

## Point

A point uses two instance variables to represent a dot's location. X represents the column (horizontal) coordinate and y represents the row (vertical) coordinate. The `@` message is sent to an integer to create a point. For example:

```
5 @ 6
```

Three important features of point operations are

- `x:` and `y:` messages can be sent to alter the coordinates of a point.

  ```
  (10 @ 120)  X: 60 =>60 @ 120
  (10 @ 120)  y: 100 =>10 @ 100
  ```

- `x` and `y` messages can be sent to retrieve the coordinates of a point.

  ```
  (10 @ 120) x =>10
  (10 @ 120) y =>120
  ```

- Points can be compared and point operations performed arithmetically.

  ```
  (-1 @ 50) < (0 @ 60) => true
  (-1 @ 50) max: (-2 @ 60) =>(-1 @ 60)
  (-1 @ 50) + (-2 @ 60) => (-3 @ 110)
  (-1 @ 50) dotProduct: (-2 @ 60) => 3002
  (-1 @ 50) Transpose => (50 @ -1)
  ```

## Rectangle

A rectangle is represented by two points: the *original* (the upper left point) and the *corner* (the lower right point). Its width and height can be calculated by

```
width := corner x - origin x
height := corner y - origin y
```

The above expression can be used to represent the extension of the rectangle from the original point as follows:

```
extent := corner - origin
```

A rectangle is created by sending the `corner:` or `extent:` message to a point.

```
0 @ 1 corner: 50 @ 50

0 @ 1 extent: 50 @ 49
```

Major Rectangle operations include `top`, `bottom`, `left`, `right`, `center`, `width`, `height`, `origin`, `corner`, `containsPoint:`, `expandedBy:`, `insetBy:`, `intersect:`, `merge:`, `translateBy:`, `moveBy:`, and `moveTo:`. Consider the rectangles *Box1* and *Box2* to illustrate some of these messages.

```
Box1 := 10 @ 5 corner: 100 @ 125

Box2 := 50 @ 60 corner: 180 @ 120
```

Examples of Rectangle operations using these two rectangles are given below.

```
Box1 top =>5

Box2 bottom =>120

Box1 left =>10

Box2 right =>180

Box2 containsPoint 100 @ 100 =>true

Box1 merge Box2 =>10 @ 5 corner: 180 @ 125

Box2 moveTo: Box1 corner => 100 @ 125: 230 @ 185
```

## Form

Class *Form* is a subclass of class *DisplayMedium,* which is a subclass of class *DisplayObject.* Both parent classes are abstract classes and contain no data. A form is used to provide a two-dimensional view for a Bitmap. The three major variables in Form operations are `bits`, `width`, and `height`. The variable `bits` contains a Bitmap, the content of the form that is represented by the other two variables as follows:

```
0 @ 0 extent:(width @ height)
```

Major messages that can be sent to class Form to create new forms are

`width: w height: h`—Answers a white form whose width is `w` and whose height is `h`, and allocates its bit map with the appropriate size.

`displayAt: clippingBox`—Displays the contents of a form on a restricted screen area.

`outputToPrinter`—Prints the contents of a form on a printer.

`copyForm:` or `copy: From: to: rule:`—Copies the contents of one form onto another form.

Examples of these messages include:

```
white:= Form width: 60 height: 120  "This example creates a
     white Form of (60 @ 120)"

white displayAt: 50 @ 50 clippingBox: aRectangle "To display
     the white box at 50 @ 50 within aRectangle."

(Form new width: 100 height: 100 initialByte: 16rF0)
outputToPrinter      "To create a new Form and display at the
                     printer."
```

# BitBlt

Class BitBlt has two subclasses: CharacterScreen (for writing text) and Pen (for drawing). BitBlt is used to move a rectangular area of bits from one portion of a form or display screen to another. The source rectangle is defined as

```
sourceX  @ sourceY extent: width @ height
```

The destination rectangle is defined as

```
destX @ destY extent: width @ height
```

and the clipping rectangle to restrict your bit transfer to a designated rectangle is defined as

```
clipX  @ clipY extent: clipWidth @ clipHeight
```

The source form must be either nil or an instance of Form or its subclasses.

The following messages are used to move one form to another:

`destForm: sourceForm`—Specifies the destination and source form.

`copyBits`—Moves bits from one place to another.

`drawLoop X: xDelta Y: yDelta`—Draws a line from the destination origin to a point of Delta distance to the original.

A sample code that employs some of these messages to move the top left quarter of the screen to the right is shown in Example 6-36.

*Example 6-36*

```
(BitBlt destForm: Display sourceForm: Display) "Display used
   as both the source and destination Form"
sourceRect: (0 @  0 extent: Display extent / / 2); "The top
   left quarter of Display is the source rectangle"
destOrigin: (Display width / / 2 @ 0); "The top center point
   is the destination origin"
copyBits  "Move the bits"
```

A gray tone effect can be created by using messages such as `Form gray`, `black`, `darkGray`, and `lightGray` as shown in Example 6-37.

*Example 6-37*

```
(BitBlt destForm: Display sourceForm: nil)
mask: Form gray;
destRect: (0 @ 0 extent: 100 @ 100);
copyBits
```

Note that in the second line of the example, `gray` can be changed to any of the shades mentioned in the message, such as `black` or `darkGrey`.

Class CharacterScanner, a subclass of BitBlt, can be used to write text. To allow various styles of writing, the instance methods of class Font are used. Some useful messages are

`Font: aFont`—Specifies `aFont` as the current font.

`setFont: aFont`—Changes the font to `aFont`.

The following sample program displays *`I love you.`* at the top left corner of the screen using an initial font of 8 lines height (8 by 8 pixels) and then switching to a font of 14 lines (8 by 14 pixels).

*Example 6-38*

```
"Display ' I love you.'"
CharacterScanner new
initialize: Display boundingBox
font: Font eightLine
display:'I love you.' at 0 @ 0;
setplay: Font fourteenLine;
display: 'I love you.' at: 40 @ 0
```

Class Pen is used to draw pictures. It has three parameters: `location`, `direction`, and `downState`.

`location`—Tells the pen where to start the next movement.

`direction`—Calculates the ending point when the `go:` message is used.

`downState`—When true, the pen draws as it moves; otherwise, the pen moves without drawing

Useful messages include:

`black`—Changes the pen color to black.

`gray`—Changes the pen color to gray.

`white`—Change the pen color to white.

`direction: aNumber`—Sets the direction to `aNumber` degrees.

`home`—Centers the pen on the destination form.

`north`—Sets the direction to 270 degrees.

`place: aPoint`—Positions the receiver pen at `aPoint`.

`go: distance`—Moves the receiver pen for the length of `distance`.

`goto: aPoint`—Moves the receiver pen to `aPoint`.

`down`—Sets down the pen.

`up`—Lifts up the pen.

These messages are employed to create `aForm`, which is executed by either of the following expressions:

```
Pen new aForm

Pen new
```

`aForm` contains parameters about location and direction. Its `downState` is equal to true. `Pen new` draws on `display` rather than on `aForm`.

The use of these messages is illustrated in Example 6-39.

*Example 6-39*

```
pen
  home;
  north.
side timesRepeat:[
  pen
     up;
     go:length / / 2;
     down;
     go: length. "length is a local variable"
  side - 1 timesRepeat: [
          pen
```

```
                turn: 360 // sides; "side is a local variable"
                go: length]]
```

Class Pen has a subclass called Animation, which contains several collections of images of the objects in motion, and displays forms continuously to create the illusion of a moving object, as in a cartoon. Useful messages include:

`tell: name bounce: increment`—Tells the object with the `name` to bounce for `increment` distance.

`tell: name direction: anInteger`—Tells object `name` to change its direction to `anInteger`.

`tell: name go: distance`—Tells object `name` to go for `distance`.

`tell: name place: aPoint`—Tells object `name` to be placed at `aPoint`.

`tell: name turn: anInteger`—Tells object `name` to turn by `anInteger` degrees.

`speed: anInteger`—Changes the distance between consecutive copies to `anInteger`. The larger the distance, the faster the object moves.

`shiftRate: anInteger`—Displays the current picture `anInteger` times before going to the next picture.

Examples of sending these messages are:

```
tell: 'David' bound 800;

tell: 'Lise' go: 360;

tell: 'Eileen' direction: -180;

tell: 'Emily' place 0 @ 50;

speed: 24; "each picture is displayed 6 pixels apart."

shiftRate: 4
```

## *Classes for Manipulating Windows*

The window operation is one of the most useful features in Smalltalk. Windows facilitate the man-machine interface. A window requires the working of three types of classes: the *application* classes such as ClassBrowser or DiskBrowser, to synchronize panes; the *Pane* class to display the window on the screen; and the *dispatching* classes to process mouse and keyboard inputs. Each of the three types of classes contains several subclasses. The main functions of the three types of classes can be summarized as follows:

1. Application classes

   a. Remember the current state
   b. Create panes
   c. Initialize contents of panes
   d. Carry out communication and synchronization
   e. Define menus for panes

2. Pane class, contains two subclasses (TopPane and SubPane), which serve slightly different purposes.

   a. TopPane

      - Display the window frame and evoke each subpane to display its pane contents.
      - Save, display, and highlight the window label.
      - Activate the window and all subpanes.
      - Answer whether the window contains a certain point.
      - Close the top pane and invoke each subpane to close itself.

   b. SubPane (with three subclass, Graph Pane, ListPane, and TextPane)

      - Display the pane frame.
      - Activate itself.
      - Answer whether the pane contains a certain point.
      - Display a portion of its data in the pane.
      - Scroll data in four directions.
      - Make a selection on a piece of data.
      - Close itself.

3. Dispatching classes, such as Dispatch, Prompter, and DispatchManager

   a. Dispatch

      - Activate or deactivate the corresponding pane.
      - Return the cursor to the upper left corner of its pane.
      - Open or close the window.
      - Cycle windows or panes in the window.

   b. Prompter

      - Show the intended question.
      - Edit the answer.

   c. DispatchManager

      - Schedule all windows.

You generally need to be concerned only with application classes because they must be written for each application. The Pane and dispatching classes and their subclasses are predefined building blocks in the system. The remaining discussion in this section concerns use of existing standard windows and creation of new windows.

## Using Standard Windows

Standard windows can be used to perform the following tasks:

- Display and edit files on a given directory by opening a *disk browser window.*
- Display and edit the interrelationship of classes by opening a *class hierarchy browser window.*
- Examine and edit objects by opening an *inspector window.*
- Review and debug a program at the point of error by opening *walkback* and *debug windows.*

### *Display and Edit Files*

You can browse the files on a disk drive to display and edit them, by activating a *disk browser window.*

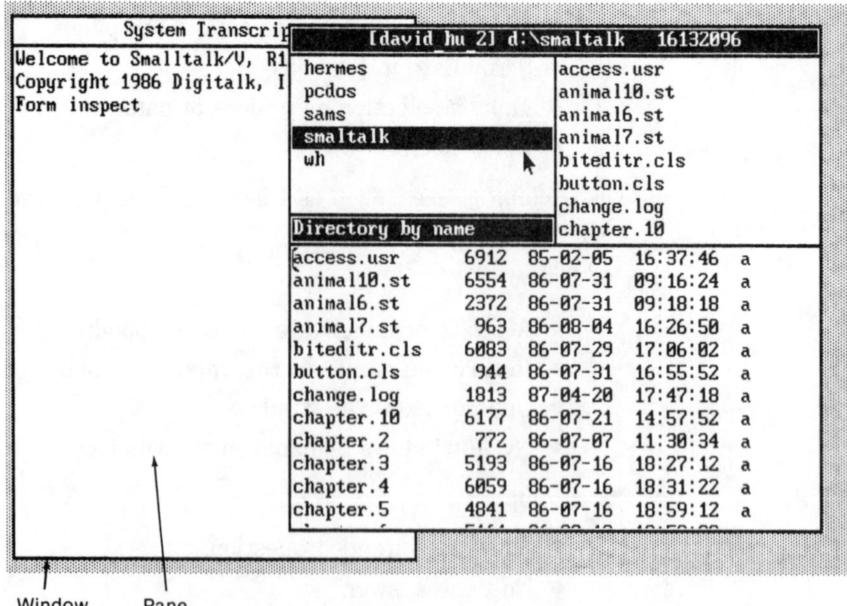


**Figure 6-3**
***The structure of a disk browser window***

A disk browser window contains four panes, as shown in Figure 6-3. They are

- The *directory hierarchy list pane*, located in the upper left corner, lists the names of all files in the directory selected.
- The *file list pane*, located to the right of the directory hierarchy list pane, displays the files under the subdirectory selected in the directory hierarchy list pane.
- The *contents (text) pane*, located in the bottom of the window, displays the text of a selected file.
- The *directory order pane*, located between the directory hierarchy list pane and the contents pane, contains a statement regarding the order of subdirections.

The following tasks can be performed to display and edit files:

To open a disk browser window:

- Select *browse disk* on the system menu.
- Input the disk drive name at the prompt.
- Size the window by fixing the upper left and lower right corners.

To select a directory to browse:

- Move the cursor into the directory hierarchy list pane.
- Press the right mouse button when the cursor is on top of the target directory, to display directory operation choices:

  *remove* eliminates a subdirectory and its file from the disk.

  *update* browses another disk in the same drive. If the disk is a hard disk, it merely reinitializes the disk.

  *create* creates a new directory as a subdirectory of the target directory.
- Select the desired choice and press the right mouse button.

To select a file to browse:

- Move the cursor into the file list pane (the upper right pane).
- Press the left mouse button to select the target file.
- Press the right mouse button to display file operation choices:

  *remove* eliminates the selected file.

  *rename* changes the file name.

  *copy* duplicates the file in another location.

  *print* prints the selected file.

  *create* generates an empty new file.
- Select the desired choice and press the right mouse button.

To edit the contents of a file:

The contents (text) pane shows the complete file for editing. The procedure for editing a text pane, discussed in the "Text Editing" section of this chapter, can be applied here.

To display a directory:

- Move the cursor into the directory order pane (between the directory list and text pane—see Figure 6-3).
- Press the left mouse button.
- Press the right mouse button to display the choices:

  *data order* orders files by data.

  *name order* orders files by name.

  *size order* orders files by size.

- Press the left mouse button to select the desired choice.

## *Display and Edit the Interrelationship of Classes*

You can use a class hierarchy browser window to display and edit the interrelationship of classes.

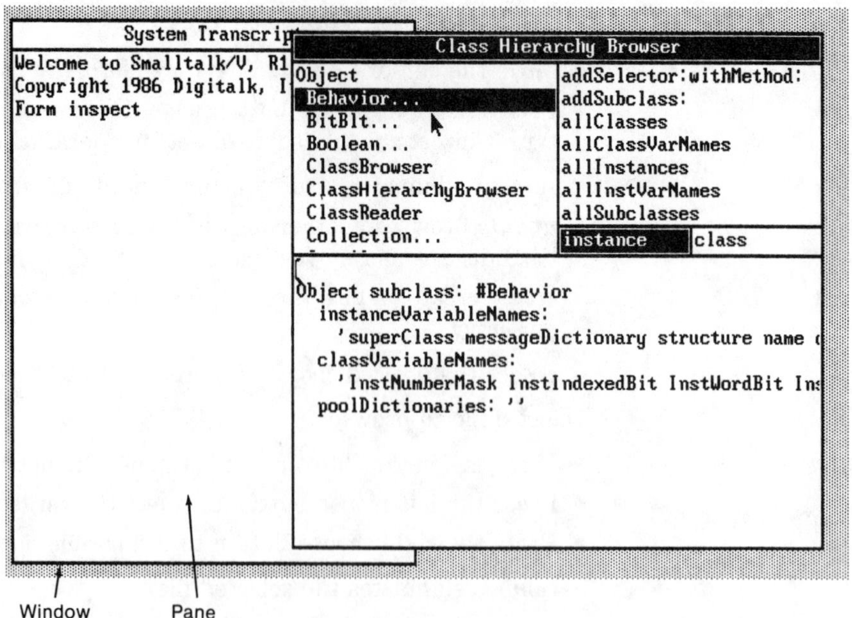


**Figure 6-4**
***Sample class hierarchy browser window***

The class hierarchy browser window in Figure 6-4 contains five panes:

- The *class hierarchy list pane*, located in the upper left, displays the names of all the classes in the system.

- The *method list pane,* located to the right of the class hierarchy list pane, displays the methods for either the class or instance selected in the class or instance pane.
- The *instance* and *class panes,* located beneath the method list pane, lets you select either the instance method or the class method, respectively.
- The *content pane,* located at the bottom of the window, displays the contents of the code selected.

The following tasks can be performed to display and edit the interrelationship of classes:

To open a class hierarchy browser window:

- Select *browse class* on the system menu.
- Size the window.

To select a class to display:

- Move the cursor into the class hierarchy list pane.
- Press the left mouse button when the cursor is on top of the target class.
- Press the right mouse button to display the following choices on the selected class:

  *file out* writes the class definition and related data to a file with the class name plus the extension `.cls`.

  *update* updates the class file.

  *hide/show* displays the subclasses of the selected class and hides those of other classes.

  *add-subclass* adds a subclass.

  *browse* displays the content of a class.

To add a subclass:

- Select the superclass from the class hierarchy list pane.
- Pop up the pane menu and select *add subclass.*
- Input the subclass name at the prompt.
- Select one of the following choices:

  *named instance variable*

  *indexed instance variable*

  *word arrays*

  *byte arrays*

To browse a class:

- Select *browse* from the class hierarchy list pane (by pressing the right mouse button when the cursor is in the class hierarchy list pane).

- Size the selected class browser window.
- Select methods to display, edit, or create.

To change a class definition—change the instance variables, class variables, etc. of a class.

- Select the target class from the class hierarchy list pane, to display the text in the contents pane.
- Edit the text in the contents pane.
- Select *save* from the contents pane menu (by pressing the right mouse button to display the choices).

To remove classes:

- Confirm the name of the class to be removed.
- Evaluate the following expression in the text pane: `nameOfClass removeFromSystem.`

To display methods:

- Move the cursor into either the instance or class pane and click the left mouse button.
- Move the cursor into the methods list and press the right mouse button to display the choices for method manipulation:

  *remove* removes a method.

  *new method* adds a new method.

  *sender* searches and displays the methods that send a message with the chosen message selector.

  *implementers* search and display the classes that implement the method of the chosen message selector.

To add a method:

- Select *new method* from the methods list pane.
- Edit an existing method or create a new method in the contents pane.
- Select *save* from the contents pane menu (by pressing the right mouse button to display all choices).
- Check whether the new method's name is added to the methods list pane.

To remove a method:

- Select *remove* from the methods list pane menu.
- Check whether the method name is deleted from the methods list pane.

To modify a method:

- Select the target method from the methods list pane to display the code in the contents pane.

- Edit the code.
- Select *save* from the contents pane menu.

## *Examine and Edit Objects*

An *inspector* window is opened to examine and change objects in the system. It is a low-level debugging aid. As shown in Figure 6-5, an inspector window has two panes: *instance variable list* and *contents*.

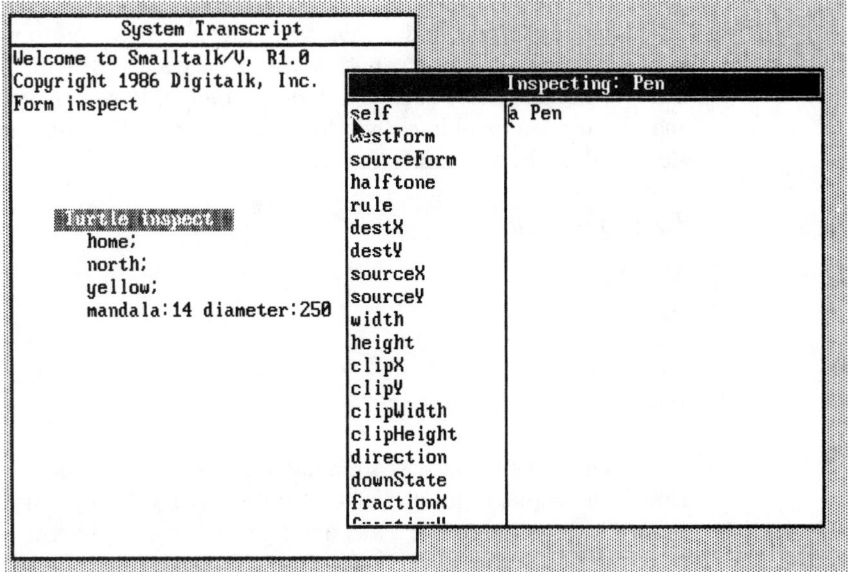


**Figure 6-5**
***Sample inspector window***

The following tasks can be performed by using an inspector window:

To open an inspector window to inspect an object other than a dictionary:

- Select the object to be inspected—for example, a global variable, `Demo`.
- Evaluate the following expression: `Demo inspect`.
- Select a variable for inspection from the instance variable list.
- Edit or evaluate the text in the contents pane to examine the object.
- Select *inspect* from the variable list pane menu to open another inspect window.

To open a dictionary inspector to inspect a dictionary:

- Select the dictionary to be inspected.

- Evaluate the following expression:
  `NameOfDictionaryInspect.`
- Select one of the following choices from the list pane:

  *remove* removes a selected key.

  *inspect* opens another inspector window.

  *add* adds a new element to the dictionary.

## *Review and Debug a Program*

A *walkback* window and a *debug* window are provided to review and debug a program. When an error is detected, a walkback window pops up automatically. You must request a debug window, however, by selecting a command from the walkback window menu. The following sample program is designed to draw a multi-mandala.

*Example 6-40*

```
Turtle
home;
north;
yellow;
mandala: a4 diameter: 250
```

When the *show it* command from the text pane menu is selected, Smalltalk/V picks the obvious error `a` and puts a highlighted "undefined" before it to indicate that `a` has been not defined. The error `a` is then changed to `1` because it was a typographical error. Following this correction, *do it* is clicked to rerun the mandala program. Another error is detected and this time a walkback window, as shown in Figure 6-6, appears on the screen, partially overlapping the original window.

The walkback window contains two panes: *label* (on the top) and *text* (on the bottom). The label describes the error (for example, `message not understood: yellow`). The text pane exhibits the methods called (or messages sent) that led to the error, in a reversed nest order (that is, the most recent send listed first). On each line of the text, the class of the receiver (for example, Pen) is given and the class in which the method is defined appears next in parentheses (for example, Object). The string follows the method, and the symbol `>>` is the message selector (for example, `doesNotUnderstand`). The message in the walkback window indicates that `yellow` is an undefined variable. At this point, you must take one of three actions to continue:

- If the walkback window has provided enough information to enable you to locate the error, move the cursor over the top pane of the window, click the right mouse button, and select *close* to close the window and correct the problem.
- Move the cursor over the text pane of the walkback window and

press the right mouse button to select *resume*, if the walkback window occurred intentionally—for example, following a control-break-interrupt (caused by typing the ⟨Break⟩ key) or a `halt` message. The walkback window closes and execution continues.

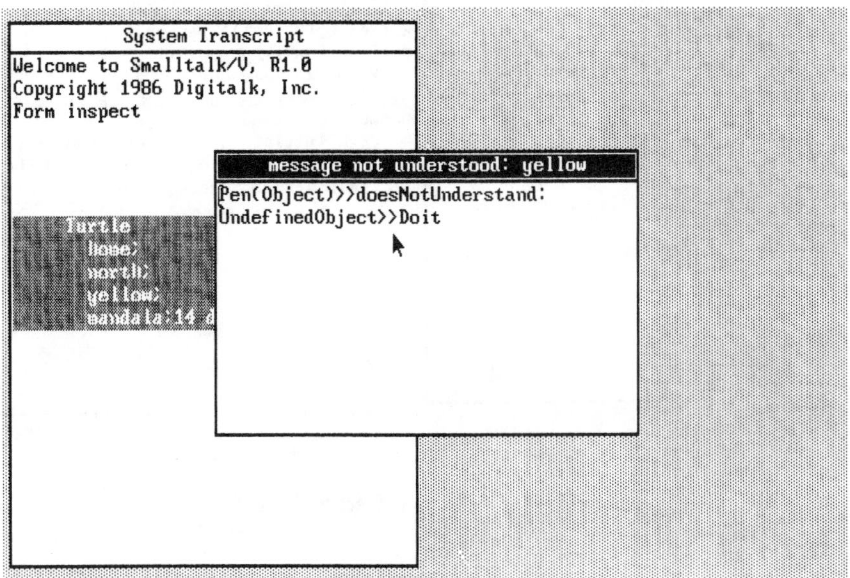


**Figure 6-6**
***A sample walkback window***

- Move the cursor over the text pane of the walkback window and select *debug* instead of *resume*, if you need more information to locate the error. The walkback window closes automatically and prompts for the two corners of the debug window.

The debug window provides an expanded view of the walkback window in four panes, as shown in Figure 6-7.

- The *list pane* (top left pane) reports the error message in the walkback window and allows you to select an error line for further examination.
- The *text pane* (bottom pane) displays the source code for the selected error method and allows you to modify the method using the procedure described in the section titled "Display and Edit the Interrelationship of Classes."
- The *variable name pane* (to the right of the list pane) contains *self*, which represents the receiver, and the names of all arguments and temporary variables for the error line selected in the list pane. You can click the right mouse button to open an inspector window and probe further on any object listed in this pane (for example, *self*).

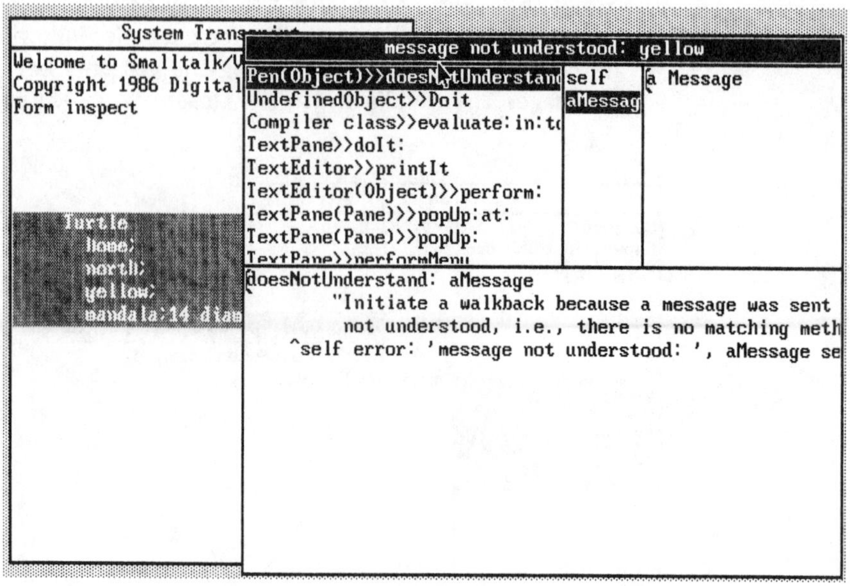

**Figure 6-7**
***A sample debug window***

- The *variable value pane* (to the right of the variable name pane) allows you to edit the value of a variable that has been selected in the variable name pane.

## Create New Windows

The three elements involved in creating new windows are (1) creating pane windows, (2) connecting panes, and (3) customizing pane menus.

### *Creating Pane Windows*

There are two types of pane windows, which are created differently—prompt windows (prompters) and other pane windows, such as text panes. To create a prompter, evaluate the following expression:

```
Prompter prompt: 'Message you want.....?'
     default: 'yes,........'
```

A window pops up with the `prompt:` argument as the window label (for example, `message you want....`) and the `default:` argument (for example, `yes,.......`) shown below it.

Two approaches can be used to create a pane window, such as text pane. The first approach is to use the message `windowLabeled: frame:` as follows:

```
PaneYouCreate :=
  TextEditor
    windowLabeled: 'pane you have created'
    frame( 0 @ 0 extent: 250 @ 200).
```

Note that `PaneYouCreate` is capitalized because a window is a global variable. `TextEditor` is used to provide the window with text editing capability. The message `windowLabeled: frame:` creates a rectangular area (`0 @ 0 extent: 250 @ 200`) on the screen with the label `pane you have created.`

The second approach is to use `openOn` or `open` as shown in Listing 6-1. The `openOn` message is sent to create a window that has a top pane and a subpane. The message `topPane:` is sent to create a top pane that encompasses the entire window as well as the label. The message `addSubpane` is used to add `TextPane` as a subpane to `TopPane`. The dispatcher of the top pane is then open to schedule the window—that is, to pick up the active pane.

**Listing 6-1**
***Sample program to create a window***

```
openOn: aString
      "Create a single pane window with aString
         as its initial script."
      | topPane |
      inputString := aString.
      topPane := TopPane new label: 'WindowName'.
      Toppane addSubpane: TextPane new.
      topPane dispatcher open scheduleWindow
```

Source: modified from Smalltalk [1].

## *Connecting Panes*

A means of communication between the panes is required. The following lines of code are added after `topPane addSubPane:` to connect the text pane to the top pane (the window):

```
(TextPane new
   model: self;
   name: #input).
```

These additional messages are

`model: self`, which instructs the text pane to send the message to the application class (`WindowName`)

`name: #input`, which gives the name `#input` to the text pane and allows the window to be initialized with the `input` message—for example:

```
input
"initialize inputPane with inputString"
^inputString
```

The window can be initialized by evaluating the following expression:

```
WindowName new openOn: 'It is a new window.'
```

## *Customizing a Pane Menu*

To customize a pane menu, the following expressions are required:

```
    (inputPane := TextPane new
     model: self;
     name: #input;
     menu: #inputMenu).
topPane dispatcher open scheduleWindow
```

The message `menu:` informs the window that it has a method called `inputMenu` to create the menu for the input pane, and that the instance variable `inputPane` is assigned to `TextPane new`.

The `inputMenu` method needs to be defined to include the desired menu list. A sample menu list of five selections is shown in Example 6-41 below.

*Example 6-41*

```
inputMenu
    "Answer a Menu for the input Pane."
    ^Menu
    label:
       ('copy\cut\paste',
       'new Menu 1\new Menu 2') withCrs
    lines: #(3)
    selectors: #(copySelection cutSelection
    pasteSelection menu1Selection menu2Selection)
```

This sample method returns a menu that contains five selections. Each selection needs to be defined. In this case, the first three selections are standard TextEditor methods that require no definition. However, the last two selections, `menu1Selection` and `menu2Selection`, need to be defined to meet the needs of the application.

More than one subpane can be created in a window. Listing 6-2 shows a sample program that combines one reply pane, one input with menu selection, and one graph pane.

**Listing 6-2**
***Sample program combining a replay pane, an input pane with menu selection, and a graph pane***

```
openOn: aString
    "Create a sample window with a string
          as its initial script."
     topPane replyPane
     inputString := aString.
     topPane := TopPane new label: 'Sample window'.
     topPane addSubpane:
         (replyPane := TextPane new
          model: self;
          name: #reply;
          framingRatio: (0@0 extent: 2/3 @(1/4))).
     topPane addSubPane:
         (GraphPane new
          model: self;
          name: #graph:;
          framingRatio: (0 @ (1/4) extent: 2/3 @ (3/4))).
     topPane addSubpane:
         (inputPane := TextPane new
            menu: #inputMenu;
            model: self;
            name: #input;
            framingRatio: (2/3 @ 0 extent 1/3 @ 1)).
     topPane reframe:
     (Display boundingBox insetBy: 16@16).
    replayStream := replyPane dispatcher.
    topPane dispatcher openWindow scheduleWindow
```

Source: modified from Smalltalk [1].

Note in Listing 6-2 that the message `framingRatio` is used. It defines the position and size of each pane relative to its window. Coordinates of the rectangle argument to `framingRatio:` are a fraction of the width or height of the window. For example, if the window rectangle is:

```
50 @ 100 extent: 210 @ 160
```

then a framing ratio of `(0 @ 0 extent: 2/3 @ 1/4)` yields a rectangle of `(50 @ 100 extent: 140 @ 40)`, using the following calculation:

```
(50 @ 100) + (210 @ 160) * (0 @ 0))  extent:
           (210 @ 160) * (2/3 @ 1/4)
=> 50 @ 100 extent:140 @ 40
```

The window operation and menus are powerful in making an expert system user friendly.

# Summary


- Smalltalk is an object-oriented language environment that consists of windows.
- The main features of Smalltalk include menu/window operations, text editing, system operations, classes and methods, graphics, and debugging.
- Windows consist of labels and panes; a window menu contains at least three choices, such as *frame, cycle,* and *move.*
- Text editing includes functions such as inserting, selecting, cutting, and pasting.
- A basic Smalltalk program employs objects, messages and methods, and classes.
- The concept of classes is one of the most distinctive features of Smalltalk. Classes describe data structures (objects), algorithms (methods), and external interfaces (messages).
- Windows, menus, and graphics can be created by changing variables of relevant classes.


# References


[1] Digital, Inc., *Smalltalk/V: Tutorial and Programming Handbook* (Los Angeles, 1986).

# SECTION 3

# Building Expert System Tools

Chapters 4, 5, and 6 reveal three major expert system programming languages on which an expert system or tool can be built. Among the three languages, LISP is the most primitive and consequently provides the most freedom to build fairly basic functions, such as mouse or menu operations. Prolog has its own backtracking reasoning mechanism but requires extensive work on knowledge representation and menu, window, and mouse operations. Smalltalk has built-in functions for creating window, menu, graphics, and mouse operations; however, significant effort is still required to develop an environment for expert system development because it has no knowledge representation and reasoning mechanisms. Figure III-1 shows the structure of an expert system tool. To illustrate how each of the expert system tool components is built, LISP is selected to implement the methodologies discussed. Prolog and Smalltalk can also be used to build most of these components.

As discussed in Chapter 1, the power of an expert system resides in its knowledge and how it is represented. Because the knowledge is often abstract and ambiguous, a well-specified language to represent and encode this knowledge becomes essential. This language is called *knowledge representation language*. The knowledge representation language may employ any one or a combination of frames, rules, and logic to represent facts explicitly. However, an expert system must also provide access to facts, implicit in the knowledge represented, that can be derived through its inference mechanism (including user interface). Finally, an expert system would remain empty if no particular domain knowledge were extracted and encoded in it. In essence, the three major components of expert system technology to be addressed in the remainder of this book are the knowledge representation language, inference engine (plus user interface), and specific domain knowledge. Section 3 presents methods for building the first two components. These components provide a user-friendly environment that

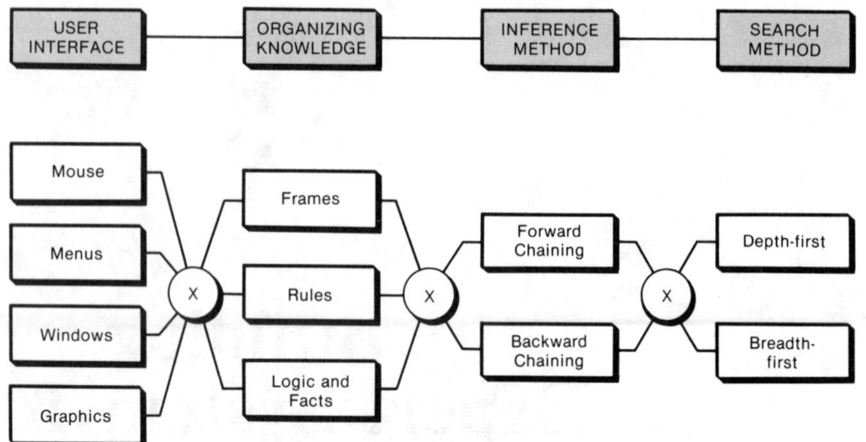


**Figure III-1**
***Structure of an expert system tool***

allows programmers or experts/specialists to record explicit descriptions of how they solve real-world problems.

The knowledge representation language is used to build the knowledge base of an expert system. An inference engine in the expert system then probes the knowledge base and infers the implicit data in the base. As discussed in Chapter 1, however, a critical element of an expert system is the user interface. Without a friendly man-machine interface, the expert system becomes essentially "deaf" and "dumb." Methods for building the knowledge base are discussed in Chapter 7. Methods for constructing the inference engine and user interface are discussed in Chapter 8. Note that each sample program may not work by itself because it often calls upon other programs to perform certain functions. The sample programs need to be organized correctly for execution.

# 7

# Building Knowledge Representation Language Structures

This chapter discusses methods for building knowledge representation language (KRL) structures. Chapter 8 examines approaches to building an inference engine that interprets these structures and infers implicit information, and a user interface that connects the user with the expert system.

Most current PC expert system tools employ a singular KRL structure (or representation architecture), such as rules, frames, or logic. Rules are best for representing knowledge that enables decision making. For a sophisticated problem, a singular KRL structure may be inconvenient and ultimately inefficient for representing knowledge. This chapter discusses a structure that combines all three languages to provide the user with all conveniences available for representing various types of knowledge.

This chapter covers the following topics: (1) building frame structures, (2) building rule structures, and (3) building logic structures.

## Building Frame Structures

Frame structures are also called *units* or *schemas* in some AI workstation tools (for example, KEE, distributed by IntelliCorp.). A frame structure can provide a uniform set of representation services for complex data collections or data bases. A frame is more than a structure that is used in other computer languages such as C or PASCAL. It is a generalized property list that contains rooms (called *slots*), which specify more than property value. For example, slots can in turn contain a default value, a restriction of value to be added, a procedure activated to compute a needed value, or a rule activated when certain conditions are met. Furthermore, a frame is a *generalization* hierarchy in which information is inherited from its superclass.

This chapter section discusses the fundamental assumptions, advantages, disadvantages, and methods for designing frame structures.

## Fundamental Assumptions

A fundamental assumption about the frame representation language is that frames can be used to unify and denote a loose collection of related ideas, concepts, facts, experiences, and so forth. Frames can be linked into a classification system. Each frame represents a class of objects that is connected to a superclass or subclass. A frame contains slots that can be filled with other expressions such as frames, names, identifiers, specifications, relationships between slots, or procedural attachment.

Clearly it is assumed that both declarative knowledge ("knowing that," such as facts and relationships) and procedural knowledge ("knowing how," such as when to do something and how to do it) can be represented in a frame. A frame of the AI programmer is shown in Tables 7-1 and 7-2. Table 7-1 shows the declarative knowledge of the AI programmer frame and Table 7-2 demonstrates the procedural knowledge of the programmer frame. The two tables clearly indicate the combined and powerful features of a frame.

**Table 7-1**
***Declarative knowledge of the AI programmer frame***

| Slot | Description |
|---|---|
| Languages-tools-used | LISP, Prolog, shells* |
| Educational-background | General plus AI courses |
| Programming-approach | "Heuristic" programming** |
| Major-tasks | Acquiring domain knowledge |
| | Defining and structuring the problem |
| | Interviewing experts |
| | Encoding knowledge |
| | Prototyping the system |
| | Testing the program |
| | Refining the system |

*LISP and Prolog are AI languages. A shell is defined in Chapter 2.
**Programming by experience; no specific guidelines.

**Table 7-2**
***Procedural knowledge of the AI programmer frame***

| Slot | Procedure |
|---|---|
| Languages-tools-used | When-apply |
| Educational-background | Test-qualification |
| Programming-approach | Test-applicability |
| Major-tasks | How-to-perform |

It is further assumed that the operation of classifications is one basic reasoning method—that is, the property of an object in the superclass is passed down to the object in the subclass if no restriction is specified in the object of the subclass. Through this operation, you can apply a set of specific knowledge in a particular class to objects in the downstream classes, guide your search for specific facts about the object in the frame, or make assumptions about properties that must be true for the entire class of frames, without checking specific slots.

## Advantages and Disadvantages

The advantage of frame structures lies in the powerful features of a frame, which support hierarchical knowledge representations—for example, default values, declarative knowledge, and procedural attachments that are available to experts/specialists to extract their knowledge. In particular, the concept of a classification system is analogous to the real world structure of facts and organization. It is natural to relate the concept of frame to daily activities. Properties, relationships, and events can easily fit into slots of an object from conditions and situations. Restrictions can also be attached to the slots to trigger a sequence of actions to be taken by the program.

Two disadvantages arise in the design of a frame structure. First, the theoretical foundation of the frame to support the assumption that can contain both declarative and procedural knowledge requires further research to be cost effective. Some experts even suggest that the frame is only an organized extension of logic representation [1].

Second, the implementation of frames in the context of class deserves attention for two reasons. The class structure to which a frame belongs should allow the user to change the order of the hierarchy and to create subclasses or superclasses to any given class. However, because of the inheritance feature of frames, special care is needed when a superclass is inserted into an existing classification system, to ensure that the properties of the slots are properly passed down to the subclass. Furthermore, because a frame can be attached to a slot, the depth of the frame can become infinite and thus prohibit an efficient search in consultation. Frame structures are weak when representing exceptions or an object in multiple classes.

## Methods To Design Frame Structures

To design a frame structure that provides classification and inheritance, four essential elements are required: class, unit, slot, and inheritance. The functions of these elements are described briefly as follows:

*Class* — Provides a hierarchical structure that can locate the position of a frame, either a superclass (layer higher than other frames) or a subclass (layer lower than other frames).

| | |
|---|---|
| *Unit* | Provides an organization to host slots that will be used to store both declarative and procedural information on a given subject. |
| *Slot* | Provides a data structure to hold information regarding a particular attribute of a unit—that is, certainty factors, inheritance, and so forth. |
| *Inheritance modes* | Either enable or disable a class to inherit value and default value from the parent class (superclass) and pass the value and default value to the child class (subclass). |

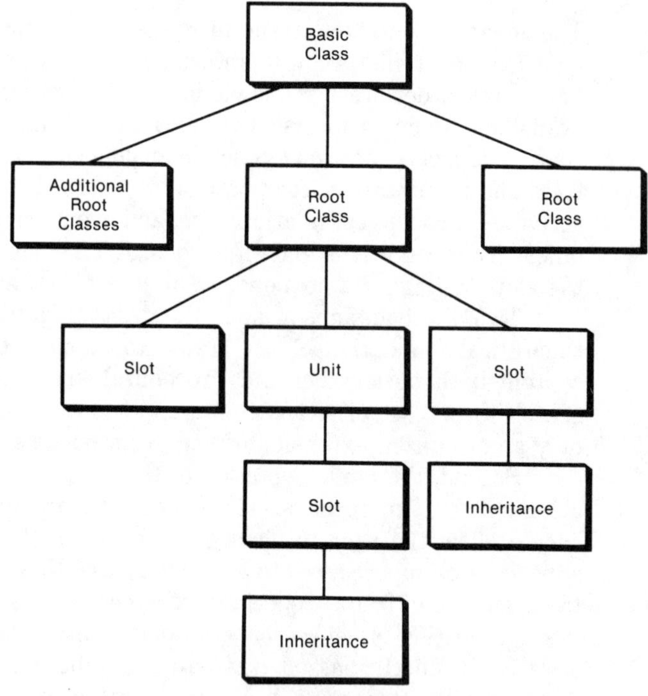


**Figure 7-1**
***Relationships among classes, units, slots, and inheritance modes***

The relationships among these four elements are shown in Figure 7-1. Here, class contains another class, a unit, or a slot. Unit in turn may contain many slots. Slots contain inheritance modes and other attributes input by the user. As shown in Figure 7-2, a class may have a superclass. A class may also contain many units, and a unit may contain as many slots as desired. Depending on whether the value of the slots can be passed down to those of the subclass, slots may be classified as *member* slots or *own* slots:

| | |
|---|---|
| *Member slots* | The value of the slot is inherited by those of the subclass. |
| *Own slots* | The value of the slot is not inherited. |

A discussion of how to program each of the four elements follows.

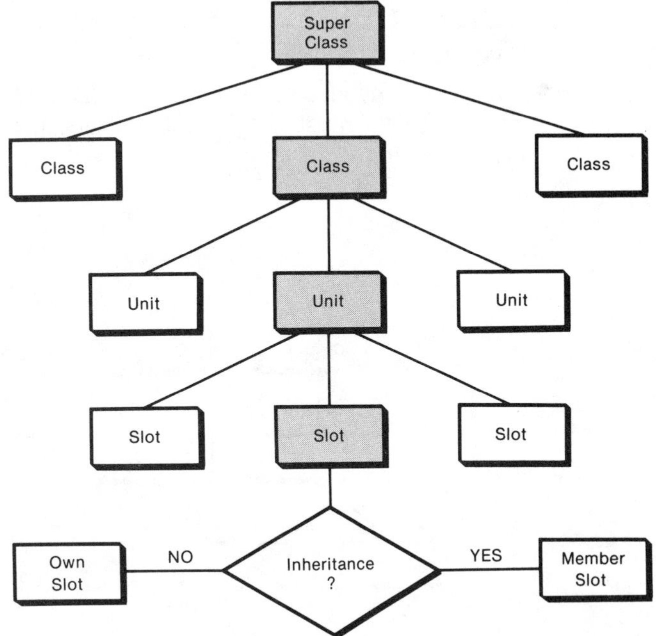


**Figure 7-2**
***The organization of a frame structure***

## Class

A class is a set of closely related objects that share the same attributes. The initial class is always the basic class to which any root class belongs; every other class created thereafter is a subclass of the root class, as shown in Figure 7-1. A class can have slots that are inherited by subclasses, other classes, or units. The values in the slots of the basic class and superclasses are also inherited by the class.

Common LISP has the capability to implement these features into a frame structure. Ideally, classes should be implemented as a separate structure from units, perhaps even including units; however, the current version (1.01) of GCLISP does not support structure inclusion. Classes should also be implemented in such a way as to allow any change of class structure to be easily incorporated. For example, if you make a mistake in creating the root class (for example, in Figure 7-3, Class 0 should be the root class instead of Class 1), the frame structure should allow you to change the hierarchy of a class. Another example is the subclass 112 shown in the same illustration. How to allow a subclass to have two parent classes is a difficult task.

Due to the current implementation of GCLISP, a simplified version of class hierarchy is discussed here with the following assumptions:

- Classes are not separated from units; that is, their structures are similar.
- A class can have only a parent class (superclass) with as many child

classes (subclasses) as desired. The root class has the same basic class as its parent class.

- The hierarchy of a class cannot be changed easily. When it is changed, care must be given to the detail of the attributes that can be inherited.

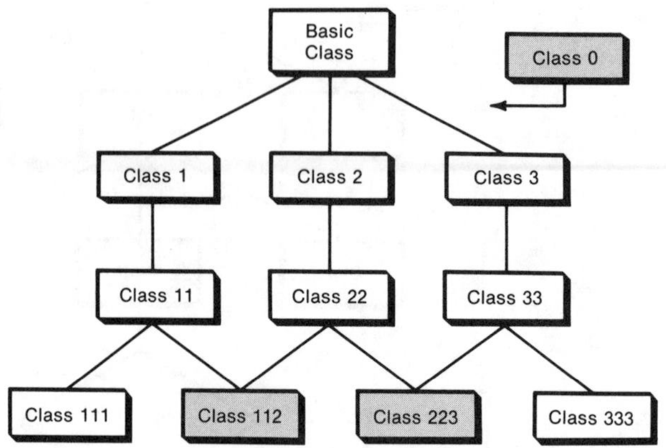


**Figure 7-3**
***Difficulties in editing the class structure***

With these assumptions, let us examine the features that are desirable in a frame structure. These features include:

Display class
Describe class
Create class
Delete class
Edit class
Create slot
Delete slot

The first five features are used to operate on the class itself. The last two features (*create slot* and *delete slot*) are used to operate in the slots of the class, that is, to enable the class to receive attributes that can be inherited by the subclasses.

LISP can be used effectively to write subroutines that contain these features. The most useful LISP macros for writing these subroutines include `defparameter`, `defstruct`, and `defun`. `Format`, `let`, `cond`, `setq`, `if`, `dolist`, and `progn` are functions often employed in making a class structure.

`Defparameter` is used at top level (the very beginning of the program) to assign a global value to the variable, `*class-operations-item-list*`. This variable includes the slots of features such as *display class* and *delete class*. As shown in Listing 7-1, these features can be selected by the user. The value of the variable is set by the user before program execution.

**Listing 7-1**
***Sample program to define features for a frame structure***

```
(defparameter *CLASS-OPERATIONS-ITEM-LIST*
             '(("Display Class"
                (display-unit (EKO-menu-choose :class
    "display"))
                :doc "Pops up a menu of classes to
    display")
               ("Describe Class"
                (describe-unit (EKO-menu-choose :class
    "describe"))
                :doc "Gives an internal description of a
    unit")
               ("Create class" (user-create-class)
                :doc "Allows creation of a class")
               ("Delete class" (user-delete-class)
                :doc "Allows deletion of a class")
               ("Edit class" (edit-class)
                :doc "Allows editing of a class")
               ("Create Slot" (create-class-slots)
                :doc "Allows creation of slots in an
    existing class")
               ("Delete Slot" (delete-class-slots)
                :doc "Allows deletion of a slot in an
    existing class")))

(defmode Class-Operations-Mode "Class Operations"
              *Class-Operations-Item-List*
              (graph-classes))
```

Note that in contrast to conventional programming language, `*class-operations-item-list*` contains a list of functions, each corresponding to an operation that the user performs on a class hierarchy:

`Display-unit` (class)

`Describe-unit` (class)

`User-create-class`

`User-delete-class`

`Edit-class`

`Create-class-slot`

`Delete-class-slot`

Comments as well as documentation for these functions are also included. Because one of the programming rules is modularity (object-oriented programming), functions that are written for other purposes are used to reduce the number of lines of code. For example, `display-unit` and `describe-unit` (functions used in unit operations, discussed next) are employed. Furthermore, `EKO-menu-choose` (a macro written for user-interface operations, to allow the user to choose menus) is also employed. Except for those functions defined in other operations in other files that can be called during execution, all of the functions need to be defined in this program.

As discussed in the beginning of this chapter, `defstruct` is a powerful function for use in defining a structure such as class, unit, or slot. Listing 7-2 provides a partial sample of how a class structure is defined using `defstruct`.

**Listing 7-2**
***Sample program to define a class structure using defstruct***

```
(defstruct (CLASS (:print-function 'print-unit))
  (Name nil)
  (Slots nil)            ; Meaningful when type is :unit or
     :class
  (Documentation nil)    ; Meaningful when type is not :unit
  (Type nil)     ; this should be one of (:unit :class
     :rule :rule-class)
  (Class nil)
  (SuperClass nil)       ;
  (SubClasses nil)       ; Meaningful when type is :class or
     rule-class
```

Ideally, a generic structure is initially defined using `defstruct`, which can then be modified for the various attributes of class and unit. However, because the current GCLISP (version 1.01) does not support `defstruct` slot-options such as `:include` (discussed in Chapter 4), the structure defined by `defstruct` cannot be used to make a generic structure that fits both class and unit. For this reason, a structure that combines class and unit as well as rule classes (discussed in "Building Rule Structures") is defined by `defstruct`, as shown in Listing 7-3. The combined structure is also renamed to `unit`.

**Listing 7-3**
***Sample program to define a structure that combines class and unit using defstruct***

```
(defstruct (Unit (:print-function 'print-unit))
  (Name nil)
  (Slots nil)            ; Meaningful when type is :unit or
     :class
```

```
(Documentation nil)    ; Meaningful when type is not
   :entity
(Type nil)    ; this should be one of (:unit :class
   :rule :rule-class)
(Class nil)
(SuperClass nil)       ;
(SubClasses nil)       ; Meaningful when type is :class
   or rule-class
(Units nil)            ; Meaningful when type is :class
(Rules nil))           ; Meaningful when type is
   :rule-class
```

An examination of Listing 7-3 indicates that `print-unit` is a function that needs to be defined. `Print-unit` is defined in Listing 7-4, using `defstruct` functions such as `unit-type` and `unit-name`. These two functions retrieve the type and value of the structure given in Listing 7-3:

```
(unit-type unit)
(unit-name unit)
```

**Listing 7-4**
***Sample program to print a unit structure***

```
(defun Print-Unit (unit stream ignore)
  (format stream "<~A unit ~A>" (unit-type unit) (unit-name
    unit)))
```

After defining parameters and the structure for class, you must then define the example functions that allow the user to operate on class. These two functions are `display-unit` (class), which is used to display class, and `user-create-class`, which allows the user to create a class. You can then write the remaining functions through these examples.

## *Display Class*

As indicated in Listing 7-3, the structure of class is combined with that for unit and rule; `display-unit` is also used to display class as defined under the context of this structure. A sample program for `display-unit` is shown in Listing 7-5.

**Listing 7-5**
***Sample program for the display-unit (class) function***

```
;;; Unit Operations
(defun Display-Unit (&optional (unit (EKO-menu-choose
    :entity "display")))
  (unless (abortp unit)
    (let ((unit-obj (eval unit))
          (stream *main-window*))
      (clear-screen)
    (on-main-screen
      (center-string "~A:~&" stream unit) (terpri)
      (case (unit-type unit-obj)
      (:entity
        (format stream "Class: ~A~%" (unit-class unit-obj))
        (dolist (slot (unit-slots unit-obj)) (display-slot
     unit slot)))
      (:class
        (format stream "Documentation: ~A~%" (unit-
     documentation unit-obj))
        (format stream "Superclass: ~A~%" (unit-SuperClass
     unit-obj))
        (format stream "Subclasses: ~A~%" (unit-SubClasses
     unit-obj))
        (format stream "Units: ~A~%" (unit-Units unit-obj))
        (dolist (slot (unit-slots unit-obj)) (display-slot
     unit slot)))
      (:rule-class
        (format t "Documentation: ~A~%" (unit-documentation
     unit-obj))
        (format t "Superclass: ~A~%" (unit-Superclass unit-
     obj))
        (format t "Subclasses: ~A~%" (unit-SubClasses unit-
     obj))
        (format t "Rules: ~A~%" (unit-rules unit-obj)))
      (:rule
        (format t "Rule-Class: ~A~%" (unit-class unit-obj))
        (format t "  If: ~A~%" (rule-premise unit))
        (format t "  Then: ~A~%"  (rule-conclusion unit))
        (format t "  Explanation: ~A~%" (rule-explanation
     unit))
        (format t "  Certainty: ~A~%" (rule-certainty unit))
        (if (rule-askable? unit)
            (format t "  Premise of rule is user-askable")
            (format t "  Premise of rule is not user-
     askable"))))
     (user-pause))))
```

A scan of the sample program indicates that the following functions and global variable need to be defined:

`EKO-menu-choose` A macro that specializes `menu-choose` to differentiate between unit and class lists.

`clear-screen` A function that clears the screen.

`on-main-screen` A macro that specially binds `*terminal-io*` to the main window.

`*main-window*` A global variable that designates the main window of an expert system shell.

As a good programming practice, `EKO-menu-choose` should be defined in the user interface operation; `clear-screen`, `on-main-screen`, and `*main-window*` should be defined in the window operation. Chapter 8 covers the details of these operations and explains how to define these macros and variables to meet your needs.

## *User-Create-Class*

The procedure of `user-create-class` takes input from a user-selected menu, and determines whether the class name is a ⟨CR⟩ (that is, abort) or a class that already exists. If the class name is a ⟨CR⟩, stop creating a class. If the class name already exists, tell the user to edit the class rather than create it. Otherwise, push the new class name into the bottom of the class hierarchy and provide users with prompts to obtain attributes about the class. A sample program for implementing this procedure is shown in Listing 7-6. The following functions and variables need to be defined for the sample program to run.

`Menu-input` A function that allows input from the menu.

`Notify` A function that notifies the user with a specific message.

`Abortp` A function that tests whether the class is aborted.

`Push-last` A function that pushes the new class name into the bottom of the class list.

`Make-unit` A construction defined through the structure of unit.

`Inherit-slot` A function that allows the attribute to be passed down.

`Create-class-slot` A previously discussed function that creates one of the features for operating on class.

**Listing 7-6**
***Sample program for user-create-class***

```
(defun User-Create-Class (&optional superclass)
  (let ((class (menu-input "Name of class to create (<CR>
     aborts)")))
```

**Listing 7-6 (cont.)**

```
    (ifn class
         (notify "~&Class not created")
    (if (member class *class-list*)
        (notify "~&That class already exists!  Edit class
     instead.")
        (let ((superclass (or superclass
                                (EKO-menu-choose :class
     "use as a Superclass"))))
          (if (abortp superclass)
              (notify "Class not created")
              (let ((doc (menu-input (format nil "Enter
     documentation for ~A" class)
                                                    'string)))
                (create-class class :doc doc :superclass
     superclass)
                (create-class-slots class))))))))
```

Most of these functions are fairly simple and are not elaborated on further here. Only `inherit-slot` is discussed, in the slot structure.

## Unit

The unit structure is similar to the class structure. `Defparameter` is employed to define a global variable, `*unit-operation-item-list*` as shown in Listing 7-7, which is a list of functions that represent features for use in operating units. These features include *display unit, describe unit, create unit, delete unit, edit unit, create slot, delete slot,* and *edit slot.* `Display-unit` has been discussed in the previous section, "Class." `Create-unit` is similar to that discussed in Class. `Create-slot` and `edit-slot` are functions in the slot operation, which is discussed later. `Delete-unit` and `edit-unit` are discussed below to illustrate the method of programming these features.

**Listing 7-7**
***Sample program for defining a global variable for unit operations***

```
(defparameter *UNIT-OPERATIONS-ITEM-LIST*
              '(("Display Unit" (display-unit)
                 :doc "Pops up a menu of units to display")
                ("Describe Unit" (describe-unit)
                 :doc "Gives an internal description of a
     unit")
                ("Create Unit" (user-create-unit)
                 :doc "Allows creation of a unit")
```

```
                ("Delete Unit" (user-delete-unit)
                 :doc "Allows deletion of a unit")
                ("Edit Unit" (edit-unit)
                :doc "Allows editing of a unit")
                ("Create Slot" (user-create-slots)
                :doc "Allows creation of slots in an
     existing unit")
                ("Delete Slot" (user-delete-slot)
                 :doc "Allows deletion of a slot in an
     existing unit")
                ("Edit Slot" (user-edit-slot)
                :doc "Allows editing of a slot in an
     existing unit")))

(defmode Unit-Operations-Mode
         "Unit Operations"
         *unit-operations-item-list*
         (graph-units))
```

## *Delete-Unit*

`Delete-unit` is an internal function that deletes a unit; the user may not be aware of the deletion process. The `delete-unit` procedure is initially to receive the name of the unit to be deleted, delete the contents of each slot, and pull the name of the unit out of the `*entity list*`. A sample program is shown in Listing 7-8. An examination of Listing 7-8 indicates that the following functions and variables need to be defined.

| | |
|---|---|
| `Delete-slot` | A function that deletes a slot. |
| `Slot` | A `defstruct` function that defines the slot structure. |
| `Pull` | A macro utility function that is defined to remove a name from a given name list. |
| `*Entity-list*` | A global variable for the list of entities of a slot or unit. |

The slot operation is discussed in the next section. Both `pull` and `*entity-list*` can be defined to perform the desired task.

## *Edit-Unit*

The menu of `edit-unit` accepts commands from the user and then modifies the unit requested. The `edit-unit` procedure is to determine initially whether the user wants to abort the command. If so, it aborts the editing process and notifies the user that `nothing is edited`. Otherwise, it retrieves the slots of the unit and allows the user to modify them one by one and then save the modified entities. A sample program is shown in Listing

7-8. An examination of this listing indicates that the following functions need to be defined:

| | |
|---|---|
| `EKO-menu-choose` | A macro that specializes `menu-choose` to differentiate between unit and class lists to be defined in the menu operation. |
| `Choose-slot-values` | A function that updates slot values. |
| `Assert-entity` | A function that updates entity values. |

These functions or macros can be written by reviewing materials in this chapter and Chapters 4 and 8.

**Listing 7-8**
***Sample program for delete-unit and edit-unit***

```
(defun Delete-Unit (unit-name)
  "Internal function to delete a unit"
  (let ((unit-obj (eval unit-name)))
    (dolist (slot (unit-slots unit-obj))
      (delete-slot unit-name (slot-name slot)))
    (pull unit-name (unit-units (eval (unit-class
     unit-obj))))
    (pull unit-name *entity-list*)))

(defun Edit-Unit (&optional (unit (EKO-menu-choose :entity
     "edit")))
  (if (abortp unit)
      (notify "~&Nothing Edited")
      (progn
        (choose-slot-values (unit-slots (eval unit)) unit)
        (assert-entity unit))))
```

## Slot and Inheritance

A slot is an object that holds information regarding a particular attribute of a unit. A unit can have as many slots as desired. The primary items of information include:

- Slot name—name of the slot
- Slot value—value given by the user
- Slot type restriction—restriction on the type of value that can be input for this slot
- Slot source—where the attribute is inherited
- Slot destination—where the attribute is passed
- Slot inheritance—inherit value or not
- Slot default value—the value used, if no value is given

- Slot certainty—how sure the user feels about the information
- Slot prompt—used by the user to enter value
- Slot documentation—documents the purpose, function, etc. of the slot
- Slot assertable?—whether the value of the slot can be asserted

Slot `name` and `value` are self-explanatory. Slot `type-restriction` is used to restrict the value of the slot that can be accepted when input by the user. To restrict a slot value, set its `type-restriction` to:

| | |
|---|---|
| `Expression` | The value can be any expression. |
| `Number` | The value can be any number. |
| `String` | The value can be any string. |
| `Boolean` | The value must be yes or no. |
| `(member (<atom>*))` | The value must be one of the atoms in the list. |
| `(predicate <predicate>)` | The value must satisfy the LISP predicate. |
| `(class <classname>)` | The value must be an entity of class classname. |
| `Name` | The value must be a name. |

Slot `source` and slot `destination` are used for inheritance to indicate the unit that the slot originates from and the slot to which it is destined. Slot `default-value` is used if the user does not input a value. Slot `certainty` indicates the confidence level that the user feels about the value he/she is inputting. For the purpose of probability calculation, it is selected to range between zero and one. Slot `prompt` allows the user to input value. In a more sophisticated tool, a procedure name can be input to compute the appropriate value. The procedure is called a method or a demon. However, this procedure can also be implemented in the rule structure. Slot `documentation` is provided for the user to input desirable information regarding the slot for future users. Slot `assertable?` is either yes or no. It is activated when the value must be asserted for future reasoning. If the slot is nonassertable, when reasoning is evoked, the information it contains is not checked, but considered merely a document.

## *Implementing Slot Features*

`Defstruct` can be used to create a slot structure that contains all features discussed in the previous section. This use is shown in Listing 7-9. The automatically defined construction function implied in `defstruct` is then used to specify the detailed characteristics of the slot structure with the aid of various `defstruct` options, such as `:value` and `:prompt`.

**Listing 7-9**
***Sample program to define a slot structure***

```
(defstruct (Slot (:print-function 'print-slot))
  (name nil)
  (value nil)
  (type :value)          ; type of slot (value, method,
    etc..)
  (type-restriction :expression)
  (source nil)           ; unit from which slot is inherited
  (destination :member) ; slot can only be :member if
    unit is a class
  (inheritance :inherit-value)
  (default-value nil)
  (certainty 1.0)
  (prompt nil)          ; used for asking a value of the user.
    Defaults to name
  (documentation nil)
  (assertable? t)
  (attributes nil))     ; the attributes of a slot that can be
    changed by user.

(defun Make-Slot1 (&rest keys-and-vals)
  "Makes a slot with an attributes slot so that Choose-Slot-
    Values can
  choose the attributes of the slot.  Attributes that can be
    changed are:
  value, documentation, type-restriction, inheritance,
    default-value,
  certainty, prompt, assertable?, destination"
  (let ((keys-and-vals (list-quote keys-and-vals))
        (slot-name (string-capitalize (second (member :name
    keys-and-vals)))))
    (eval
      '(make-slot
         :attributes
         (make-slot-item-list
           '((value :value nil
                 :type-restriction :expression :prompt "Slot
    Value: ")
              (documentation :value "" :type-restriction
    :string
                             :prompt "Slot Documentation: ")
              (type-restriction :value :expression
    :type-restriction :expression
                             :prompt "Slot Value Type
    Restriction: ")
```

```
        (inheritance :value inherit-value
:type-restriction
                                (member (inherit-value
not-inherit))
                            :prompt "Inheritance mechanism:
")
        (default-value :value nil :type-restriction
                            :expression :prompt "Slot
Default Value: ")
        (certainty :value 1.0 :type-restriction :number
                            :prompt "Certainty Factor: ")
        (prompt :value ,(format nil "~A: " slot-name)
                            :type-restriction :String
:prompt "Slot Prompt: ")
        (assertable? :value yes :type-restriction
(member (yes no))
                            :prompt "Should slot be
assertable?: ")
        (destination :value :member :type-restriction
           (member (member own)) :prompt "Destination
of slot: ")))
    ,@keys-and-vals))))

(defun Print-Slot (slot stream ignore)
  (format stream "#<Slot ~A>" (slot-name slot)))
```

Note that in the slot items of inheritance and destination the following options exist:

- Inheritance: `inherit-value, not-inherit`
- Destination: `member, own`

`Inherit-value` indicates value is inherited from the unit or superclasses, and `not-inherit` is the opposite. `Member` indicates that the value of the slot is passed down to slots in the subclasses, and `own` is the opposite. These options affect inheritance, which is discussed next.

## *Inheritance*

The method of implementing inheritance involves copying appropriate values from the superclass and passing certain values to subclasses. The two types of inheritance are:

- Class inheritance—the slot values of the subclass are inherited from those of the superclass universally
- Slot inheritance—the slot value of the parent class is passed down to the child class

***Copying Slots***—`Defstruct` provides a neat way to copy slots. `Make-slot` is employed in using `defun` to define the function `copy-slot`, as shown in

Listing 7-10. The structure of `slot` is copied item by item through `make-slot`. For example, the name of the slot is copied from the name of the originating slot by calling the function:

```
(slot-name slot)
```

**Listing 7-10**
***Sample program for inheritance features***

```
(defun Inherit-slot (class-name slot)
  "Inherits slot to class, and to its subclasses
     recursively."
  (let ((new-slot-obj (copy-slot slot)))
    (push-last new-slot-obj (unit-slots (eval class-name)))
    (dolist (subclass (unit-subclasses (eval class-name)))
      (inherit-slot subclass slot))))

(defun Inherit-Slots (parent-name son-name)
  "Takes the member slots of parent and copies
     them into son"
  (do ((member-slots (get-slots parent-name :member) (cdr
     member-slots))
        new-slot-obj (son (eval son-name)))
      ((null member-slots))
    (setq new-slot-obj (copy-slot (car member-slots)))
    (when (member (unit-type son) '(:rule :entity))
        (setf (slot-destination new-slot-obj) :own)
      (unless (slot-value new-slot-obj)
        (setf (slot-value new-slot-obj) (slot-default-value
     new-slot-obj))))
    (push-last new-slot-obj (unit-slots son))
    (when (equal :not-inherit (slot-inheritance new-slot-
     obj))
      (setf (slot-value new-slot-obj) nil))))

(defun Inherited-Slotp (unit slot-obj)
  (not (equal (slot-source slot-obj) unit)))

(defun Copy-slot (slot)
  (make-slot :name (slot-name slot)
             :value (slot-value slot)
             :type (slot-type slot)
             :type-restriction (slot-type-restriction slot)
             :source (slot-source slot)
             :destination (slot-destination slot)
             :inheritance (slot-inheritance slot)
             :default-value (slot-default-value slot)
             :certainty (slot-certainty slot)
             :prompt (slot-prompt slot)
```

```
:assertable? (slot-assertable? slot)
:attributes (slot-attributes slot)))
```

***Class Inheritance***—Class inheritance uses a recursive function to pass its slot values to a class and its subclasses. The procedure of the function is to duplicate the slot values of the current class (unit) to the corresponding slots of all subclasses, until all subclasses have received the same slot values. The sample program in Listing 7-10 uses the functions `Inherit-slot` and `Inherit-slots`. In the program, `push-last` is a function that pushes the slot into the stack of the unit that is called.

***Slot Inheritance***—In slot inheritance, the values of a slot may or may not pass down to the slot of its child class, depending on whether it is a `member` slot or an `own` slot. If it is a `member` slot, copy the content of its parent's `member` slots to those of the children. Otherwise, they will not be copied. If the slot is designated as `not-inherit`, then the items of that particular slot will not be copied either. This is shown in Listing 7-10, above.

# Building Rule Structures

Rule structures—also called "production rules," "production systems," or "rule-based systems"—are the most often used and simplest form of knowledge representation. Most PC tools fall in this category. Examples include M.1, Personal Consultant, and EXSYS. In this form of knowledge representation, every piece of knowledge or experience is expressed. Fundamental assumptions, advantages/disadvantages, and methods to design rule structure are discussed below.

## *Fundamental Assumptions*

A rule structure in its simple form consists of templates that enable programmers or experts/specialists to input IF-THEN rules to build expert systems. The five fundamental assumptions about a rule structure or even the basic rule are

- Acceptance of rule formalism
- Modus ponens
- Limited interaction between factors in rules
- Limited attributes of a given object
- Common understanding between various users

Acceptance of rule formalism by the user or the expert/specialist is the most important assumption. Experts/specialists must be able to transform their knowledge into rules; that is, they must be able to recognize and then formalize chunks of their knowledge and experience, and express these chunks in rules. Unfortunately, not every field supports this assumption. It appears to require a field which has attained a certain level of formalization but has not yet achieved a thorough, scientific formalization of the problem-solving process. The fields that are inclined to accept rules in representing knowledge generally have a broadly recognized set of conceptual, primitive factors and a minimum understanding of basic processes, such as diagnostics and configuration. It is further assumed that the IF-THEN format of rules is sufficiently simple, expressive, and intuitive that it can provide a useful knowledge representation language for use by experts in expressing their knowledge.

The implication of modus ponens, as discussed in Chapter 1, is that a simple, basic logic rule allows new facts to be deduced from other facts as follows:

| | |
|---|---|
| IF A, THEN B, and | (Rule 1) |
| IF B, THEN C | (Rule 2) |
| IF A, THEN C | (Rule 3) |

From rules 1, 2, and 3, if both A and B are known, then C can be deduced. However, for rule structures to be useful in representing knowledge, their simple modus ponens chaining must appear natural enough that a user can readily identify with it.

Limited interaction between factors in rules entails three assumptions:

1. Only a small number of factors (about six clauses) in the premise can simultaneously trigger an action in the consequence.
2. The presence or absence of each of these clauses can be determined without adverse effects on the others.
3. The clauses of rule premises connected by AND/OR can be set up toward nonconflicting subgoals so that action clauses in the consequence do not depend on the order in which the evidence is collected.

Limited number of attributes for a given object prevents an exponential growth in search time when the number of rules in the knowledge base grows substantially. Thus newly acquired rules reference only to established attributes of a given object, and the use of these rules does not cause further branching because the attributes appearing in the premises of these rules have already been traced.

Common understanding between users assures that the same representation language communicates among different classes of users—that is, the domain experts, who "train" the expert system, and the users who possess little knowledge of the expert system but who wish to use it to gain its knowledge. We assume that common understanding is feasible.

## *Advantages and Disadvantages*

The advantages of the rule structure are in three areas: modular coding, ease in explanation, and ease in knowledge acquisition.

Each rule in the rule structure is a simple conditional statement in which the premise consists of a limited number of conditional clauses, the action contains one or more conclusions, and each statement is modular and independent of all others. Such modular coding provides an easy way to identify contradiction and subsumption in the knowledge base. Individual rules can be manipulated to facilitate automatic detection and correction of undesirable interactions among rules. Since rules are retrieved only when they are relevant to a specific goal (that is, the goal appears in their action part), the addition of new rules becomes easy. The premise and action parts of rules can be systematically scanned to search the desired goals, and the rules can then be added to the appropriate internal lists according to the parameters found in their actions. These rules can simply be added to the rule set in the knowledge base without changing other rules, because rules in the knowledge base are relatively independent; that is, one rule never directly calls another. This advantage is particularly significant when you compare an addition of rules to the addition of a new procedure to a typical FORTRAN program.

Ease in explanation is another benefit. Inquiries of an expert system can be answered by retrieving rules whose premise and action (consequence) contain the relevant items. The reason for these actions can then be easily explained by tracing the passage of rules fired. Explanation involves the tracing of the consultation process through an AND/OR goal tree. In general, inquiries are of two types: *how* a conclusion is reached and *why* a question is asked. In *how* type inquiries, rules are traced from the top down as shown in Figure 7-4a. For example, if you ask the expert system, "*How* is C11 obtained?" the system answers that C11 is obtained because of

```
Rule A and B1
```

However, in *why* type inquiries, rules are traced from the bottom up, as shown in Figure 7-4b. If you ask "*why* C11 is obtained," the answer is

```
Rule E1121 and D112
```

Ease of knowledge acquisition lies in the fact that rules are a reasonably intuitive way of expressing chunks of inferential knowledge and experience that are significant without the prerequisite of acquaintance with any programming language. Because it may be impossible to write a complete set of rules, the rule structure provides a capability for incremental improvement of competence in response to new research that produces new results and modifications of old principles and rules. The rule structure further facilitates the explanation of errors in the conclusion process. This tracing facility supplies subsequent clues for fixing

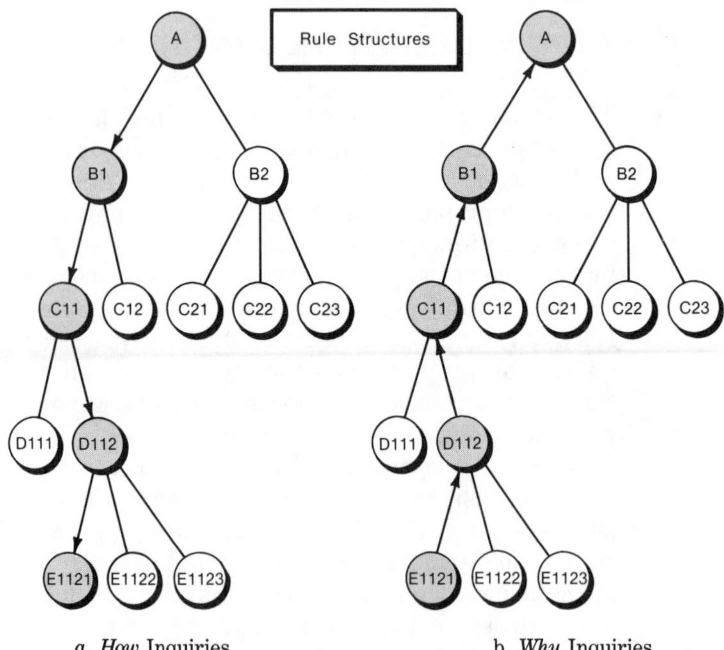


a. *How* Inquiries

b. *Why* Inquiries

**Figure 7-4**
***Rule tracing: how and why***

errors and a set of expectations about the form and content of the anticipated correction.

The disadvantages of the rule representation language include inflexibility of rule expression, sequence of rules, and insufficient power.

Inflexibility of rule expression—that is, a predetermined format—reduces freedom in expressing the expert's knowledge and experience and at times appears difficult to the inexperienced user. All contextual information must be stated explicitly in the premise and the consequence in order to meet the requirement of modularity. This requirement often results in rules with long and complicated premises that entail many subgoals. Furthermore, rule structures are suitable in supporting flat domains but are weak in representing hierarchical knowledge.

Sequence of rules affects the efficiency of production systems in consultation. The requirement of correct sequence for either backward or forward chaining means substantial effort is needed to arrange rules to meet the appropriate sequence.

The rule structure provides insufficient power for expressing complex, large, or dynamic concepts because rules are simple conditional statements. In particular, mapping a sequence of events to a set of rules has at times proven extremely difficult. Goal-directed chaining may require excess human effort to structure the appropriate sequence for large chunks of knowledge that cannot easily be subdivided into separate pieces. The rule structure is weak in detecting rule conflicts or duplications; clever knowledge engineers are then required to validate rules.

## Methods To Implement Rule Structures

To implement a rule structure is relatively easy once the frame structure has been implemented. (See "Methods To Design Frame Structures.") Similar to the frame structure discussed, a rule structure consists of rule classes and rules. The rule class operation is provided to allow the user to group rules together for improved knowledge acquisition, for memorization of rule usage, and most important of all, for speedy search of relevant rules in a rule class. For the convenience of the user in manipulating rules, the rule class operation includes the following features:

- Display rule class
- Create rule class
- Delete rule class

These features enable the user to operate on the entire class of rules. For example, if it is desirable to delete the entire class, then `Delete Rule Class` can be called on to perform this task. It is necessary to use `Create Rule Class` to create a rule class hierarchy initially because each individual rule belongs either to a class named by the user or to the basic rule class (the root of all rule classes). The features of rule operations after a rule class has been established include:

- Create rule
- Display rule
- Edit rule
- Delete rule

`Create Rule` allows the user to create rules initially. After a rule has been created, `Display Rule` is used to display the rule; `Edit Rule` is used to edit the attributes of the rule; and `Delete Rule` is used to delete the rule entirely. The attributes of a rule needed to enable the user to extract knowledge generally include:

- `Rule premise`
- `Rule conclusion`
- `Rule action`
- `Rule explanation`
- `Rule certainty`
- `Rule askable?`

`Rule premise` provides the facility to record the premise of a rule. The premise can contain conjunctive (`and`) and disjunctive (`or`) phrases, and can be an arbitrary logical expression. `Rule conclusion` is the rule's "then" part; it can contain conjunctive and disjunctive phrases, and also can be an arbitrary logical expression. `Rule action` indicates the set of actions to be taken if the rule is invoked. `Rule explanation` contains an explanation for the rule that is an English-language description of why the rule is true. `Rule certainty` indicates the likelihood of the conclusion, given that the premise is true. It represents the degree of confidence in a rule or a fact. In determining the confidence factor of a conjunction of rules or facts, the minimum confidence factor among the factors for the rules or facts is given. For a disjunction, the maximum confidence factor is used. Once the confidence factor of the premise of a rule is determined, the confidence factor of the conclusion is then calculated as the product of the confidence level of the premise and that of the rule. `Rule askable?` indicates whether the premise of the rule can be obtained from the user if it cannot be determined internally by the system in achieving a goal.

**Listing 7-11**
***Sample program to define rule operation parameters***

```
(defparameter *Rule-Operations-Item-List*
              '(("Display Rule"
                 (display-unit (EKO-menu-choose :rule
     "display"))
                 :doc "Display a rule")
                ("Create Rule" (user-create-rule)
                 :doc "Add a rule to the rule database")
                ("Delete Rule" (user-delete-rule)
                 :doc "Delete a rule")
                ("Edit Rule" (edit-rule)
                 :doc "Edit an existing rule")
                ("Display Rule Class"
                 (display-unit (EKO-menu-choose :rule-class
     "display"))
                 :doc "Display a rule class")
                ("Create Rule Class" (user-create-
     rule-class)
                 :doc "Add a rule class to the rule
     database")
                ("Delete Rule Class" (user-delete-
     rule-class)
                 :doc "Delete a rule class")
                ("Meta Level" (meta-level-mode)
                 :doc "Perform meta level operations")))

(defmode Rule-Operations-Mode "Rule Operations"
     *rule-operations-item-list*
          (graph-rules))
```

As in the unit operation, `defparameter` is used to define all operations in rules and rule classes. Listing 7-11 shows a sample program using `defparameter`. The structures and functions defined in the frame operations (unit and slot) are used in the rule operation. To take advantage of the structure of unit, the parameters of the rule operation (such as name, rule-class, premise, conclusion, certainty, and so forth) are defined in a make-rule function to differentiate the rule operations from the unit operation. A sample program of make-rule is shown in Listing 7-12. Note that keys-and-vals is used to enable the program to match keywords such as :name, to select the appropriate name for the rule operation. Furthermore, the slot value is redefined for the rule slot so the slot operation can be applied to the rule operation in modifying rule attributes, such as explanation, premise, askable? or certainty. Listing 7-13 shows a sample program for defining access functions for rule slots.

**Listing 7-12**
***Sample program for make-rule in rule operations***

```
(defun Make-Rule (&rest keys-and-vals)
  "Supports keywords :name, :rule-class, :premise,
     :conclusion, :action
  :certainty, :askable?"
  (let ((rule-name (second (member :name keys-and-vals)))
        (rule-class (or (second (member :rule-class
     keys-and-vals))
                        'basic-rule-class)))
    (push-last rule-name (unit-rules (eval rule-class)))
    (push-last rule-name *rule-list*)
    (set rule-name (make-unit :name rule-name :class rule-
     class :type :rule))
    (inherit-slots rule-class rule-name)
    (dolist (rule-slot
             '(explanation premise conclusion action
     certainty askable))
     (let ((value (second (member (keywordize rule-slot)
     keys-and-vals))))
        (when value
          (set-unit-slot-value rule-name rule-slot
     value))))))
```

**Listing 7-13**
***Sample program for rule slots***

```
(defun Rule-Explanation (rule-name)
  (unit-slot-value rule-name 'explanation))
(defun Rule-Premise (rule-name)
  (unit-slot-value rule-name 'premise))
(defun Rule-Conclusion (rule-name)
  (unit-slot-value rule-name 'conclusion))
(defun rule-certainty (rule-name)
  (unit-slot-value rule-name 'certainty))
```

**Listing 7-13 (cont.)**

```
(defun Rule-Askable? (rule-name)
  (unit-slot-value rule-name 'askable?))
```

## *Meta Rules*

In implementing a rule, the rule can be designated as a forward chaining rule that can be used in forward chaining only, a backward chaining rule that can be employed in backward chaining only, or a bidirectional rule that can be called upon in both chaining directions. This feature is called *Meta Level*, as defined in Listing 7-11. An even more advanced concept is the meta-level rule, which is a rule describing the feature of all rules in a given rule class.

The meta-level rule, also called *meta rule*, can refer to object rules by description rather than by name. Meta rules express strategies for using other knowledge in rules, frames, or other sources in the knowledge base, to invoke subsequent rules in a situation where more than one chunk or source of knowledge may be applicable. For example, meta rules can reduce search space. Given a problem solvable by either a forward chaining search through rules first or a tree search through the frame structure first, a meta rule might indicate which approach to take, based on the characteristics of the problem domain and other specifications of the desired solution, such as speed of search and accuracy of solution.

A meta rule makes a conclusion about other rules. It either makes deductions about the likely use of certain groups of rules or determines a partial ordering among subsets of rules or among rule classes. A meta rule makes conclusions about rule classes in rule groups, but does not indicate circumstances under which some rule classes are invalid. A sample meta rule is shown in the box below.

**A sample meta rule**

| | |
|---|---|
| IF: | 1. You are attempting to identify a new chemical compound |
| | 2. There are rules which mention online data bases |
| | 3. There are rules which mention library reference |
| THEN: | It is very likely (0.9) that the former should be used before the latter. |

Implementing meta rules requires only a minor change to the control structure; that is, before the system attempts to retrieve the entire class of rules relevant to the current goal, it first determines if there are any meta rules relevant to that goal. If so, these meta rules are invoked first to determine the likely utility and relative ordering of rule classes and rules.

As a result, the search space can be pruned or the branches of the search tree can be reordered to increase system efficiency.

# Building Logic (Predicate Calculus) Structures

Logic can be used to represent facts about objects and their relations, properties, and functions, as shown in Figure 7-5. These facts can be expressed in a formula such as:

(For-all(x) (Feathers (x)) (Animal (x)) => (Bird (x))

The equation above is used to indicate the fact that all animals that have feathers are birds. It is a formula in which *feathers*, *animal*, and *for-all* are predicates that express relations or properties between objects such as $x$. $X$ in this equation represents only objects but not relations (predicates). Consequently, this type of logic is called first-order logic or first-order predicate calculus. Times, events, kinds, organizations, worlds, and physical objects can be treated as logic individuals (facts). Predicate calculus provides methods that allow the user to assert these facts.

Predicate calculus is a powerful addition for knowledge representation, but it also has advantages and disadvantages. Logic expressions are usually concise and universally understood. Logicians have over the centuries proven rigorously and structurally what we can achieve with knowledge in certain domains, such as mathematics. On the other hand, logic has serious drawbacks. Because of its traditional focus on the methodology, it can deceive us into concentrating on the mathematics of logic and deflect attention away from the really important task of representing the key pieces of knowledge that are the source of power.

Another drawback is the abstractness of logic expressions, which may discourage experts/specialists from comprehending the true meanings behind the symbols. Obviously, for expert system tools to be useful to experts and specialists, logic expressions need to remain simple and expressive.

## *Methods for Implementing Logic Structures*

The logic structure for expressing facts is implemented in an unstructured knowledge and variable base (unstructured knowledge base). A fact can be a partial fact regarding a unit specified in the frame structure, a mathematical operation, or a special relationship between classes. Facts are expressed in predicate calculus internally and can be input through the translation of natural language, if a natural language template is implemented.

All knowledge that cannot be encoded in either the frame structure or the rule structure is encoded in the unstructured knowledge base. The features available to the user to operate on the logic structure include:

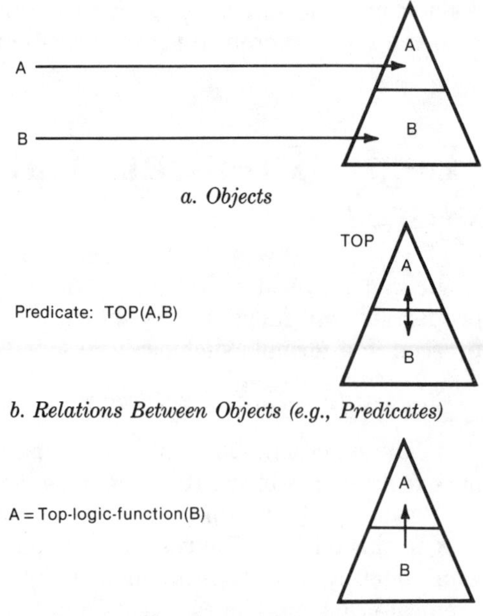


*a. Objects*

*b. Relations Between Objects (e.g., Predicates)*

*c. Functions of Objects*

**Figure 7-5**
***Logic in representing facts about objects, relations, and functions***

| | |
|---|---|
| Display | Allows the user to display the unstructured knowledge base. Each of the facts are followed by their certainty factors. |
| Assert | Allows the user to insert a fact into the knowledge base. Forward chaining is performed and any rules whose antecedent matches the facts are triggered. The user is prompted for the certainty factor. |
| Stash | Allows the user to stash a fact into the knowledge base. No forward chaining is performed. The user is prompted for the certainty factor. |
| Delete | Allows the user to delete a fact from the knowledge base. |
| Edit | Allows the user to edit a fact in the data base. |
| Clear | Allows the user to delete all facts from the knowledge base. Clear requires confirmation. |

As with other structures, `defparameter` is used to define the features for the knowledge base. Listing 7-14 shows a sample `defparameter` program for the unstructured knowledge base. Because this structure is significantly different from the other two, the functions available for units or slots are not used in the program. Except for *assert* and *stash*, the other features are similar to those in the frame or rule structure. Assert and stash are discussed below.

**Listing 7-14**
***Sample program to define unstructured knowledge base operations***

```
(defparameter *Kb-Operations-Item-List*
              '(("Display" (display-kb)
                 :doc "Display the Knowledge Base currently
     in Workhorse")
                ("Assert" (user-assert-fact) :doc
                 "Assert a fact into the unstructured
     knowledge base")
;               ("Unassert" (user-unassert-fact) :doc
;                "Unassert a fact from the unstructured
     knowledge base")
                ("Stash" (user-stash-fact) :doc
                 "Add a fact to the kb, without triggering
     any rules")
                ("Delete" (user-delete-fact) :doc
                 "Delete a fact from the unstructured
     knowledge base")
;               ("Find" (user-find-fact)
;                :doc "Find a proposition in the knowledge
     base")
                ("Clear" (user-empty-kb)
                 :doc "Delete all facts from unstructured
     knowledge base")))

(defparameter *Unstructured-Kb* Nil
              "Unstructured Knowledge Base.  Currently
     implemented as a list:
             ((fact . certainty)*).  Needs more efficient
     implementation.")
```

# *Assert and Stash*

*Assert* triggers forward chaining to be performed and invokes any rules whose antecedent matches the facts. The procedure of assert is as follows:

1. Choose the value of the attributes of the fact that is given by the user.
2. Compare the fact. If the fact is null, then inform the user, ***Nothing asserted.*** If the fact is already in the knowledge base, inform the user, ***Fact is already in the knowledge base.*** Otherwise, assert the fact and certainty factor through forward chaining.
3. Push the fact into the knowledge base. A sample program for

*Assert* is shown in Listing 7-15. Some of the variables and functions are

| | |
|---|---|
| `Choose-slot-value` | A function that chooses the slot value that has appeared in the slot operation. |
| `*Fact-items-list*` | A global variable defined with `defparameter` in Listing 7-15. |
| `In-KB` | A function that tests whether a fact is in the knowledge base. |
| `Assert` | A function that asserts the fact and certainty factor, using forward chaining. |
| `User-pause` | A function that requests the user to hit any key to continue the consultation. |

**Listing 7-15**
***Sample program to define user-assert-fact***

```
(defun User-Assert-Fact ()
  (choose-slot-values *fact-item-list* "Enter fact to
     assert")
  (let ((fact (get-item *fact-item-list* 'fact))
        (certainty (get-item *fact-item-list* 'certainty)))
    (cond ((null fact) (notify "Nothing asserted"))
          ((in-kb fact) (notify "Fact already in kb"))
          (t (assert fact certainty)
             (format *monitor-stream*
                     "~&~A [CF=~A] asserted into unstructured
     kb."
                     fact certaiy)
             (user-pause)))))
```

*Stash* is slightly different from *assert.* Rather than asserting the fact, *stash* adds it to the knowledge base without performing forward chaining, by using the function `add-fact`. This function pushes the fact and its certainty factor into the last of the stack in the knowledge base. Listing 7-16 shows a sample program for *stash.*

**Listing 7-16**
***Sample program to define user-stash-fact***

```
(defun User-Stash-Fact ()
  (choose-slot-values *fact-item-list* "Enter
     fact to stash")
  (let ((fact (get-item *fact-item-list* 'fact))
        (certainty (get-item *fact-item-list* 'certainty)))
    (cond ((null fact) (notify "Nothing stashed"))
```

```
        ((in-kb fact) (notify "Fact already in kb"))
        (t (add-fact fact certainty)
           (format *monitor-stream*
                   "~&~A [CF=~A] stashed into unstructured
kb."
                   fact certainty)
           (user-pause)))))
```

# Summary

- LISP, Prolog, and Smalltalk can be used to build knowledge representations and reasoning mechanisms for expert system tools.
- LISP is used to demonstrate the methodology of building expert system tools.
- The three knowledge representation structures are rule, frame, and logic (predicate calculus). The rule structure is needed to capture experts' rules of thumb experience; the frame structure is needed to organize complex data collections; and the logic structure is needed to receive the remaining knowledge that cannot be expressed in either rules or frames.
- Fundamental assumptions, advantages, and disadvantages of the three structures have been discussed.
- The four essential elements required for designing a frame structure are class, unit, slot, and inheritance.
- A rule structure consists of rule classes and rules.
- An unstructured knowledge and variable base is required to implement a logic (predicate calculus) structure.

# References

[1] P. Hayes, "The Logic of Frames," in *Readings in Knowledge Representation*, ed. R. Brachman and H. Levesque (Los Altos, CA: Morgan Kaufmann Publishers, 1985).

# 8

# Building the Inference Engine and User Interface

Chapter 7 discussed approaches to the design of the first component of an expert system and tools—a knowledge base that uses frames, rules, and predicate calculus. This chapter concerns the design of the remaining two components—the inference engine and user interface. The inference engine, as introduced briefly in Chapter 1, empowers an expert system or tool with a reasoning mechanism and search control to solve problems. The user interface provides the user with a convenient means to use the expert system or tool. The inference engine and user interface are discussed in separate sections of this chapter.

## Designing an Inference Engine

An inference engine can be either simple or complicated, depending on the structure of the knowledge base. For example, if the knowledge base consists of simple rules (no rule classes structured) and facts, forward chaining suffices. However, for a knowledge base that consists of structured frames and rules and unstructured logic (facts, data, and variables), both sophisticated forward and backward chaining with a well thought-out search strategy may be required. The main elements of an inference engine are forward chaining, backward chaining, justification, and search strategy.

### *Forward Chaining*

Forward chaining in its simple form is an interactive program that performs a loop. It steps through the rule list until it finds a rule whose premise matches the fact or situation. The rule is then used or "fired" to assert a new fact. As discussed in Chapter 1, once the rule has been used, it is not used again in the same search; however, the fact concluded as the result of that rule's firing is added to the knowledge base. This cycle of finding a matched rule, firing it, and adding the conclusion to the knowledge base is repeated until no more matched rules can be found. Variations of the simple forward chaining form can be suggested to enrich the inference mechanism. The next section discusses the implementation of a simple forward chaining form, followed by a variation of the form.

## Implementation of a Simple Chaining Form

Forward chaining is used to assert a fact that matches the premise of a rule, and can be applied to determine further facts. The detailed procedure for forward chaining is as follows:

1. A fact or facts are asserted.
2. The fact or facts match the premise of a rule.
3. The system computes the substitution that unifies the fact and the premise.
4. The substitution is applied to the conclusion of the rule.
5. This result is asserted into the knowledge base, and is available for further forward chaining.
6. Steps 1 through 5 are repeated.

For example, assume that the knowledge base consists of rules and facts in Example 8-1.

*Example 8-1*

Rule 1: IF you lose the key and the gas tank is empty,
THEN the car is not running.

Rule 2: IF the car is not running and you have no cash,
THEN you are going to be late.

Fact 1: You lost the key.

Fact 2: The gas tank is empty.

Facts 1 and 2 ("you lost the key" and "the gas tank is empty") are asserted and found to match the premise of Rule 1. The forward chaining system computes the substitution and results in a new fact: "the car is not running." The new fact is asserted into the knowledge base as Fact 3 and is now available for use in Rule 2.

Listing 8-1 shows a sample forward chaining program.

**Listing 8-1**
***Sample program for forward chaining***

```
;;; Forward Chaining Stuff
(defun Forward-Chain (fact &optional (certainty 1.0))
```

```
  (let (substitution)
  (when-debug  "Forward-chaining on ~A..." fact)
    (dolist (rule *rule-list*)
      (when (setq substitution (unify fact (rule-premise
     rule)))
        (when-debug  "Forward-chaining successful with ~A"
     rule)
        (assert (substitute (rule-conclusion rule)
     substitution)
                        (* certainty (rule-certainty rule)))))
    (unless substitution
      (when-debug  "No applicable rules found."))))
(defun Assert (proposition &optional (certainty 1.0))
  "Incorporates proposition into the knowledge base, doing
forward chaining as
   appropriate"
  (when-debug  "Asserting ~A" proposition)
  (if (ConjunctionP proposition)
      (dolist (prop (cdr proposition))
        (assert prop certainty))
      (stash proposition certainty))
  (forward-chain proposition certainty))
```

As shown in Listing 8-1, the implementation of this forward chaining procedure involves three elements:

- `Unify`
- `Substitute`
- `Assert`

The purpose of *unify* is to return a substitution that unifies the fact with the rule premise—that is, tests the compatibility of the fact and the premise. You can either design `unify` in a narrow sense that exactly matches the fact and the premise, or you can design it in broad terms that enable substitution of parts of the fact and the premise to make them compatible. For example, if the fact is that the size of an engine order can be any number and the premise is that the size of any order is 10, you can unify the two statements as shown in Example 8-2.

*Example 8-2*

```
Unify (( Order-size Engine $x) (Order-size $y 10)
==> (($x . 10) ($y . Engine))
```

The two statements are combined to obtain the size of an engine order —10. The new statement can then be used to derive a conclusion from the rule whose antecedent matches it.

A sample program for a broadly defined `unify` is shown in Listing 8-2.

The program initially determines whether the two expressions, p1 and p2, are equal. If not, it tries to substitute the components of the two expressions and compose a new statement that combines both expressions.

Note that the program uses *substitute* to replace components. Substitute is used to compute the substitution that unifies the fact and the premise. It performs a variable substitution on the proposition, as shown in Example 8-1.

**Listing 8-2**
***Use of unify and substitute for forward and backward chaining***

```
(defun Unify (p1 p2)
  "Returns a substitution that unifies p1 and p2, if there
     is one."
  (if (or (atom p1) (atom p2))
      (progn
        (when (not (atom p1))
          (switch p1 p2))                    ; makes p1 the atom of
     the two
        (cond ((equal p1 p2) '((t . t)))
              ((variablep p1)
               (unless (member p1 p2)
                  '((,p1 . ,p2))))
              ((variablep p2)
               '((,p2 . ,p1)))
              (t nil)))
      (let* ((f1 (car p1))
             (f2 (car p2))
             (t1 (cdr p1))
             (t2 (cdr p2))
             (z1 (unify f1 f2)))
        (if (not z1)
            nil
            (let* ((g1 (substitute t1 z1))
                   (g2 (substitute t2 z1))
                   (z2 (unify g1 g2)))
              (if (not z2)
              nil
              (compose z1 z2)))))))
(defun Substitute (proposition substitution)
  "Performs a variable substitution on proposition"
  (do ((substitutions substitution (cdr substitutions))
        this-subst
        (new-prop proposition))
       ((endp substitutions)
        new-prop)
    (setq this-subst (car substitutions))
```

```
    (setq new-prop (subst (cdr this-subst) (car this-subst)
     new-prop))))

(defun ConjunctionP (proposition)
  (and (consp proposition)
       (equal (car proposition) 'and)))
```

`Assert` is needed to incorporate the proposition (conclusion) into the knowledge base. Because the conclusion may include a conjunctive or disjunctive statement, each statement as well as its certainty factor needs to be asserted. The certainty factor for a conjunctive statement is simply copied from that of the premise. Listing 8-1 shows a sample program that implements `assert` to handle conjunctive propositions.

## Enhancement of Simple Forward Chaining

The simple forward chaining form can be enhanced in two ways: (1) by using a conflict resolution method (a tie-breaking procedure) to select one of the eligible rules when premises of more than one rule match the fact and (2) by considering the combination of conjunctive and disjunctive propositions in the premise or conclusion. A detailed discussion of the first enhancement follows. For the second enhancement, you can expand the `assert` program in Listing 8-1 to include the case of disjunctive propositions.

The first enhancement involves two operations: (1) discarding those rules that add only duplicates to the knowledge base and (2) executing a conflict resolution method to select one of the eligible rules. The enhanced procedure is as follows:

1. Make eligible all rules whose premises unify with the facts.
2. Substitute the premises.
3. Discard rules whose conclusions have a nullifying effect.
4. If no eligible rules remain, stop.
5. Use a conflict resolution method to select one of the eligible rules if more than one rule is eligible.
6. Assert the conclusion proposition to the knowledge base.
7. Repeat the previous six steps.

The procedure is similar to that in the previous section. The only difference is that all eligible rules are first stored in the group `eligible-rules`, and a conflict resolution method indicates the way in which these rules are selected. If no other methods are preferred, a first-in-last-out method is used to break ties among all eligible rules, as shown in Example 8-3.

*Example 8-3*

```
(defun resolve-conflict (*eligible-rules*)
Let best-rule (car *eligible-rules*)
```

```
(pull best-rule *eligible-rules*)
(return best-rule)))
```

In Example 8-3, pull is used to pull a rule out of the stack of *eligible-rules. Pull is a macro that is defined in Chapter 7 as follows:

```
(defmacro Pull (item list)
   '(setf ,list (remove ,item ,list :test 'equal)))
```

## *Backward Chaining*

Backward chaining is employed when the user queries whether a certain fact is true, and a rule exists that can determine the query from known information in the knowledge base or from answers given by the user.

In other words, backward chaining attempts to prove the hypothesis from facts. If the current goal is to determine the fact in the conclusion (hypothesis), then it is necessary to determine whether the premises match the situation. The sample knowledge base given earlier in Example 8-1 can be used again to show the logic of backward chaining:

Rule 1: IF you lose the key and the gas tank is empty,
THEN the car is not running.

Rule 2: IF the car is not running and you have no cash,
THEN you are going to be late.

Fact 1: You lost the key.

Fact 2: The gas tank is empty.

For instance, if you want to prove the hypothesis that "you are going to be late," given the facts and rules in the knowledge base (Facts 1 and 2, Rules 1 and 2), backward chaining may be applied to determine whether the premises match the situation. Rule 2, which contains the conclusion, is fired first to determine whether the premises match the fact. Because the knowledge base does not contain the facts in the premises of Rule 2, "the car is not running" and "you have no cash," "the car is not running" becomes the first subgoal. Rule 1 is then fired to assert whether the premises "you lost the key" and "the gas tank is empty" match the facts. Because the facts (Facts 1 and 2) in the knowledge base match the premises of Rule 1, the subhypothesis is proven. However, the system still has to prove that "you have no cash," which is not contained in the knowledge base and cannot be asserted through rules because no rule is related to it. The system then asks "IS IT TRUE THAT: you have no cash?" If the answer is "yes," then the second subgoal is also satisfied and the original hypothesis is proven. The conclusion is that "you are going to be late."

In summary the procedure for backward chaining is

1. A request is made to achieve a fact (the goal).
2. The goal does not match any known fact.

3. The goal matches the conclusion of a rule.
4. The system computes the substitution that unifies the goal with the conclusion.
5. The substitution is applied to the premise of the rule.
6. This result becomes a new goal of the system.
7. This new goal can:

   - Match a fact in the knowledge base
   - Match a conclusion of a rule, leading to further backward chaining
   - Ask the user for the needed information
   - Fail, in which case the original goal fails

8. Repeat steps 1 through 7

**Listing 8-3**
***Sample program for backward chaining***

```
(defun Backward-Chain ()
  (let ((goal (car *goal-list*))
        substitution antecedent-subs consequent-subs)
    (when-debug  "Backward-chaining on ~A..." goal)
    (dolist (rule *rule-list*)
      (setq consequent-subs (unify goal (rule-conclusion
     rule)))
      (when consequent-subs
        (push-last (list goal consequent-subs :rule rule
     (rule-premise rule))
                          *last-goal-achievement*)
        (when-debug "Match achieved with conclusion of ~A
     using ~A"
                             rule consequent-subs)
        (incf *debug-level*)
        (setq antecedent-subs
              (or (achieve-goal (substitute (rule-premise
     rule)
     consequent-subs))
                  (and (rule-askable? rule)
                       (ask-user (rule-premise rule)))))
       (decf *debug-level*)
       (when antecedent-subs
         (return (setq substitution
                       (compose consequent-subs
     antecedent-subs))))))
    (unless substitution
```

**Listing 8-3 (cont.)**

```
     (when-debug  "No Matching Conclusion for goal ~A."
    goal))
   substitution))
```

A sample program for backward chaining is given in Listing 8-3. As shown in the program, the implementation of a backward chaining procedure involves the following major elements:

- `Unify`
- `Substitute`
- `Achieve-goal`
- `Ask-user`

The first two elements are discussed in the earlier section on forward chaining. `Achieve-goal` and `ask-user` are discussed below.

The objective of ***achieve-goal*** is to achieve the goal inquired by the user and return a substitution by checking if the substitution is

- a conjunction or a disjunction
- a fact in a unit, or a proposition in the unstructured knowledge base

These two issues are discussed sequentially.

As demonstrated in the example of "whether you are going to be late," the difference between a conjunctive and a disjunctive statement is the requirement of achieving the subgoals. When a conjunction appears in the subgoals, all of the subgoals have to be proven true in order for the final goal to be true. In the case of disjunction, only one subgoal must be true. A sample program to handle conjunctive subgoals is shown in Listing 8-4. This program uses recursion to reach the deep "nest" of conjunctive propositions which need to be substituted one by one.

**Listing 8-4**
***Sample program to handle conjunctive subgoals***

```
(defun Achieve-Conjunction (conjunction)
  (let ((conjuncts (cdr conjunction)))
    (case (length conjuncts)
      (0 '((t . t)))
      (1 (achieve-goal (car conjuncts)))
      (t (do* ((substitution (achieve-goal (car conjuncts))
                      (achieve-goal (car conjuncts)
    prev-substs))
               (prev-substs (list substitution)
                                 (cons substitution
    prev-substs))
               (rest-subst
                 (when substitution
```

```
                (achieve-conjunction
                  (cons 'and (cdr (substitute conjuncts
substitution)))))
              (when substitution
              (achieve-conjunction
                (cons 'and (cdr (substitute conjuncts
substitution)))))))
        ((or (not substitution) (and rest-subst
substitution))
         (and substitution (compose rest-subst
substitution)))
     (when-debug "~A failed on ~A, backtracking..."
                         substitution (cons "and (cdr
conjuncts)))
       (pop-last *last-goal-achievement*))))))
```

The second issue is to determine whether the new goal can match the fact in the knowledge base. This fact can be either a proposition in the unstructured data base or structured information in the frame structure; for example, a slot of a unit or class. A sample program to unify the new goal with the proposition in the unstructured data base is shown in Listing 8-5.

**Listing 8-5**
***Sample program to unify the new goals with the proposition in the unstructured knowledge base***

```
(defun Unify-With-Kb (goal &optional prev-substs)
  "Attempts to unify goal with some fact in the data base"
  (let (substitution fact)
    (dolist (fact1 *unstructured-kb*)
      (setq fact (car fact1))
      (when (and (setq substitution (unify goal fact))
           (not (member-1 substitution prev-substs)))
        (push-last (list goal substitution :fact fact)
                        *last-goal-achievement*)
        (return substitution)))))
```

*Ask-user* is called when no fact in the knowledge base can be matched and no rule can be applied to derive new facts. The user is asked whether the fact is true, as shown in the sample program in Listing 8-6.

# Justification

Justification provides a tracing facility to indicate the history of goal substitution regarding the last conclusion and the achievement method via rules, units, facts in the unstructured data base, or user-provided answer. It gives the source name of the rule, unit, or fact used, as well as the fact in the rule or unit that has been used. Justification combines `car` and `cdr` to retrieve the history of goal achievement, and employs `case` to print out the tracing results. A sample program for justification, called *justify*, is shown in Listing 8-6.

**Listing 8-6**
***Sample program for ask-user and justification***

```
(defun Ask-User (fact)
  (if (menu-input (format nil "Is ~A true?" fact) :boolean)
     '((t . t))))
(defun Justify ()
  (clear-screen)
  (on-main-screen
    (dolist (achievement *last-goal-achievement*)
      (let* ((goal (car achievement))
             (subs (subst-abbrev (cadr achievement)))
             (achievement-method (caddr achievement))
             (source-name (cadr (cddr achievement)))
             (args (car (last achievement))))
        (format t "~&~A was achieved by using" goal)
        (format t "~&  the substitution ~A with" subs)
        (case achievement-method
          (:rule (format t "~&  the rule ~A," source-name)
                 (format t "~&  and the fact ~A." args)
                 (format t "~&  The explanation is: ~A"
                        (rule-explanation source-name)))
          (:fact
                 (format t "~&  the fact ~A in the
     unstructured kb." source-name))
          (:user-provided
             (format t "~&  the user-provided fact ~A"
     source-name))
        (:entity (format t "~&  the unit ~A, because"
     source-name)
               (format t "~&  the ~A of ~A is ~A."
                      (car args) source-name (car (last
     args))))))))
  (user-pause))
```

# *Search Strategy*

The three common search strategies are *depth-first, breadth-first,* and *best-first.* Each of the three strategies uses a slightly different approach to search for the target solution.

## Depth-First Search

In the discussion of forward and backward chaining, we have used an implied search strategy—depth-first. In both forward and backward chaining, there is always a starting point (either a fact or a goal). The starting point is called the *root node.* There are choices (*branch nodes*) after the starting point and more subbranches at each branch, as the matching and substitution process goes along. This decision process is called a *tree* because every branch has a unique parent with only one exception (the root node).

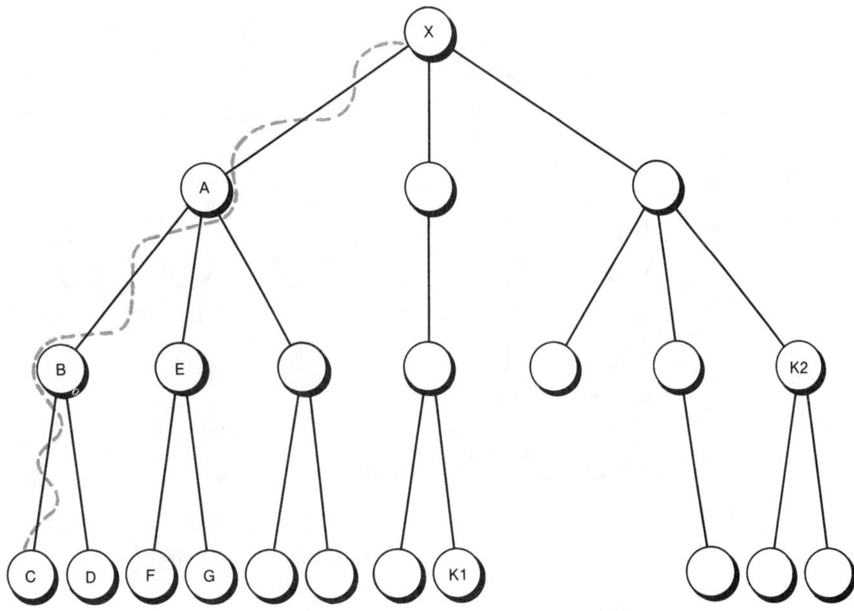


**Figure 8-1**
***Depth-first search***

In a depth-first search, as illustrated in Figure 8-1, the search starts at X and moves down to A, B, and C. Only the leftmost child of each node is examined. If it is not the desired node, the process goes down to the next level and picks the leftmost child of that node, always moving downward. If it reaches the bottom level without finding the desired choice, the process returns to the last node where there was a choice. Then the downward motion is repeated. For example, if the target node for search in Figure 8-1 is K2, the depth-first strategy requires a great effort to reach the target node. The process has to go through almost all nodes, down from X to C, returning from C to B and moving down again to D, returning to A, descending to E and F and so on to get to K2.

The depth-first search entails a recursive procedure in which the recursion occurs for movement down one tree branch and then across all the branches. This recursion is implemented in both sample forward and backward chaining programs, as discussed previously.

## Breadth-First Search and Best-First Search

In breadth-first search, movement is performed level by level. The process examines all nodes on each level, one by one. If the target node is not found, then the process looks at those on the next level, as shown in Figure 8-2.

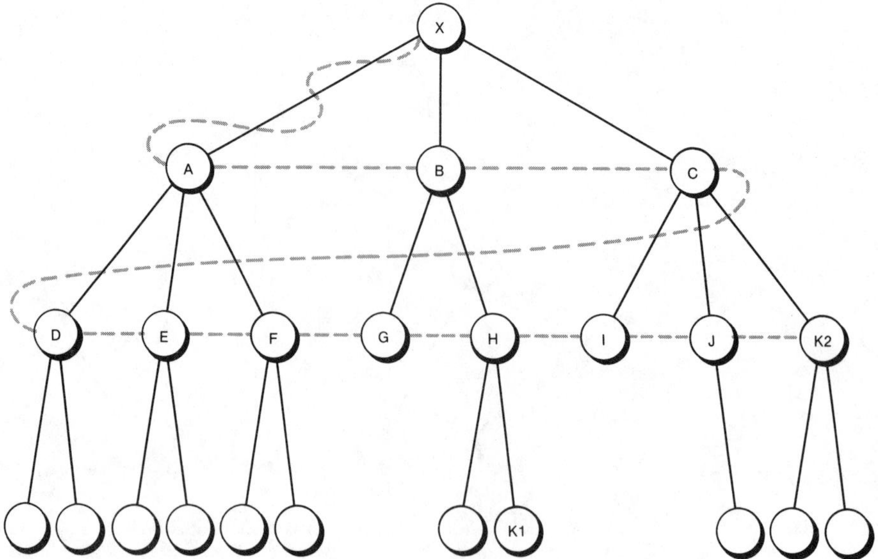


**Figure 8-2**
***Breadth-first search***

The same example of searching for K2 is used to compare the difference in efficiency. Because K2 is on the third level, the search process has to examine only ten nodes to reach K2, in comparison with nineteen nodes in the depth-first search. Whether the breadth-first search is more efficient than the depth-first search depends on where the target node is. Consequently, it sometimes pays to make a good guess about how far the target node is from the current node and select the shortest path leading to the target node. This strategy is called best-first search.

The two elements required in a best-first search are (1) complete ordering of the paths and (2) a method to determine the distance remaining between the current node and the target node. In theory, the ordering of the paths can be undertaken by using `Sort`, and the straight-line distance between the target node and the current node can be used as the starting point if the locations of these nodes can be identified. The straight line distance is estimated as follows:

$$\text{Distance} = \text{SQRT}\ ((N1-X)\ (N1-X) + (N2-Y)\ (N2-Y))$$

where (N1, N2) is the position of the target node and (X,Y) is the location of the current node on a travel map.

The implementation of breadth-first and best-first search into the forward and backward chaining programs requires a careful estimation of the tradeoff between complexity and efficiency for the actual application of the expert system and tool. It is left to you to explore the possibility of implementing these two strategies in actual applications.

# Designing a User Interface

User interface includes mouse, window, and menu operations and natural language front ends. The mouse, window, and menu operations are familiar to most programmers and are system- and language-dependent. They are discussed within the context of the GCLISP environment for the IBM PC. These elements are interrelated and all are required for an effective user interface mechanism.

## *Mouse Operation*

The mouse operation requires a three-button mouse and involves designing the following elements: structure, environment, utility function, and documentation of the mouse operation. For programs written in Smalltalk, a two-button mouse operation is equipped automatically.

The mouse structure is designed to pop up menus in a designated area on the screen, to allow the user to select the desired menu, which is highlighted when the mouse passes over it, and to hide the mouse when the keyboard is used for inputting. As shown in Listing 8-7, `defstruct` is used to define the mouse structure, which includes:

- Sensitive text (menu) shown on screen
- Documentation
- Value to return from the screen
- Starting column position for the menu area
- Starting row position for the menu area
- Mouse starting (X,Y) position
- Other features such as text highlighting

**Listing 8-7**
***Sample program to define mouse structure***

```
;;; Mouse Sensitive TEXT.  These are items that will be
     highlighted when
;;; the mouse cursor is over the sensitive area on the
     screen.
(DEFSTRUCT (STEXT (:PRINT-FUNCTION 'PRINT-STEXT))
  TEXT                      ; the sensitive text
  (doc "")                  ; documentation
  value                     ; value to return
  color
  COLUMN                    ; starting column position
  ROW                       ; starting row position
  MIC-X                     ; mickeys for the mouse, starting x
     position
  MIC-Y                     ; starting y position
  MIC-END-X                 ; ending x position
  (ON-P NIL))               ; whether the text item is
     highlighted or not
(DEFUN PRINT-STEXT (OBJ STRM IGNORE)
  (FORMAT T "<Mouse Sensitive Item ~A>" (STEXT-TEXT OBJ)))
```

**Listing 8-8**
***Sample program to design mouse operations***

```
;;; This global variable holds the current sensitive text
     item or NIL
;;; if the mouse cursor is not over one.
(defvar *CURRENT-STEXT* NIL)
;;; The screen mode in effect when we are using the mouse.
(DEFVAR *MOUSE-SCREEN-MODE* 6)
;;; The color for any line drawing that is done during mouse
     tracking.
(DEFVAR *MOUSE-PEN-COLOR* 1)
;;; The function for any mouse drawing functions
(DEFVAR *MOUSE-PEN-FUNCTION* 1)
```

A sample program for designing a mouse operation is shown in Listing 8-8. To design the environment for the mouse operation, you need to define the color for any line drawing during mouse tracking, the color of menu items, and the color of the backward screen. The function used for these definitions is `defvar`. Utility functions required for the mouse to operate smoothly include functions for initializing the mouse, showing or hiding the mouse, and highlighting the menu text with a given color. Many of these functions use low-level system functions, such as `%sysint`, that generate a software (internal) interrupt. Listing 8-9 shows sample programs for the following utility functions:

| | |
|---|---|
| `Mouse-init` | To initialize the mouse by putting the screen in graphics mode |
| `Mouse-show` | To show the mouse to the user |
| `Mouse-hide` | To hide the mouse from the user |
| `Highlight` | To highlight the menu text item with a given color when the mouse passes over it |

**Listing 8-9**
***Sample program to define mouse operation utilities***

```
;;; UTILITY AND INTERNAL FUNCTIONS
;;; Set the mouse cursor to be CHAR.  COLOR is the attribute
    used when
;;; writing the mouse cursor character.
(DEFUN SET-MOUSE-CURSOR (CHAR COLOR)
  (SYS:%SYSINT #X33 0 0 0 0)
  (SYS:%SYSINT #X33 10 0 0 (LOGIOR (LSH COLOR 8) CHAR))
  (SYS:%SYSINT #X33 1 0 0 0))
;;; Initialize the mouse putting the screen in graphics
 mode.
(DEFUN MOUSE-INIT ()
  (SYS:%SYSINT #X10 *MOUSE-SCREEN-MODE* 0 0 0)    ; graphics
    mode
  (SYS:%SYSINT #X33 1 0 0 0))
;;; Show the mouse.
(DEFUN MOUSE-SHOW ()
  (SYS:%SYSINT #X33 1 0 0 0))
;;; Hide the mouse.
(DEFUN MOUSE-HIDE ()
  (SYS:%SYSINT #X33 2 0 0 0))
;;; Move the mouse to the X and Y position specified.
(DEFUN MOUSE-WARP (X Y)
  (SYS:%SYSINT #X33 4 0 X Y))
;;; Highlight the sensitive text item X with the color
    COLOR.
(DEFUN HIGHLIGHT (X &optional COLOR)
  (unless color (setq color (stext-color x)))
  (WITH-MOUSE-HIDDEN                                ; hide the
    mouse
   (SEND *TERMINAL-IO* :SET-CURSORPOS (STEXT-COLUMN X)
    (STEXT-ROW X))
   (LET ((A (SEND *TERMINAL-IO* :ATTRIBUTE)))
    (SEND *TERMINAL-IO* :SET-ATTRIBUTE COLOR)
    (SEND *TERMINAL-IO* :WRITE-STRING (STEXT-TEXT X))
```

**Listing 8-9 (cont.)**

```
(SEND *TERMINAL-IO* :SET-ATTRIBUTE A))))      ; bring
the mouse back
```

Documentation of the mouse operation is required to inform the user of the function of the mouse button; that is, the meanings of the right, middle, and left buttons. Listing 8-10 shows a partial sample program for documentation of the mouse operation at the bottom of the screen.

**Listing 8-10**
***Sample program for mouse documentation***

```
;;; Mouse documentation stuff
;;; convention: left chooses, middle aborts, right exits
(defun buttons-translate (buttons)
  (cond ((leftp buttons) 'left)
        ((rightp buttons) 'right)
        ((middlep buttons) 'middle)))
(defun leftp (buttons)
  (oddp buttons))
(defun Rightp (buttons)
  (member buttons '(2 3 6 7)))
(defun Middlep (buttons)
  (> buttons 3))
(defun Mouse-Doc (button)
  (get-item-doc (assoc button *buttons-operation*)))
(defparameter *buttons-operation*
      '((left :choose :doc "Choose") (middle nil) (right
     :exit :doc "Exit")))
```

# *Window Operation*

The window operation organizes the screen skillfully to provide the user with maximum visual comfort and convenience. The designing of a window operation involves two major tasks: making windows and operating windows. This window operation is built upon the GCLISP window system. In programs written in Smalltalk, windows are created differently, as discussed in Chapter 6.

## Making a Window

A GCLISP window is an abstraction of a character input/output terminal that produces and consumes characters. The characters that a window produces are generated by a keyword and those that a window consumes are displayed in an associated rectangular region of the screen. ***Make-window-stream***, a GCLISP function (nonstandard), is used to create a window. Arguments to `make-window-stream` specify the size and shape of the window, its position on the physical display, the initial X,Y coordinate of the window's cursor, and so forth, as shown in Example 8-4.

*Example 8-4*

```
Make-window-stream   &key :height :width  :top  :left
     :status
:page :cursorpos-x :cursorpos-y :attribute => stream
```

Because this function creates a new window stream, all stream operations and functions, such as `*terminal-io *`, `close`, and `send`, may be used with window operations.

Keyword arguments set the attributes of a window and need not be specified. Default values are used for those attributes that are not specified by the user. The main keywords are

`:height` Sets the initial height (in lines) of the window. An integer between 1 and 25. Default: 24.

`:width` Sets the initial width (in columns) of the window. An integer between 3 and 80. Default: 80.

`:top` Sets the initial offset (in lines) from the top of the physical display to the top line of the window. An integer between 0 and 24. Default: 0.

`:left` Sets the initial offset (in columns) from the leftmost column of the physical display to the leftmost column of the window. An integer between 0 and 79. Default: 0.

`:status` Sets behavioral attributes of the window. An integer used to represent a bit vector with the value 0,2,4 or 6. Default: 4. The bits are used as follows:

- Bit 0 Current window-p
  This bit is read-only to the user. Only one window ever has this bit set.
- Bit 1 Wrap lines-p
  If 1, the cursor is wrapped to the top line of the window. If 0, the lines in the window are scrolled up one line and the cursor is left on a blank line at the bottom of the window.
- Bit 2 Auto-newline-p
  If 1, a newline is automatically inserted. If 0, the last column is overwritten.

`:page` Sets the display page upon which the window is displayed. An integer between 0 and 3. When in alphanumeric mode, the color/graphics monitor adapter provides enough storage for four separate 25-row/80-column display pages or eight separate 25-row/40-column display pages.

`:cursorpos-x` Sets the initial offset (in columns) of the cursor from the leftmost column of the window. An integer between 0 and 79. Default: 0.

`:cursorpos-y` Sets the initial offset (in lines) of the cursor from the top of the window. An integer between 0 and 24. Default: 0.

`:attribute` Sets the display attribute of the characters displayed in the window. An unsigned integer (used to represent a bit vector) between 0 and 65535. Default: 7. The bits have the following meanings:

| | |
|---|---|
| Bits 0–2 | Foreground color |
| Bit 3 | Intensity |
| Bits 6–4 | Background color |
| Bit 7 | Blinking |

Listing 8-11a shows two sample programs, one for the main window and the other for the menu window. Note the following features in the programs:

- `Defparameter` is used to define `*main-window*` and `*menu-window*`, which are global variables to be used in other files.
- The width of the main window is the difference between 78 and the width of the menu window.
- The attribute is a function that defines the foreground color, intensity, background color, and blink.

**Listing 8-11**
***Sample programs for defining and resetting windows***

```
;;; Main window
(defparameter *main-window*
              (make-window-stream :height 20 :width
     *main-window-width*
                                  :top 1 :left 1
           :attribute (make-color-attribute :brown :bright
     :black :off)))

;;; *******************************************************
;;; Menu Window
(defparameter *menu-window*
              (make-window-stream :height 23 :width
```

```
          (make-window-stream :height 23 :width
*system-menu-width*
                              :top 1 :left (- 79
*system-menu-width*)
 :attribute (make-color-attribute :lavender :bright
:blue :off)))
```

*a. Sample Programs for Defining a Main Window and Menu Window*

```
(defun Reset-Screen ()
  "Writes out border and clears main window"
  (let* ((a (send *terminal-io* :attribute)))
    (set-screen-color :lavender :bright :blue :off)
    (set-cursorpos 0 0)
    (send *terminal-io* :write-char 201)
    (dotimes (i 78)
      (send *terminal-io* :write-char 205))
    (send *terminal-io* :write-char 187)
    (set-cursorpos 0 0)
    (center-string " Expert Knowledge Organizer "
     *terminal-io*)
   (dotimes (i 23)
      (set-cursorpos 0 (1+ i))
      (send *terminal-io* :write-char 186)
      (set-cursorpos 79 (1+ i))
      (send *terminal-io* :write-char 186))
    (send *terminal-io* :set-attribute a))
  (send *main-window* :clear-screen)
  (refresh-menus)
  (send *monitor-stream* :clear-screen))
```

*b. Sample Program for Writing a Border and Clearing the Main Window*

---

The same method can be applied to make a window beneath the main window to show notices, a mode line at the bottom of the screen to show mouse document, or a mode line at the top of the screen to show the logo of the expert system or tool.

## Operating Windows

Because windows are streams, stream functions can be used to operate a window. The most frequently used function is ***Send***, as shown in Example 8-5.

*Example 8-5*

```
(send *main-window*: clear-screen)
```

`Send` in the above expression sends a message to the main window to clear the screen, using an object-oriented programming format.

`:Clear-screen` is a window operation that is employed to clear the entire window and set the window's cursor position to 0,0.

The specification of major operations accepted by a window, its arguments, and the window's response (shown after =>) are as follows:

`:clear-input => nil`
Clears the window's character input buffer up to the next Newline character.

`:clear-screen=> nil`
Clears the entire window and sets the window's cursor position to 0,0.

`:cursorpos => x-pos y-pos`
Returns the current x-position (column) and y-position (row) of the window's cursor.

`:set-position left top => nil`
Repositions the window on the physical display so that the window's leftmost column is offset `left` columns from the physical display's leftmost column and the window's top line is offset `top` lines from the physical display's top line.

`:set-size width height => nil`
Modifies the size of the window so that it is `width` columns wide and `height` lines high.

`:set-attribute integer => nil`
Sets the character display attributes of the current window.

`:write-string string =>string`
Successively outputs the characters in a string (using `:write-char`) to the window stream.

`:write-char character => nil`
Outputs characters to the window stream. The character is displayed at the current cursor position and the cursor position is updated.

Listing 8-11b shows a sample program for writing a border with the logo of the expert system shell (e.g., "Expert Knowledge Organizer") and clearing the main window. Note that `set-screen-color` is a function written to define foreground color, intensity, background color, and blink option. `Dotimes` is a macro that provides simple iteration over a sequence of integers—for example, `(i 78)` means doing an operation 78 times, from 77 to 0.

## Menu Operation

The menu operation integrates the mouse and window operations, receiving input from the mouse as well as the keyboard, and returning output streams to windows. Because the number of menu items and restrictions and the type of each item are different for every individual menu group (such as classes, units, rules, unstructured data base, and variables), common menu operations need to be defined to enable the user to select menus in those menu classes. The main menu operations include:

- Create menus
- Initialize menu windows
- Erase menus
- Choose menus
- Display menus
- Menu input

## Create Menus

The command `create-menu` is used to create a menu structure that can house a given number of menu items. The procedure is to (1) define the location of the menu and (2) make a menu structure correspondent to its width, length, location, and other attributes. A sample program for creating a menu structure is given in Listing 8-12.

**Listing 8-12**
***Sample program for creating a menu structure***

```
(defun Menu-Choose-Initialize (item-list label)
  (let* ((width (+ 2 (apply 'max (mapcar 'length
                                          (mapcar
     'get-item-string
                                          (cons label
     item-list))))))
        (length (1+ (length item-list)))
          (menu (make-menu1 width length))
          (char-x (car (menu-location menu)))
          (char-y (cadr (menu-location menu))))
    (setf (menu-label menu) (make-sens-item label char-x
     char-y width))
   (do ((items item-list (cdr items))
          (char-y (1+ char-y) (1+ char-y)))
         ((endp items))
     (push-last (make-sens-item (car items) char-x char-y
     width)
              (menu-sens-item-list menu)))
    menu))
```

## Initialize Menu Windows

The purpose of initializing menu windows is to allow the user to fit menu items and the menu label into the main menu window and other secondary menu windows, if any. As shown in Listing 8-13, the procedure of initializing the menu list is to (1) define the width, length, and location of the menu window space that is required, on the basis of the number of menu items and the label provided by the user, (2) put the item into the menu window slots, one by one, and (3) enable the item to be highlighted when the mouse passes through it.

**Listing 8-13**
***Sample program to initialize the main menu window***

```
(defun Make-Menu1 (width length)
  "Creates a menu structure where the mouse is, initializing
     its size"
  (multiple-value-bind (mouse-x-pix mouse-y-pix ignore)
    (mouse-pos)
    (let ((char-x (get-menu-pos (round (/ mouse-x-pix 8))
     width
                                (- 79 *system-menu-width*) 1))
        (char-y (get-menu-pos (round (/ mouse-y-pix 8))
     length 20 1)))
     (make-menu :width width :length length
           :location (list char-x char-y)
                     ))))
```

The location needs to be changed when another menu window is to be initialized at a different location in the screen. Otherwise, the method is applicable to other menu windows.

## Erase a Menu

The purpose of erasing menus is to clear the menu window. It is required to assure that only the desired menus in the screen are erased. The command is essentially the window operation `send *terminal-io*` with a blank string to clear the menu window space. A sample program for erasing menus is shown in Listing 8-14.

**Listing 8-14**
***Sample program for erasing menus***

```
(defun Erase-Menu (menu)
  (unless (eq menu *system-menu*)
  (do ((y-offset 0 (1+ y-offset))
       (x (car (menu-location menu))))
      ((= y-offset (menu-length menu)))
    (send *terminal-io* :set-cursorpos
          x (+ y-offset (cadr (menu-location menu))))
```

```
    (send *terminal-io* :write-string
          (blank-string (menu-width menu))))))
```

## Choose a Menu

The objective in choosing a menu is to select an item from the menu and return the value of the chosen item. The procedure is as follows: if `item-list-or-menu` (the input from the user) is `item-list`, a menu is created and an item is chosen from it; if the input is `menu`, then the menu is used. The reason for the IF condition is that some menus in the main menu system may contain submenus, and only one submenu can be chosen at a time. Listing 8-15 shows a sample program for choosing menus. Note that `track-highlighting` is a function written to return the value of the menu highlighted and clicked by the mouse. You may need to use information in the mouse operation to write such a function.

**Listing 8-15**
***Sample program for choosing menus***

```
;;; Menu-Choose Facility

(defun Menu-Choose (item-list-or-menu &optional label)
  "If item-list-or-menu is an item-list, creates a menu and
     chooses an item
   from it.  If it is a menu, then uses it.
  Returns the value of the chosen item."
  (let* ((menu (if (menu-p item-list-or-menu)
                         item-list-or-menu
                         (Menu-Choose-Initialize
     item-list-or-menu label)))
        result)
    (setq *current-stext* nil
          *temporary-menu-sensitive-items*
     (menu-sens-item-list menu)
        result (track-highlighting)
        *temporary-menu-sensitive-items* nil)
    (erase-menu menu)
    result))
```

## Display a Menu

`Display-Menu` is a function that combines both mouse and window operations. It employs `highlight`, which is defined in the mouse operation, to highlight with a designated color the menu text item that the mouse has passed over. If there are submenus, the submenu also is displayed. Listing 8-16 shows a sample program for displaying menus.

**Listing 8-16**
***Sample program for displaying menus***

```
(defun Display-Menu (menu)
  (highlight (menu-label menu) *label-color*)
  (let ((items (menu-sens-item-list menu)))
    (dolist (item items)
      (highlight Item))))
```

## Menu Input

The purpose of menu input is to allow the user to prompt input from the keyboard as well as to give commands from the mouse. The procedure of menu input is as follows:

- Clear input buffer.
- Initialize the mouse position, the menu window position, and the length of the prompt string.
- Highlight the query (menu) for input with a designated color.
- Receive a prompted value from the user.
- Reset the window cursor's positions.
- Return the prompted input value.

A sample program for menu input is shown in Listing 8-17. Note that `multiple-value-bind` is a Common LISP function used to bind the mouse's position. `Menu-read-value` is a function that you need to define to allow your user to be prompted for the right input information in the right format.

**Listing 8-17**
***Sample program for menu input***

```
;;; Menu-Input
;;; there should be no max input length
(defun Menu-Input (prompt &optional (type 'expression))
  (send *terminal-io* :clear-input)
  (multiple-value-bind (mouse-x-pix mouse-y-pix ignore)
    (mouse-pos)
    (let* ((width (max (length (string prompt)) 30))
           (char-x (get-menu-pos (round (/ mouse-x-pix 8))
     width
                               (- 79 *system-menu-width*) 1))
        (char-y (get-menu-pos (round (/ mouse-y-pix 8)) 2
     20 1))
        (prompt-si (make-sens-item prompt char-x char-y
     width))
        value)
```

```
 (highlight prompt-si *label-color*)
 (setq value (menu-read-value char-x (1+ char-y) width
type))
(set-cursorpos char-x char-y)
 (princ (blank-string width))
 (set-cursorpos char-x (1+ char-y))
 (princ (blank-string width))
 value)))
```

# *Natural Language Front Ends*

Natural language (in comparison to computer language) front ends translate the query or prompt from natural language to the predicate calculus that is used efficiently by AI professionals. Predicate calculus (PC) enables you to conveniently calculate the truth of propositions, because it consists of a language for expressing propositions and rules for inferring new facts from facts that exist in the knowledge base. However, a PC form is not as apparent to the user as natural language. Consequently, natural language front ends can provide a useful service to the user in communicating with the expert system and tool. An unconstrained natural language front end can be extremely complicated. Fortunately, the PC form is fairly concise, because it is used to express the following relationships:

1. Class
   - A fact about the own-slot value of a class. The format is *(<slot-name> <class name> <value>).*
   - A fact about the memberships of a class in another class. The format is *(subclass <class-name1> <class-name2>).*
2. Units
   - A fact about the slot value of a unit. The format is *(<slot-name> <unit-name> <value>).*
   - A fact about the class of a unit. The format is *(in-class <unit-name> <class-name>).*
3. Variable
   - A fact about the value of a variable. The format is *(value <variable-name> <variable-value>).*

A preliminary natural language front end can be used to add appropriate terms such as “the,” “of,” “is,” “a,” and “all” to those relationships, so they can be more apparent to the user. The preliminary front end allows the following simple translation of the above PC formats:

1. Classes
   - The own-slot value of a class: *the <slot-name> of <unit-name> is <value>.*
   - Membership of a class in another: *all <class-name1> are <class-name2>.*
2. Units
   - Slot value of a unit: *the <slot-name> of <unit-name> is <value>.*
   - The class of a unit: *<unit-name> is a type of <class-name>.*
3. Variables
   - The value of a variable: *<variable name> is <variable-value>.*

To translate this natural front end to the PC form, a simple parsing of the input string is required to delete the add-on English words such as "the," "of," and so forth. Listing 8-18 shows a sample program for translating the natural language front end to predicate calculus.

**Listing 8-18**
***Sample program for translating the natural language front end to predicate calculus***

```
(defun Nl-Translate (string)
  "Takes a string and makes it into predicate calculus"
  (parse-unit-string string))
(defun Parse-Unit-String (string)
  (let ((exp (read-from-string (format nil "(~A)" string))))
    (cond ((and (= 6 (length exp))
                (string-equal "the" (string (first exp)))
                (string-equal "of" (string (third exp)))
                (string-equal "is" (string (fifth exp))))
      '(,(second exp) ,(fourth exp) ,(sixth exp)))
        ((and (= 4 (length exp))
                (string-equal "is" (string (second exp)))
                (string-equal "a" (string (third exp))))
      '(type-of ,(first exp) ,(fourth exp)))
        ((and (= 7 (length exp))
                     (string-equal "the" (string (first
    exp)))
                     (string-equal "of" (string (third
    exp)))
                     (string-equal "all" (string (fourth
    exp)))
                     (string-equal "is" (string (sixth
    exp))))
```

```
          '(,(second exp) ,(fifth exp) ,(seventh exp)))
            ((and (= 3 (length exp))
                  (string-equal "is" (string (second
exp))))
          '(value-of ,(first exp) ,(third exp)))
            (t exp))))
```

# Summary

- The implementation of the inference engine and the user interface has been discussed.
- An inference engine can be either simple or complicated, depending on the structure of the knowledge base.
- The main elements in an inference engine are forward chaining, backward chaining, justification, and search strategy.
- Forward chaining is used to assert a fact that matches the promise of a rule to determine a new fact.
- Backward chaining attempts to prove a hypothesis from facts.
- The three search strategies are depth-first, breadth-first, and best-first.
- Justification provides the user with a tracing facility to indicate the history of goal substitution.
- Facilities to enhance user interface include mouse, window, and menu operations and natural language front ends.

SECTION

# 4

# Building and Delivering Expert Systems

Section 4 discusses methods for building expert systems by extracting and organizing the expert's knowledge, using the tools developed in Section 3. Chapter 9 provides an overview of applications and approaches to expert system technology. Chapter 10 examines example cases in selected domains.

Methods and examples are used in the discussion and design rules for building expert system tools and expert systems are followed closely. Note that the two important rules in writing code, which are discussed in previous chapters, are modularity and object-oriented programming.

# 9

# Expert System Technology Applications and Approaches

The initial application of expert systems was in the diagnosis and treatment of human physical disorders. The basic purpose of these systems is to determine what various symptoms indicate and what remedial treatment is appropriate. One example is MYCIN, which identifies the type of infection in a patient and prescribes corrective treatment. This type of expert system was subsequently applied to the diagnosis and repair of equipment failure. The application of expert systems was further expanded to cover situation analysis and understanding (e.g., military operations), manufacturing and engineering (e.g., floor layout), geological exploration (e.g., mineral assessment), nuclear power plant operations (e.g., crisis management), software development (e.g., automatic programming), and financial services (e.g., bank loan applications).

Not every problem, however, can be solved with expert systems; expert systems have their own limitations. For example, current expert systems are slow, cost much to develop, and are unable to recognize their own knowledge boundaries.

## Statistics of Historical Applications

The primary historical application areas can be classified into industrial applications (including chemistry, computer systems, electronics, engineering, geology, manufacturing, and manufacturing-related areas, such as space technology), medicine, military, information management, law, and agriculture. Table 9-1 shows the distribution of expert systems over these five areas [1] [2] [3].

Of the 257 expert systems known to me, about 35 are either in daily use or field test. More than a hundred new expert systems have been

**Table 9-1**
***Distribution of expert systems over primary application areas***

| Application | Number of Applications as of 1985 |
|---|---|
| Industrial | 129 |
| Medicine | 60 |
| Military | 38 |
| Information management | 15 |
| Law | 11 |
| Agriculture | 4 |
| TOTAL | 257 |

developed and tested in the past year but are not included. From these statistics, it is clear that approximately half of the existing expert systems have been developed for industrial applications. Only thirty-eight expert systems have been developed for military purposes, fewer than expected. However, many military expert systems may be classified in nature and thus not publicly known. Information management and law applications have become increasingly important and now account for 10 percent of all expert systems.

# Tasks in Which Expert System Technology May Be Helpful

As discussed in the previous section of this chapter, expert system technology has been applied to many fields of science and liberal arts. The most successful task types are control/monitoring, debugging, design, diagnosis, instruction, interpretation, planning, and prediction.

## *Control/Monitoring*

Control and monitoring systems usually perform sequential tasks and are closely integrated. Monitoring is required for effective control, and control is usually the ultimate objective of monitoring. The function of control/monitoring is the continuous interpretation of signals and actuation of alarms when intervention is needed. Expert systems have been developed to perform control and monitoring for computer systems, nuclear power plants, and medicine. Examples include PTRANS [4], YES/MVS [5], and REACTOR [6].

PTRANS, developed jointly by Digital Equipment Corporation and Carnegie-Mellon University, assists managers in controlling the manufacture and distribution of Digital Equipment computer systems [4]. It monitors the progress of technicians in the implementation of assembly plans in accordance with customer orders, diagnoses problems, predicts shortages or surpluses of materials, and prescribes solutions. YES/MVS, developed at the IBM T.J. Watson Research Center, assists computer operators on a real-time basis in monitoring and controlling the IBM MVS (multiple virtual storage) operating system [5]. REACTOR, developed by EG&G Idaho, helps reactor operators diagnose and treat nuclear reactor accidents by monitoring instrument readings on a real-time basis [6].

The limitation with expert systems in regard to this task is that requirements and conditions for monitoring and control vary according to the process monitored, and are time and situation dependent. Current expert technology cannot deal effectively with real-time problems.

## *Debugging*

Debugging is performed to identify remedies for malfunctions in a physical system, such as a machine. The search space for remedies is usually limited; therefore, debugging can be performed admirably by expert systems. Debugging usually accompanies diagnosis, which is the best understood application area. The debugging task is usually employed for chemistry, computer systems, electronics, engineering, geology, and medicine. Examples are TQMSTUNE (chemistry [7]), TIMM/Tuner (computer systems [8]), ACE (electronics [9]), DRILLING ADVISOR (geology [10]), and BLUE BOX (medicine [11]). The purposes of these expert systems are summarized in Table 9-2.

**Table 9-2**
***Examples of expert systems specialized in debugging***

| Expert System | Application | Function(s) | Status |
|---|---|---|---|
| TQMSTUNE [7] | Chemistry | Fine tune a triple quadruple mass spectrometer | Demonstration prototype |
| TIMM/Tuner [8] | Computer system | Tune VAX/VMS computers | Production systems |
| ACE [9] | Electronics | Troubleshoot faults in telephone networks | Production systems |
| REACTOR [6] | Nuclear power | Treat nuclear reactor accidents | Research prototype |
| DRILLING ADVISOR [10] | Geology | Correct oil rig "drill stitching" problems | Research prototype |
| BLUE BOX [11] | Medicine | Treat various forms of depression | Research prototype |

The limitation with regard to the debugging task is that a single fault is usually assumed and an appropriate correction is prescribed for it. It may be difficult to develop expert systems capable of identifying remedies for multiple, sequential, or intermittent faults, because the system anatomy may not be fully understood and represented in expert systems.

## Design

The function of design is to establish specifications to configure objects that satisfy particular requirements and constraints. Design expert systems are developed mostly for chemistry (e.g., organic molecules), computer systems (e.g., configuration of computers), electronics (e.g., VLSI circuits), and the military (e.g., map labeling). Table 9-3 summarizes one example for each application area and its function. The systems listed in the table are research prototypes, with the exception of XCON [12].

XCON was developed by Carnegie-Mellon University for Digital Equipment Corporation. It configures VAX family computer systems at a very detailed level. XCON performs configuration at a level equal to that of an experienced technical editor but at a speed 20 times faster than the editor. Details of XCON are discussed in a later section of this chapter.

**Table 9-3**
***Examples of expert systems specialized in design***

| Expert System | Application | Function(s) | Status |
|---|---|---|---|
| SECS [28] | Chemistry | Synthesize organic molecules | Research prototype |
| XCON [12] | Computer systems | Configure VAX computers | Production system |
| PALLADIO [29] | Electronics | Design new VLSI circuits | Research prototype |
| ACES [30] | Military | Design map labeling | Research prototype |

The limitation of using expert systems specialized in design is that the problem scope may be so large that assessment of the consequences of design decisions is precluded. Subproblems may be consequently partitioned and subproblem interdependency difficult to resolve. Because of the complexity of the system, it may be difficult to evaluate the impact of design changes or to record design decisions because design decisions are made by expert systems sequentially during the design process.

## Diagnosis

Expert systems specialized in diagnosis troubleshoot faults in a system, based on interpretation of data. This task is the best understood and most highly developed of all expert system applications. These expert systems also perform debugging, as discussed previously. They have been developed for computer systems (e.g., to locate defects in computers), electronics (e.g., to diagnose faults in telephone networks), nuclear power plants (e.g., to diagnose nuclear reactor accidents), geology (e.g., to locate problems related to drilling fluids used in drilling operations), and medicine (e.g., to diagnose lung diseases). Table 9-4 provides five examples. The three systems listed that have reached either the field test or production system stage are ACE [9], MUD [13], and PUFF [14].

**Table 9-4**
***Examples of expert systems specialized in diagnosis***

| Expert System | Application | Function(s) | Status |
|---|---|---|---|
| IDT [31] | Computer systems | Locate defective units in PDP 11/03 computers | Research prototype |
| ACE [9] | Electronics | Diagnose faults in telephone networks | Production system |
| REACTOR [6] | Nuclear power | Locate nuclear reactor accidents | Research prototype |
| MUD [13] | Geology | Troubleshoot drilling fluid problems | Field-test prototype |
| PUFF [14] | Medicine | Diagnose lung diseases | Production system |

The limitation with expert systems specialized in diagnosis is similar to that of debugging. These systems tend to be based on single fault assumption and may not consider sequential, combined, or intermittent faults. Many times, the faults originate with the diagnostic equipment rather than with the physical system. The complexity of the physical system often precludes a full understanding of the system. In some cases—for example, nuclear power plants—diagnostic data is expensive and unavailable for test.

# Instruction

Instructional expert systems train students by diagnosing, debugging, and correcting student behavior or knowledge in a particular field. These systems develop a basis of the student's acquired knowledge in a particular field, diagnose his/her deficiencies, and prescribe training drills to correct the deficiencies. These instructional systems are used in electronics (e.g., to teach the use of a CAD system), plant operation (e.g., to train operators of a steam propulsion plant), and medicine (e.g., to instruct in methods of anesthesia management). Table 9-5 summarizes examples of instructional expert systems. Most of these systems have not yet reached the production system stage.

One limitation with instructional expert systems lies in the complexity of interaction between teachers and students and the learning process of

**Table 9-5**
***Examples of expert systems specialized in instruction***

| Expert System | Application | Function(s) | Status |
|---|---|---|---|
| CAD HELP [32] | Electronics | Teach the use of a CAD subsystem for digital circuit design | Research prototype |
| STEAMER [33] | Plant operation | Instruct naval engineering students in operating a steam propulsion plant | Field test |
| ATTENDING [34] | Medicine | Teach medical students in anesthesiology | Research prototype |

students. It is still too early to evaluate the effectiveness of the instructional expert systems.

## *Interpretation*

Expert systems for interpretation perform analysis of sensor data to determine its meaning. These systems deal with real data measured from sensing instruments in the form of data streams, waveforms, or pictures. Because of the real environment, this data may be flawed by noise and may be incomplete, unreliable, or erroneous.

Interpretational expert systems are developed for chemistry (e.g., to infer a compound's molecular structure from mass spectral data), nuclear power plants (e.g., to infer accidents from reactor data), geology (e.g., to interpret dipmeter logs), medicine (e.g., to interpret scanning densitometer data for inflammatory conditions), and the military (e.g., to interpret sonar sensor data for detecting and identifying ocean vessels).

The main purpose of these systems is to explain what is taking place and to determine what the signals mean. Table 9-6 summarizes examples of expert systems specialized in interpretation. Data interpretation is also a well-understood and well-developed expert system task. DENDRAL [15] and SPE [16] are both commercial systems.

The drawback with interpretational expert systems is that the interpretation may be based on partial information or conflicting data from various sensors. These systems also require real-time processing of data that is still under development for the current technology.

## *Planning*

Expert systems specialized in devising plans and programs to achieve given goals develop an entire course of action and occasionally reject a portion of a

**Table 9-6**
***Examples of expert systems specialized in interpretation***

| Expert System | Application | Function(s) | Status |
|---|---|---|---|
| DENDRAL [15] | Chemistry | Infer the molecular structure of unknown compounds from mass spectral and nuclear magnetic response data | Production system |
| REACTOR [6] | Nuclear plants | Interpret instrument readings to evaluate system deviations | Research prototype |
| DIPMETER ADVISOR [35] | Geology | Infer subsurface geological structure by interpreting dipmeter logs | Research prototype |
| SPE [16] | Medicine | Interpret scanning densitometer data to diagnose inflammatory conditions | Production system |
| HASP/SIAP [36] | Military | Interpret sonar sensor data to detect and identify ocean vessels | Research prototype |

plan after implementation because it violates constraints. These systems are used in chemistry (e.g., to develop experiments in molecular genetics), computer systems (e.g., to develop plans for assembling and testing the computer system on order), electronics (e.g., to synthesize integrated circuit layouts of nMOS cells), and military operations (e.g., to develop plans for attacking enemy airfields). Table 9-7 summarizes examples of expert systems specialized in planning. Planning expert systems are new and relatively time consuming to develop. All systems listed in the table are in the research prototype stage.

The disadvantage in using expert systems in planning is the possible explosion of system complexity due to problem size and the consequences of actions. These systems often contain highly detailed actions and relationships among actions, and thus require substantial coordination among multiple players and subgoals.

## Prediction

Expert systems specialized in prediction forecast the future from models or programs of the past and present that mirror real-world activity. Predictive expert systems combine traditional models and programs with knowledge about the processes that originated them, to form the basis of predictions. These systems can be used in military applications (e.g., to forecast when

**Table 9-7**
***Examples of expert systems specialized in planning***

| Expert System | Application | Function(s) | Status |
|---|---|---|---|
| GA1 [37] | Chemistry | Develop experiments in DNA structure | Research prototype |
| PTRANS [4] | Computer systems | Develop plans for assembling and testing the ordered computer system | Research prototype |
| TALIB [38] | Electronics | Synthesize integrated circuit layouts for nMOS cells | Research prototype |
| TATR [39] | Military | Develop a plan for air targeteer to attack enemy airfields | Research prototype |

and where a major armed conflict will next occur), agricultural applications (e.g., to foretell damage due to the black cutworm), and economic applications (e.g., to predict effects of a change in economic policy).

Few predictive systems have been developed. One system, I&W, was developed through a joint effort by ESL, Inc. (Sunnyvale, CA) and Stanford University [17]. I&W assists an intelligence analyst in forecasting where and when an armed conflict will occur by analyzing incoming intelligence reports on troop locations, activity, and movements.

Another predictive system, PLANT/cd, was developed by the University of Illinois to foretell black cutworm damage to corn, using a combination of rules and a set of black cutworm simulation programs. By employing knowledge about a given field, such as moth trap count, weed density, larval age, soil condition, and corn variety, PLANT/cd produces predictions on the degree of damage the cutworm will cause in said field. The system has reached the research prototype stage [18].

The limitation with prediction expert systems lies in the integration of incomplete information, multiple possibilities of future courses, and diversity of data sources and reasoning methods.

# *Example Expert Systems—XCON, DELTA*

XCON, a design system, configures VAX systems at a very detailed level based on its task-specific knowledge. It determines necessary modifications on each order, produces diagrams of spatial and logical relationships between hundreds of components in a complete system, and defines cable lengths between components. Rules and frames (e.g., templates) are used to represent knowledge of components. For example, the rule DISTRIBUTE-MB-DEVICES-3 for the distribution of massbus devices among massbuses in the VAX computer systems is expressed as follows:

IF: The most current active context is distributing massbus devices,

And there is a single port disk drive that has not been assigned to a massbus,

And there are no unassigned dual port disk drives,

And the number of devices that each massbus should support is known,

And there is a massbus that has been assigned at least one disk drive and that should support additional disk drives,

And the type of cable needed to connect the disk drive to the previous device on the massbus is known,

THEN: Assign the disk drive to the massbus.

This rule shows that there are six conditions to be met before one of the single port disk drives on the order is assigned to one of the massbuses. The first condition indicates that the task relevant to this rule is distributing massbus devices. The remaining five conditions specify constraints that must be satisfied before a disk drive can be assigned to a massbus.

The cabinet template that describes what space is available in a particular CPU cabinet template (CPU-CABINET) is shown as follows:

Template: CPU-CABINET

Class: Cabinet

Height: 60 inches

Width: 52 inches

Depth: 30 inches

SBI module space:

CPU Nexus-2 (3 6 23 30)

4-inch-option-slot 1 Nexus-3 (23 6 27 30)

Memory Nexus-4 (27 6 38 30)

4-inch-option-slot 2 Nexus-6 (38 5 42 30)

4-inch-option-slot 3 Nexus-5 (42 5 46 30)

3-inch-option-slot Nexus-6 (46 5 49 30)

Power supply space:

FPA Nexus-1 (2 32 1 0 40)

CPU Nexus-2 (10 32 18 40)

4-inch-option-slot 1 Nexus-3 (18 32 26 40)

Memory Nexus-4 (26 32 34 40)

4-inch-option-slot 2 Nexus-5 (34 32 42 40)

Clock-battery (2 49 26 52)

Memory-battery (2 46 26 49)

SBI device space: 10 (2 52 50 56).

This template displays information regarding the CPU cabinet's class, weight, width, depth, module space, power supply space, and device space requirements.

DELTA is a rule-based diagnostic system that consists of relatively simple rules. For example, the Fuel System Faulty rule is expressed as follows:

IF: EQ (engine set idle) and
EQ (fuel pressure below normal) and
EQ (fuel-pressure-gauge used in test) and
EQ (fuel-pressure-gauge status OK),
THEN: WRITE (fuel system faulty) 1.0

This rule indicates that there is definitely (with a certainty of 1.0) a fault in the fuel system only if the four conditions are met. The first condition is that the engine must be set idle. The second condition is that the fuel pressure must be below normal. The third condition is that the readings must have been taken from a fuel pressure gauge. The fourth condition is that the status of the fuel pressure gauge must be all right.

## *Expert System Limitations*

The limitations to expert system development may originate from technology inheritance, environment, and cost.

Because current expert system technology is still evolving, limitations include inherent shortcomings such as narrowness of expertise, inability to recognize knowledge boundaries, limited explanation facilities, and difficulty in validation.

Because building and maintaining a large knowledge base requires substantial effort, most expert systems cover a narrow range of expertise. Part of the reason is due to current computing facilities which limit the speed and capability of search in expert systems. Even when an expert system achieves a broad coverage of knowledge (for example, INTERNIST, which covers some 500 diseases [23]), it becomes shallow in representing associations between elements in the knowledge base. With the current limitations to technology, it seems that we must be satisfied with a narrow scope of knowledge in building expert systems.

The inability of expert systems to recognize their knowledge boundaries is a serious problem. Most expert systems do not deal competently with problems at the boundaries of their knowledge. They do not have the knowledge built in to determine when a problem is beyond their capabilities or outside their fields. Expert systems may need constant maintenance to reduce mistakes in complex or derived cases that are not fully represented in the knowledge base. The explanations are primitive and a human expert may need to explain again what the expert system has explained.

Although validation of software programs is time consuming, the effort required to validate expert systems is many factors greater than that for conventional software programs. Expert systems can be validated by human experts in actual use. Very few employees have both domain expertise and knowledge engineering expertise. Communications between human experts and knowledge engineers in identifying and correcting mistakes in an expert system can be a formidable task.

The environment in which an expert system is developed or employed is significant. The three potential limitations that exist within an environment are *hardware, software,* and *organization.* Current computing architectures are slow and not equipped for symbolic processing; they were built primarily for number crunching. Special AI workstations—for example, LISP machines—may be required to develop expert systems. These workstations are not only expensive, they usually cannot execute existing software programs.

Except for large, expensive tools such as KEE, expert system tools have limited knowledge representation methods. Most of them use rule-based approaches that are not well suited to represent structural knowledge that has no immediate IF-THEN consequences.

The third area is organization. Because expert system technology is new, management in organization expects either too much or too little from the technology. Initiating an expert system project can be a major undertaking.

Cost is the final source of problems for developing expert systems. At present, a knowledge engineer extracts knowledge from human experts and laboriously builds it into the knowledge base. The effort is time consuming and the knowledge engineers' services are costly due to supply shortage. Most expert system prototypes require three man-months to develop, and a usable system requires about one man-year to build.

# System Development Rules

The four rules regarding system development learned from the two case studies are

1. It is unwise to keep an expert system from regular use until its knowledge is complete.
2. As in the case of the human specialist, expert systems always make mistakes and require time to advance from apprentice to expert.
3. A useful expert system advances incrementally over a long period of time.
4. Selection of application fields is essential because it affects programming language, knowledge source, knowledge representation, and inference engines used.

The developers of XCON found that they did not have to wait until the system was near perfection; it was providing significant assistance to technical editors during the field test prototype stage. It took 80,000 orders to uncover some of the deficiencies in XCON's configuration knowledge. Because the configuration task is continually redefined as new products are introduced, XCON will never have all the knowledge it needs and will require continual refinement. Refinement can be undertaken when the system is used and deficiencies are identified.

Unlike finished conventional software programs, which have few bugs, expert systems always make mistakes. Expert systems must pass through a lengthy apprenticeship stage (more than one or two years) to become experts. Even after they become experts, they (like all human experts) occasionally make mistakes. Fortunately, expert systems do not cover up their mistakes; these mistakes can be traced and corrected.

The developers of XCON and DELTA found that building a useful expert system is an unending process because it evolves with new task additions. Knowledge is continually added either to correct or complement existing knowledge or to augment knowledge of new products. Many additions result from expert systems needing to obtain the knowledge to perform new tasks. Some of these tasks are the consequences of new product introduction or the decision to include related products. The rest result from the user's requirement for improved expert system performance to accomplish additional tasks. Because of these additions, an expert system is likely to become too large to manage.

The selection of application types may consequently determine the programming language, knowledge source, knowledge representation method, and inference engine that can best fit the application. The developer of XCON found that the configuration problem was a good application choice because it entailed the appropriate degree of difficulty and allowed for use of a reasonable approach and computer language. The task allowed the research team to show sufficient progress from time to time, to anyone who was interested. Selection rules for application types are discussed in detail in the next section of this chapter.

## *Hardware Requirements*

Two rules in selecting hardware are

1. Use available hardware equipment.
2. Select simple equipment.

The experience of both XCON and DELTA indicates that the hardware equipment selected should be available and familiar to the user. XCON used DEC computers, which were available and familiar to DEC employees; thus, no computer training was needed. DELTA initially also used DEC computers, but its users (mainly mechanics) lacked knowledge of the computer. Training was therefore required for use of both the computer and the expert system. Problems of adjusting to new tools were compounded, the learning speed rate slowed, and the degree of user anxiety increased. DELTA was subsequently converted to the IBM PC environment and barriers to its use were somewhat reduced.

In the case of DELTA, the Sony videodisk player, color terminal, and

Epson printer were integrated with a hardened DEC computer. The idea was ingenious but a great impediment was encountered in system integration and implementation. Selecting simple equipment may be mandatory for expert system acceptance by mechanics in the repair shop.

# *Application Selection Rules*

The best candidate problems for expert systems are those that are small but important and for which the knowledge and experience of human experts, data, and test cases are available as a basis for development and for validation after development.

An expert system is more likely to succeed if two necessary conditions and at least one sufficient condition are met. These requirements are briefly described below.

## Necessary Conditions

The two necessary conditions are

1. The application (problem) area must be well bounded and understood.
2. At least one human expert must be available to explain the knowledge required for the expert system being built.

Expert systems have been more successful in scientific and technical tasks, where a well-bounded field of knowledge and application results exist. The first necessary condition requires that technical vocabularies can be enumerated and that search space for a solution is relatively small, so computers can examine all feasible combinations and reach a conclusion. This can be illustrated by the diagnostic problem that has been most often dealt with by various expert systems in different fields—diagnosing the fault in a machine. The number of possible faulty areas in a machine is limited, and these areas are understood and can be identified. Computers can be instructed to check feasible combinations and reach a conclusion on the faulty part.

Unbounded problem areas, such as linguistic concepts, take on relatively unlimited variations in meaning, depending on the context—for example, language translation. This type of problem is difficult for today's computational technology to resolve, due to limited speed and memory. That is, the computer has to examine almost endless combinational possibilities and cannot accommodate the search space that is required.

The second necessary condition is that at least one human expert is available to explain the special knowledge and experience required, and the methods used to apply them to particular problems. If no human expertise has yet evolved—such as is the case with "Star Wars"—then an expert system for the task cannot be expected to fare any better than the human sources.

### Sufficient Conditions

In addition to the two necessary conditions, one or more of the following sufficient conditions must exist for any expert system to be worthy of development:

- Shortage of human experts/specialists
- Need to preserve the experts' expertise
- High cost of expert advice or wrong decisions
- Critical requirement of expert advice
- Routine, detail-dependent decision making processes

The presence of one or more of these elements, plus the two necessary conditions, makes an expert system commercially attractive.

## Using AI/Expert Systems To Improve Conventional Programs

The five major approaches to the use of expert system technology to improve conventional software include:

- *Intelligent "user"*—acts as the user of data bases and other software packages. Interaction with the software package/data base is not its primary objective, but merely a convenient means to access data.
- *Intelligent "representative"*—uses mathematical logic to represent general facts about data in the software package/data base, to increase the usefulness of the package/data base in responding to queries.
- *Intelligent "prober"*—supports browsing through a data base or program and also supports query modification, either to narrow or broaden the scope of the request to make it more understandable.
- *Natural language "interface"*—provides natural language interface software packages. Allows the user to search for and process information without having to learn the specialized command language of a software package.
- *Natural language text "analyst"*—processes a user's natural language input text to produce appropriate responses to user queries. The capability of the expert system to understand natural language text in a given field permits the user to enter data in a relatively flexible form.

Most of these approaches are implemented only in large AI workstations. Some examples for each type are discussed below. For more detailed examples, see reference [40] at the end of this chapter.

## *Expert Systems as Intelligent Users*

Expert systems can be developed to serve as intelligent users of complex conventional software programs such as data base management systems or mixed-integer linear programs. Two distinctive types of expert systems can be developed to accomplish this objective: expert systems that act as "assistants" and expert systems that act as "controllers."

Most commercial IBM PC packages in the joint application of expert systems and data bases employ knowledge-based systems that act as software package/data base assistants in the areas of query optimization, data access through natural language front ends, and deductive data bases. In most existing coupled systems, the expert makes direct calls to the standard DBMS through a hard-craft interface. This approach implements a tight coupling of the expert system to a designated data base. Typical examples of intelligent front end systems include GURU (by Micro Data Base Systems [41]), Javelin (by Javelin Software [42]), Paradox (by Ansa Software [43]), REVEAL (by McDonnell Douglas [44]), and Superfile ACLS (by Southdata [45]). Most of these systems are tightly coupled to a specific DBMS. Each system contains varying levels of built-in, system-specific knowledge about its data base/software packages. The coupling of standard software packages to a data base is time consuming and package dependent. A hard-craft interface is required for each new package added into the data base.

The more flexible approach is an intelligent interface between the application and the data base, where the expert system acts as a controller. The interface integrates each standard software package on an as-necessary basis without hard-craft linking, and allows each component to function independently. The intelligent interface (an expert system) can reason about components, their requirements for interface, and data communications of the packages being connected. It uses knowledge of the packages being linked to provide communication and data sharing, and uses meta knowledge regarding the capabilities of the packages to optimally select and employ software programs to meet the user's requirements. For example, a user may not be aware of the need to use a statistical package or may not know which statistical package to use. The intelligent interface connects one when it determines from past experience that a particular statistical package provides a cost-effective way to show a given aspect of the data that the user has requested or acquired.

The flexibility of this interface mechanism relies on the expert system's reasoning capability regarding the contents of the data base and the data space of standard software packages being interfaced in response to the need for data processing, and on data descriptions of the software packages.

Transformation of data representations and translation of data manipulation languages are required in communication between the data base, standard software packages, and the user/preparer. These involve mapping —*semantic* mapping for transformation and *syntactic* mapping for translation. Since each individual software package may use a different organization for equivalent data or may represent the data at different levels of detail, semantic mapping is required to transform data among software packages. Different software packages may employ their own data manipulation languages. Mapping between these data manipulation languages is a syntactic translation. For example, the algebraic and calculus query languages used for relational data bases may need to be translated syntactically for use in other software packages, such as graphics.

Two examples show how the two types of expert systems have served as intelligent users of software packages. SICAD (Standards Interfaces in CAD) acts as an expert system assistant to standards processing in CAD [46]. It employs a custom knowledge base and a hard-craft inference mechanism to gain access to design standards. The knowledge base contains three elements: classifier trees that relate engineering terminology to provisions of a standard; an information network that consists of decision tables written in FORTRAN, which represent the provisions of a standard; and mapping that relates data items in a standard to data items in a design database. SICAD was developed to assist a design program that performs compliance checking. SICAD acts as an assistant to the design program in identifying and checking applicable provisions. Compliance checking uses backward chaining to determine all data required to evaluate a provision.

KADBASE (Knowledge Aided Data Base Management System) acts as an expert system controller to data base management systems [47]. The objective of KADBASE was to develop a flexible, intelligent interface that enables multiple expert systems and multiple data bases to communicate as autonomous, self-descriptive units with a CAD system operating in a distributed computing environment.

KADBASE consists of three major parts: the knowledge-based system interface which formulates the queries and updates sent to other components and processes replies from them; the knowledge-based data base interface, which acts as an intelligent user of a DBMS that accepts queries from other components and returns appropriate replies regarding the data base; and the data base access manager, which actually performs the interface by decomposing queries, issuing the appropriate subqueries to the local data base, obtaining and processing the data, and formulating the replies.

## Expert Systems as Intelligent Representatives

Expert systems acting as intelligent "representatives" use logic to represent facts about data in the data base or a complex software program to facilitate queries. They may be integrated to complex data bases or software packages. If these intelligent "representatives" are integrated to data bases, they also may be called *intentional data bases* (IDB), which are a collection of axioms such as rules, postulates, constraints, and general facts. These axioms may be viewed alternately as data integrity constraints, data definitions, or logical inference rules. They are represented in mathematical logic.

Two examples—MRPPS [48] and DADM [49]—are discussed to demonstrate the differences between the two categories. MRPPS (Maryland Refutation Proof Procedure System) is an integrated system based on mathematical logic. Knowledge and data are combined in a semantic network that consists of a semantic graph (a classification structure), a data base (including conventional data base and the IDB), a dictionary (a listing of relations, constants, and functions), and a semantic form space (consisting of definitions of constraints to be imposed on predicates and their arguments). The elements of the semantic graph are referenced by the knowledge base index to facilitate quick access.

A query to MRPPS is a conjunction of clauses. The first step in query processing is to check that the query is consistent with the acceptable syntax and structure. The system uses a refutation proof procedure search for a solution to the query. The refutation proof procedure first assumes the negation of the desired clauses, then attempts to prove a contradiction from rules and facts in the knowledge base.

DADM (Deductively Augmented Data Management System) is an intelligent front end system that represents the combinations of a file in general knowledge with an inference engine and a file of specific knowledge with a searching mechanism [49]. The general knowledge consists of a set of domain-specific assertions expressed in first-order predicate calculus. The file of specific knowledge is supported by a single relational DBMS. The system was implemented in heterogeneous hardware environments: an inference engine running on a LISP machine, a relational data base supported by a specialized data base machine, and a query and reply translator running on a DEC VAX 11/780.

The inference engine uses the specific knowledge on the problem domain to develop search strategies for locating answers from the queries. The queries are sent to the translator for conversion to data base syntax, then are further passed to the data base machine for processing. Replies from the data base machine follow a reverse path.

The applications of DADM include "Manager's Assistant," which aids in corporate project monitoring and planning, and an intelligent assistant for information resource managers [50].

## *Expert Systems as Intelligent "Probers"*

Expert systems acting as intelligent probers provide the support capability to browse through a data base or program and probe for information that the user seeks. They also attempt to determine specific information about alternative queries that may better suit the user's need, on the basis of rules that describe relationships between predicates. For instance, if `employ (X, john)`—that is, find all persons whom John employs—fails, the intelligent prober may try the queries `teach (X, john)`, `Employ (X, mary)`, or `supervise (X, john)`, in accordance with the rules on relationships between predicates. One example is provided by Motro, who discusses a system for browsing in a loosely structured data base [51].

## *Expert Systems as Natural Language "Interfaces"*

Expert systems acting as natural language (NL) interfaces allow the user to search for information without having to learn a new, specialized command language. They can be divided into two categories: *data base front ends* and *bibliographic systems*. A variety of systems have been implemented to provide restricted natural language front ends to data bases and complex software packages. Examples include CO-OP [52] (a portable NL interface for data base systems) and XCALIBUR [53] (a domain-independent NL interface for expert systems). The CO-OP system provides several good examples of the types of queries that can be processed using current technology. For example, "Who advises projects in area 36?" Most of these systems have the capability to parse simple queries expressed in restricted conversational English into data base access requests and to request clarification when ambiguities exist.

Natural language bibliographic retrieval systems allow users to enter English language queries. These systems work by selecting keyword matching and have little understanding of the actual meaning of the queries. Examples include ANNLODE [54] and CITE [55]. ANNLODE (A Navigator of Natural Language Organized Data) is a browsing system that accesses a full text knowledge base to search for paragraphs that match a natural language query issued by the user [54]. CITE (Current Information Transfer in English) is a natural language interface for an online bibliographic retrieval system [55].

ANNLODE uses linguistic, probabilistic, and empirical techniques to determine the degree of similarity between the user's query and the candidate text. It employs three linguistic methods to process queries and candidate paragraphs:

- Common word deletion—elimination of nondescriptive words such as articles, prepositions, and conjunctions from consideration in the matching
- Word root isolation—removal of suffixes from significant words in queries and paragraphs
- Thesaurus expansion—the expansion of significant terms in the query by applicable synonyms, each having associated term weights that correspond to the degree to which the meaning of the original term and synonym overlap

ANNLODE further takes advantage of heuristically derived functions to rank paragraphs for similarity with the query:

- Term weighting—these factors are used to reduce the matching weight for synonyms.

- Number of occurrences of each term in the paragraph—absolute weight increases with the number of occurrences, while incremental weight decreases.
- Frequency of query terms in the entire knowledge base—for example, widely used terms contribute little to the search for relevant information.
- Correction for paragraph length—long paragraphs are likely to contain more of any given query term than short ones.

## *Expert Systems as Natural Language Text "Analysts"*

Expert systems acting as natural language text analysts examine a user's natural language input text to produce appropriate responses. Several prototype systems derive meaning from natural language texts in highly technical domains—for example, chemical data [56, 57]—even though one may wonder whether scientists in these domains write technical papers in natural languages. The Retrieval of Numeric Chemical Data (RNCD) [56] is discussed as an example.

Retrieval of Numeric Chemical Data is an expert system that locates specific numerical data for organic compounds in the text of chemical journal articles. It can recognize a variety of data regarding physical measurements, such as *mp* (melting point) and *ir* (infrared spectra), in the chemical description. The system may be used to search for characterization data for a known compound or to identify an unknown compound for which some of the characterization data is known. It accumulates descriptive and heuristic knowledge about how chemical characterization data is represented. Some of the knowledge is devoted to distinguishing paragraphs containing characterization from those describing compound synthesis, including keys based on style, sequence in the article, vocabulary, and so forth. Its knowledge base contains rules that distinguish the subject compound (for example, a compound name mentioned in a heading) and the characterization data (for example, synonyms for data types).

# Summary

- The most successful task types are control/monitoring, debugging, design, diagnosis, instruction, interpretation, planning, and prediction.
- Two cases in industrial applications—XCON and DELTA—demonstrate expert system development, cost, and benefits.
- The most productive use of expert system technology is to enhance conventional software programs in user friendliness and in intelligent interface of data bases.

- Expert systems are successful if two necessary conditions and at least one sufficient condition are met.
- The two necessary conditions are (1) the application (problem) area must be well bounded and (2) at least one human expert must be available to explain the knowledge required for the expert system being built.
- The sufficient condition can be one or more of five situations: (1) shortage of experts/specialists, (2) need to preserve experts' knowledge, (3) high cost of expert advice, (4) critical requirements of expert advice, and (5) routine detail-dependent decision making process.
- Expert systems can act as intelligent users, intelligent representatives, intelligent probers, natural language interfaces, or natural language text analysts to conventional software packages or data bases.

# References

[1] E. Emrich, "Expert Systems Tools and Techniques" (Oak Ridge National Laboratory, ORNL/TM-9555, August 1985).

[2] Donald A. Waterman, *A Guide to Expert Systems* (Reading, MA: Addison-Wesley, 1986).

[3] M. Fox, "Knowledge-Based Systems: Applications in the Industrial Environment" (Texas Instruments AI Satellite Symposium, November 1985), 99-124.

[4] P. Haley, J. Kowalski, J. McDermott, and R. McWhorter, "PTRANS: A rule-based management assistant" (Technical Report, Computer Science Dept., Carnegie-Mellon University, Pittsburgh, PA, January 1983).

[5] J. H. Griesmer et. al., "YES/MVS: A continuous real time expert system," *Proceedings AAAI-84* (1984).

[6] W. R. Nelson, "REACTOR: an expert system for diagnosis and treatment of nuclear reactor accidents," *Proceedings AAAI-82* (1982), 296-301.

[7] C. M. Wong and S. Lanning, "Artificial intelligence in chemical analysis," *Energy and Technology Review* (Lawrence Livermore National Laboratory, February 1984).

[8] Jim Kornell, "A VAX tuning expert built using automated knowledge acquisition," *Proceedings of the First Conference on Artificial Intelligence Applications* (IEEE Computer Society, December 1984).

[9] J. R. Wright et. al., "ACE: going from prototype to product with an expert system," *ACM Conference Proceedings* (October 1984).

[10] C. R. Hollander and Y. Iwasaki, "The drilling advisor: an expert system application," in "Fundamentals of Knowledge Engineering" (Teknowledge Report, 1983).

[11] B. Mulsant and D. Servan-Schreiber, "Knowledge engineering: a daily activity on a hospital ward," *Computers and Biomedical Research*, vol. 17 (1984), 71-91.

[12] Stephen Polit, "R1 and beyond: AI technology transfer at DEC," *The AI Magazine* (Winter 1985).

[13] G. Kahn and J. McDermott, "The MUD system," *Proceedings of the First Conference on Artificial Intelligence Applications* (IEEE Computer Society, December 1984).

[14] J. S. Aikins, J. C. Kunz, and E. H. Shortliffe, "PUFF: an expert system for interpretation of pulmonary function data," *Computers and Biomedical Research*, vol. 16 (1983), 199-208.

[15] B. G. Buchanan and E. A. Feigenbaum, "DENDRAL and Meta-DENDRAL: their applications dimension," *Artificial Intelligence*, vol. 11 (1978).

[16] S. M. Weiss and C. A. Kulikowski, "Developing microprocessor based expert models for instrument interpretation," *Proceedings IJCAI-81* (1981), 853-855.

[17] G. Kiremidjian, A. Clarkson, and D. Lenat, "Expert system for tactical indications and warning (I&W) analysis," *Proceedings of the Army Conference on the Application of AI to Battlefield Information Management* (Report AD-A139 685, Battelle Columbus Laboratories, Washington, D.C., 1983).

[18] R. S. Michalski et. al., "PLANT/ds: an expert consulting system for the diagnosis of soybean diseases," *Proceedings of the Fifth European Conference on Artificial Intelligence* (Orsay, France, July 1982).

[19] T. J. Laffey, W. A. Perkins, and O. Firschein, "LES: a model-based expert system for electronic maintenance," *Proceedings of the Joint Services Workshop on AI in Maintenance* (October 4-6, 1984), 1-17.

[20] DELTA/CATS-1, *The Artificial Intelligence Report*, vol. 1, no. 1 (January 1984).

[21] M. S. Fox, "Techniques for sensor-based diagnosis," *Proceedings IJCAI-83* (1983), 158-163.

[22] J. McDermott, "Building expert systems," in *Artificial Intelligence Applications for Business*, W. Reitman, ed. (Norwood, NJ: Ablex, 1984).

[23] R. A. Miller, H. E. Pople, Jr., and J. D. Myers, "INTERNIST-1, an experimental computer-based diagnostic consultant for general internal medicine," *New England Journal of Medicine*, vol. 307, no. 8 (August 1982), 468-476.

[24] R. M. Stallman and G. J. Sussman, "Problem solving about electrical circuits," in *Artificial Intelligence: An MIT Perspective*, P. Winston and R. Brown, eds., vol. 1 (MIT Press, 1979), 30-91.

[25] M. Fox, "Knowledge-Based Systems: Applications in the Industrial Environment" (Texas Instruments AI Satellite Symposium, a Project Management Expert System developed for DEC, November 1985), 109.

[26] M. Fox, "Knowledge-Based Systems: Applications in the Industrial

Environment" (Texas Instruments AI Satellite Symposium, November 1985), 114.

[27] J. M. Wright and M. S. Fox, "SRL/1.5 User Manual" (Robotics Institute, Carnegie-Mellon University, Pittsburgh, PA, December 1983).

[28] W. Tod Wipke, Glen I. Ouchi, and S. Krishnan, "Simulation and evaluation of chemical synthesis—SECS: an application of artificial intelligence techniques," *Artificial Intelligence*, vol. 11 (1978).

[29] H. Brown, C. Tong, and G. Foyster, "PALLADIO: an exploratory environment for circuit design," *IEEE Computer* (December 1983), 41-55.

[30] EXSYS, Inc., "EXSYS Product Description" (Albuquerque, NM, 1985). EXSYS is written in C, using backward chaining, simple production rules, and uncertainty factors.

[31] H. Shubin and J. W. Ulrich, "IDT: an intelligent diagnostic tool," *Proceedings AAAI-82* (1982), 209-295.

[32] R. E. Cullingford et. al., "Automated explanations as a component computer-aided design system," *IEEE Transactions on Systems and Cybernetics*, vol. SMC-12, no. 2 (April 1982), 168-181.

[33] J. D. Hollan, E. L. Hutchins, and L. Weitzman, "STEAMER: an interactive inspectable simulation-based training system," *The AI Magazine*, vol. 5, no. 2 (1984).

[34] P. Cohen and M. D. A. Liberman, "Report in FOLIO: An expert assistant for portfolio managers," *Proceedings IJCAI-83* (1983), 212-214.

[35] R. G. Smith, "On the development of commercial expert systems," *The AI Magazine*, vol. 5, no. 3 (Fall 1984).

[36] H. P. Nii et. al., "Signal-to-symbol transformation: HASP/SIAP case study," *The AI Magazine* (Spring 1982), 23-35.

[37] M. Stefik, "Inferring DNA structures from segmentation data," *Artificial Intelligence*, vol. 11 (1978), 85-114.

[38] J. Kim and J. McDermott, "TALIB: an IC layout design assistant," *Proceedings AAAI-83* (1983).

[39] M. Callero, D. A. Waterman, and J. R. Kipps, "TATR: a prototype expert system for tactical air targeting" (Report R-3096-ARPA, Rand Corporation, June 1984).

[40] H. C. Howard and D. R. Rehak, "Knowledge Based Database Management for Expert Systems," *ACM Sigart Newsletter* (Special Interest Group on Artificial Intelligence, Association for Computing Machinery, Spring 1985).

[41] Micro Data Base Systems, *Guru Product Description* (Lafayette, IN, 1985).

[42] Javelin Software, *Javelin Product Description* (Cambridge, MA, 1985).

[43] Ansa Software, *Paradox Product Description* (Belmont, CA, 1985).

[44] McDonnell Douglas, *REVEAL Product Description* (1985).

[45] South Data, *Superfile ACLS Product Description* (U.K., 1985).

[46] L. A. Lopez, S. L. Elam, and T. Christopherson, "SICAD: A Prototype Implementation System for CAD," *Proceedings, ASCE Third Conference on Computing in Civil Engineering* (San Diego, CA, American Society of Civil Engineers [ASCE], April 1984), 84-94.

[47] D. Rehak and H. Howard, "Interfacing Expert Systems with Design Databases in Integrated CAD Systems," *Computer-Aided Design*, vol. 17, no. 9 (November 1985).

[48] J. Minker, "Search Strategy and Selection Function for an Inferential Relational Database," *ACM Transactions on Database Systems*, vol. 3, no. 1 (Association for Computing Machinery, March 1978), 1-31.

[49] C. Kellogg, "The Transition from Data Management to Knowledge Management," *Proceedings, International Conference on Data Engineering* (Los Angeles, CA, Institute of Electrical and Electronics Engineers, IEEE Computer Society Press, April 1984), 467-472.

[50] D. Kogan, "The Manager's Assistant—An Application of Knowledge Management," *Proceedings, International Conference on Data Engineering* (Los Angeles, CA: IEEE Computer Society Press, April 1984), 592-595.

[51] A. Motro, "Browsing in a Loosely Structured Database," *ACM SIGMOD*, vol. 14, no. 2 (June 1984), 197-207.

[52] S. J. Kaplan, "Designing a Portable Natural Language Database Query System," *ACM Transactions on Database Systems*, vol. 9, no. 1 (March 1984), 1-19.

[53] J. G. Carbonell, W. M. Boggs, and M. L. Mauldin, "The XCALIBUR Project: A Natural Language Interface to Expert Systems," *Proceedings, International Joint Conference on Artificial Intelligence*, vol. 2 (1983), 653-656.

[54] L. M. Bernstein and R. E. Williamson, "Testing of a Natural Language Retrieval System for a Full Text Knowledge Base," *Journal of the American Society for Information Sciences*, vol. 35, no. 4 (July 1984), 235-257.

[55] T. E. Doszkocs and B. A. Rapp, "Searching MEDLINE in English: A Prototype User Interface with Natural Language Query, Ranked Output, and Relevance Feedback," *Information Choices and Policies* (R. D. Meeting, American Society for Information Science, Knowledge Industrial Publications, Inc., White Plains, N.Y., October 1979), 131-139.

[56] J. J. Pollock, "Quantification, Retrieval, and Automatic Identification of Numerical Data in Organic Chemistry Journals," *Journal of Chemical Information and Computer Sciences*, vol. 24, no. 3 (August 1984), 139-147.

[57] N. Sager and M. Kosaka, "A Database of Literature Organized by Relations," *Proceedings, The Seventh Annual Symposium on Computer Applications in Medical Care*, R. E. Dayhoff, ed. (Washington, D.C., Institute of Electrical and Electronics Engineers, October 1983), 692-695.

# 10

# Real-World Expert Systems

Chapter 9 discusses the main application of expert system technologies. Even though many of these applications may be better performed with the computing power of a mainframe or minicomputer, most of the tasks can be accomplished with personal computers, particularly the Intel 80286- or 80386-based microcomputers.

This chapter presents examples of tasks that are applied in real-world situations. To illustrate the variety of tool characteristics, four tools are used: Expert Knowledge Organizer (developed in Chapters 7 and 8), Personal Consultant, M.1, and Micro-Expert. These tools are used to build expert systems that organize, accumulate, or disseminate knowledge in the areas of automobile parts inventory control, blackjack, and transportation. Finally, the delivery of an expert system for personal computers is discussed. In describing each example area, attention is paid to the illustration of programming rules and principles discussed previously, so you can understand why each area is applicable for expert system technology. Approaches that can be taken to build an expert system are then presented, followed by a sample expert system.

This chapter is divided into four sections:

1. Building an expert knowledge organizer
2. Blackjack—building a training tool
3. Accumulating and disseminating knowledge
4. Issues of delivery

# An Intelligent Information System— Building an Expert Knowledge (EKO) Organizer

This section discusses two topics: (1) how to use the components of expert shells discussed in Chapters 7 and 8 to put together a powerful expert system tool to meet a given need and (2) how to apply this tool to the development of intelligent information systems.

## *Building an Expert System Tool*

The three major components of an expert system shell discussed in Chapters 7 and 8 are

1. Knowledge representation
   - Frame structure
   - Rule structure
   - Logic structure
2. Inference engine
   - Forward chaining
   - Backward chaining
   - Reasoning/search/justification
3. User inference
   - Input/output menus
   - File operations (optional)
   - Graphics (optional)
   - Natural language interface (optional)
   - Window (optional)

These components, which are explained in Chapters 7 and 8, can be used to build expert systems. Because we have paid significant attention to the object-oriented programming rule, an expert system program should be modular, with appropriate subcomponents selected to build an expert system shell that satisfies the requirements of the situation. For example, if a small shell is required for interfacing with large conventional programs to facilitate their input/output speed and convenience, an expert system may include only the following subcomponents:

- Rule structure
- Forward chaining/reasoning/depth-first search/justification
- Input/output menus
- File operations
- Natural language interface

To make this selection process convenient for the potential user, the file of each subcomponent needs to be named meaningfully. For example:

*RULE.LSP* The file for the rule operation

*CLASS.LSP* The file for the class operation

*MOUSE.LSP* The file for the mouse operation

The two additional elements needed to build an expert system tool to perform the selection of various subcomponents are ***BOOT.LSP*** and *TOPLEVEL*:

*BOOT.LSP* Tells the computer which subcomponents are included in this program.

*TOPLEVEL* Informs the user of the program name, copyright logo, how to use the program, and so forth.

These two elements are discussed below.

# BOOT.LSP

The purpose of ***BOOT.LSP*** is to load files needed to run the expert system tool. The structure of ***BOOT.LSP*** is shown in Listing 10-1.

**Listing 10-1**
***Sample programs for BOOT.LSP and TOPLEVEL.LSP***

```
#|
        This file prepares the eko system for loading.
        The first call to (eko) will load it.
|#
(defparameter *eko-File-List*
        '(util userint slot menu choosval mouse window
     toplevel graphics
         variable unit class rule inherit nl kb otherops
     file mathops special
         meta inferenc backchn frwdchn reason debug init))
(Defvar *eko-Directory* "d:\\eko\\")
(defun eko-File-Load (file &optional compiled?)
  (load (string-append *eko-directory* file
                       (if compiled? ".fas" ".lsp"))
        :print nil))
(defvar *eko-loadedp* nil)
(defun Load-eko (&optional (start-file nil) (compiled? nil))
  "Loads eko, (starting with start-file) and starts system"
  (let ((file-list (if start-file
                        (member start-file *eko-file-list*)
                       *eko-file-list*)))
    (dolist (file file-list)
      (eko-file-load file compiled?))
    (initialize-eko)
```

**Listing 10-1 (cont.)**

```
    (format t "~&EKO System Loaded")
    (beep)
    (setq *eko-loadedp* t)))
(defun Compile-eko (&optional start-file)
  (let ((file-list (if start-file
                           (member start-file *eko-file-list*)
                          *eko-file-list*))
        file-string)
    (dolist (file file-list)
      (setq file-string (string-append *eko-directory* file
     ".lsp"))
;       (when (not (probe-file (string-append *eko-directory*
     file ".fas")))
       (compile-file file-string));)
    (format t "~&EKO System Compiled")))
(format t "~%The function (eko) invokes the E.K.O.
     System~%")
; to put eko in control key
;(let ((a (assoc "sys::ie-commands sys::*default-ie-
     options*)))
;  (setq sys::*default-ie-options* nil)
;  (push (reverse (cons '(#\C-W . (lambda (&rest ignore)
     (eko))) (reverse a)))
;       sys::*default-ie-options*))
(defun Eko ()
  (when (not *eko-loadedp*)
    (load-eko))
  (send *terminal-io* :clear-screen)
  (set-screen-color :brown :bright :black :off)
  (set-screen-color :brown :bright :black :off
     *main-window*)
  (set-cursorpos 0 5)
  (center-string "******** E.K.O. ********" *terminal-io*)
  (set-cursorpos 0 8)
  (center-string "Expert Knowledge Organizer" *terminal-io*)
  (set-cursorpos 0 13)
  (center-string "Copyright (C) 1985, 1986, 1987, Baldur
     Systems Corporation" *terminal-io*)
  (user-pause)
  (with-mouse-hidden (set-mouse-cursor 24 #XA))
  (setq *System-Menu*
     (top-menu-initialize *top-level-item-list* "System
     Menu")
     *menu-sensitive-items* nil
     *Mode-menu* nil)
```

```
  (reset-screen)
  (top-level-mode)
  (set-screen-color :gray :bright :black :off) t)
#|**********************************************************
            Top Level of eko
     This file defines the toplevel command loop and
      operations.
**********************************************************|#
(defparameter *Top-Level-Item-List*
            '(("Units" (unit-operations-mode)
               :doc "Perform operations on units")
              ("Classes" (class-operations-mode)
               :doc "Perform operations on unit classes")
              ("Rules" (rule-operations-mode)
               :doc "Perform operations on rules and rule
    classes")
            ("Knowledge Base" (kb-operations-mode)
               :doc "Perform operations on unstructured
    knowledge base")
            ("Variables" (variables-mode)
               :doc "Perform operations on system
    variables")
              ("Reasoning" (reasoning-operations-mode)
               :doc "Perform reasoning operations")
              ("Filesystem" (file-operations-mode)
               :doc "Perform operations with the
    filesystem")
              ("Others" (other-operations-mode)
               :doc "Menu of other operations to perform")
              ("GMACS" (with-mouse-hidden (on-main-screen
    (ed))
                                                (reset-
    screen))
            :doc "Run the GMACS editor on top of eko")
              ("LISP" (goto-lisp)
               :doc "Exit eko and enter LISP environment")
              ("DOS" (progn
                       (send *terminal-io* :clear-screen)
                       (format t "Type EXIT to Return to
    eko")
                    (sys:dos) (reset-screen))
               :doc "Create a DOS executive on top of
    eko")))
(defun Top-Level-Mode ()
  (setq *menu-sensitive-items* (menu-sens-item-list *system-
     menu*))
  (do ((menu-result (menu-choose *system-menu*)
                    (menu-choose *system-menu*)))
```

**Listing 10-1 (cont.)**

```
      ((abortp1 (item-execute menu-result)))
    (refresh-menus) (clear-screen))
  (setq *menu-sensitive-items* nil)
  (goto-lisp))
(defun Goto-Lisp ()
  (mouse-hide)
  (send *terminal-io* :clear-screen)
  (format t "~&Type (eko) to reenter eko") :abort)
```

The major elements of `BOOT.LSP` are as follows:

- `defparameter *EKO file-list *` defines the file list for the Expert Knowledge Organizer (EKO), which is the expert system tool we intend to build.
- `Defvar * EKO-directory * "d:\\EKO\\")` denotes that the directory for EKO is in drive `d` under the root name of `EKO`.
- `defun EKO file-load` loads a file. `string-append` is employed to concatenate copies of strings into a single string.
- `defun load-EKO` loads all files in the `*EKO-file-list*`.
- `Format` instructs the user to type **(EKO)** to start the Expert Knowledge Organizer.

# TOPLEVEL.LSP

*`TOPLEVEL.LSP`* defines the entire front end appearance for the Expert Knowledge Organizer. It provides menus for the user to select a mode of operation and organizes the screen to give the user a good first impression. The structure of *`TOPLEVEL.LSP`* as shown in Listing 10-1 consists of the following elements:

- `defparameter *TOP-LEVEL-ITEM-LIST*` defines a list of menus for the modes of operation that the user can select. For example:

  *Unit* is selected to allow operations on a unit. The function `unit-operation-mode` is called if the user chooses this operational mode.

  *Push to DOS* is chosen to create a DOS environment on top of EKO.

- `defun TOP-LEVEL-MODE` defines the top-level mode that accepts the command from the menu selected by the user, refreshes the menu, and clears the screen. Many of these functions (for example, `menu-choose`) have been discussed in Chapters 7 and 8.
- `defun EKO` sets the size, color, and window of the screen and shows the logo and copyright information.

- `defun GOTO-LISP` sets the program that allows the user to exit the EKO into the Lisp environment and return to EKO by typing **(EKO)**. The purpose of the function `hide-mouse` is to disable the mouse if there is one.

## *Using the Expert Knowledge Organizer To Build an Intelligent Information System*

Current information systems or data bases in the personal computer environment can be built with commerical data base management systems (DBMS) such as dBase III and R-base. Commands to process raw input data and manipulate the data in these systems are often unclear and cumbersome. To remedy this difficulty, expert systems have been built to act as data base assistants in the areas of query optimization, data access through natural language front ends, and deductive data bases. In most existing coupled systems, the expert makes direct calls to the standard DBMS through a hard-craft interface. This approach implements a tight coupling of the expert system to a designated data base system. A typical example of an intelligent front end system is GURU by MICRO Data Base Systems. Except for REVEAL, which is a data management system, all of these systems are tightly coupled to a specific DBMS. Each system contains varying levels of built-in, system-specific knowledge about its data base or system.

The coupling of software packages to an information system or a data base is also time consuming and package dependent. A hard-craft interface is usually required for each new package added into the data base. Two types of mapping are often needed: syntax translation of commands, such as directory and menu commands, and data transformation, such as header and points.

Furthermore, the wide dispersal of data bases to various locations within a large country such as the United States has created a problem of information system interface for users who are required to make rapid and crucial decisions. The Drug Enforcement Administration, for example, has to interface more than ten data bases located in different areas of the United States. These bases record different aspects of information on suspects, and the timely use of the data from various information sources presents a substantial challenge for many operators.

The data user/preparer is currently required to act as his own information access expert, learning the structure of the data bases as well as the DBMS, and mastering the techniques and knowledge required to retrieve, update, and interface them with other commercial software packages. This task is particularly difficult for dispersed, independent PC users who may have to use modems to communicate with various computer environments as well as data bases/systems.

If time and economics permit, an ideal intelligent information system reduces the time required for the user/preparer to learn information management systems, graphics, and statistics commercial packages, by integrating these packages into the system and automatically invoking them for use by the resident expert system when needed.

The optimum architecture of the ideal intelligent information system consists of four components, each of which responds to the need for a particular application:

- Master Expert System, the master controller, dispatches the remaining three interface modules.
- Network Interface responds to the need for a local area network application by the user.
- Data Base Interface responds to the need for a data base management system to handle the data bases.
- Software Package Interface responds to the need for standard package applications.

The Master Expert System should be designed to monitor and employ various software packages. It formulates queries and updates sent to the Network Interface by the user/preparer and processes replies from other components. Using the meta knowledge in its knowledge base about the user/preparer, software packages, and data base, the expert system performs syntactic translations for queries and replies, determines the need to apply a specific software package, and prepares data transformation for that package.

The Network Interface should be designed to be the actual expert interface with the user/preparer/operator. It communicates queries and updates between the user and the Master Expert System by identifying the need of the user, determining the level of communication skill of the user, and translating the queries into an appropriate form. The Network Interface has three major functions:

- *Meta knowledge about the user.* The system may use meta knowledge about the user, the user's experience, and the user's intentions, to refine the search. For example, if an auto parts system knowledge base includes information about users and their organization (for example, size, type of ownership, and location), then the system may give greater weight to potential responses based on automobile parts sold by similar organizations in similar environments.
- *Specialized domain knowledge.* Browsing a given domain may provide specialized knowledge about that domain to facilitate the search for information to respond to the user's query. The system may contain a set of heuristic rules about how to search for experiments that closely correspond to the query.
- *Keyword extraction.* The system selects pertinent terms from the user's query, with which to search the data base. Extraction may be limited to a list of predetermined keywords or it may include all significant words (for example, all except articles, prepositions, conjunctions, and so forth).

The Data Base Interface should be designed to act as an intelligent front end for data base management systems in querying the data base. It accepts queries from the Network Interface through the Master Expert System and performs the syntactic translation for queries and replies. The Data Base Interface contains deductive rules for use in specifying general knowledge to extract information from a set of specific facts. For instance, a user may wish to obtain data on the cost per parts order in a particular year, while the data base contains only the total cost of the orders in a given year and the order size. A very simple deductive rule to obtain the data for this is

(cost per parts order ) = (total cost ) / (parts order size)

More complex rules can be included to answer the user's queries.

Finally, the Software Package Interface should be designed to accept commands and transform data from the Master Expert System, dispatch and operate the specific software packages required, and return the appropriate results to the Master Expert System for the following functions:

- *Statistical and mathematical queries.* In a data base, users may wish to obtain data on the aggregate results of their experiments. An intelligent data base interface may provide these results by means of a knowledge-based interface to a statistical package and/or a library of mathematical routines. The knowledge-based interface contains information on how to invoke the requested functions and how to pass and receive data. For example, a user could ask for the average, maximum, minimum, and standard deviation of the total cost of past orders of a given part.
- *Interface to existing computer programs and commerical software packages.* In some cases, a user may want to apply computer models to answer the question, "What kind of track records might a supplier have experienced for my orders?" Such models can be linked through a knowledge-based interface that describes the capabilities of the model, input required, output supplied, and so forth.

The four components of the ideal intelligent information system work closely as a team to satisfy the need of the user/preparer for an intelligent information operation.

The Expert Knowledge Organizer can be employed to build a *specialty* intelligent information system that is able to handle the core of the tasks discussed above, to make data inputting and processing more manageable and less time consuming. Note that we have proposed a *specialty* intelligent data base system rather than a *general* intelligent data base system. A general intelligent data base system might lack the sophistication needed to meet the requirements of all users, due to limitations in current PC speed and memory and in intelligent information systems. General intelligent data base systems would be also inefficient due to the number of facilities required to please most types of users.

A Parts Inventory Control System (PICS) can illustrate how to use the Expert Knowledge Organizer. Two approaches can be adopted to build a PICS: the interactive mode and the batch mode. The minimum functions of the PICS and the two approaches are discussed.

## Minimum Functions of the Parts Inventory Control System(PICS)

The PICS is an intelligent information system that allows a parts dealer or shop owner to cost-effectively control inventory, maintain an optimal level of stock, record translations, reorder stock, and check at any time the condition of a given part, such as the cost, degree of customer satisfaction, and supplier's delivery schedule.

The minimum functions for such a system include:

1. Organization of parts inventory information in an easy-to-understand manner
2. Acceptance of rules governing how parts are sold, purchased, and priced, and other heuristic knowledge
3. Communication with other information systems that contain necessary information, such as dBaseIII

Implementation of the first two functions in the PICS is discussed below, using Mazda parts as examples. Because the third function is complicated and requires a lengthy discussion regarding the structure of information systems and modem communication, discussion of it is reserved for a separate publication.*

## Using the Interactive Mode of the Expert Knowledge Organizer Environment

The Expert Knowledge Organizer (EKO) is naturally suitable for use in building a Mazda Parts Inventory Control System (`Mazda-parts`). The interactive mode allows use of the mouse to select menus and change windows, and use of the keyboard to input information regarding Mazda parts. EKO can be invoked to perform the following tasks:

- Create classes of parts
- Create units of a given part
- Create unstructured facts/data
- Create rules for inventory control
- Display the parts hierarchy
- Advise the user on parts inventory control

---

*The functions of EKO can be expanded to retrieve data in other data base systems, such as dBase III, or in other nationally distributed data bases, such as Dun & Bradstreet Industrial Data Base (Cambridge, MA). For details of these capabilities, see Baldur Systems Corporation [1].

## *Create Classes and Display Hierarchy*

The structure of the classes created in EKO is similar to the hierarchy of an organization in daily life. Sequential menu commands are given to create a class—*CLASS, CREATE*. After these commands are accepted by EKO, a series of prompts appears to allow the user to create the desired number of classes. The sample classes created for `Mazda-parts` include:

- A root class of Mazda parts, called MAZDA-PARTS
- Two classes of cars, WAGON and SEDAN
- Several classes of part groups, such as ENGINE and FUEL-SYSTEM
- Several classes of fuel system elements, such as CARBURETOR and FUEL-PUMP

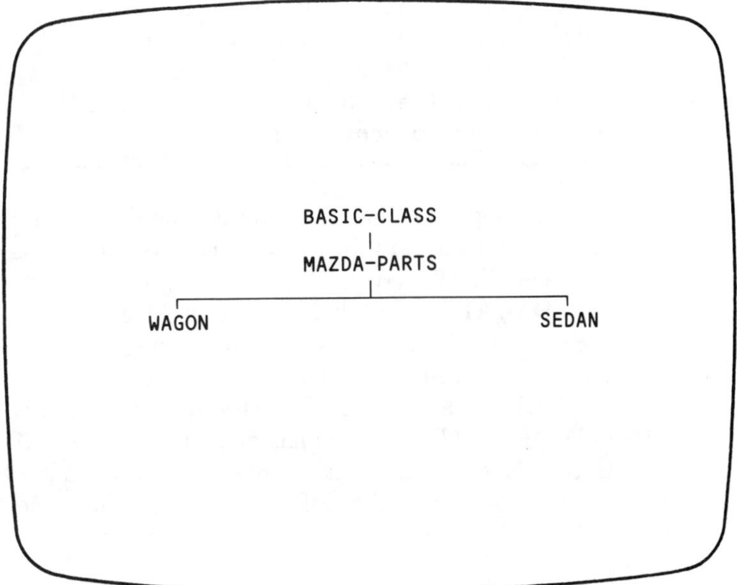


**Figure 10-1**
***The structure of the Mazda parts inventory***

This hierarchy of `Mazda-parts` is automatically exhibited in graphs, as shown in Figure 10-1. Listings 10-2 through 10-4 provide sample descriptions of the classes discussed. The root class, MAZDA-PARTS (shown in Listing 10-2), indicates the common characteristics and their default values that are inherited by the subclasses, such as DEALER-NAME and PREFERENCE (preferred supplier).

**Listing 10-2**
***Creating a class for the Mazda parts inventory***

```
Documentation: to control the inventory of Mazda parts for
 a dealer
```

**Listing 10-2 (cont.)**

```
Superclass: BASIC-CLASS
Subclasses: NIL
Units: NIL
MEMBER slot:  ICON  (Not Assertable)
  Source:  BASIC-CLASS
  Default Value:  TEXT-STRING {(MEMBER *ICON-LIST*)}
MEMBER slot:  DOCUMENTATION  (Not Assertable)
  Source:  BASIC-CLASS
  Default Value:  {STRING}
MEMBER slot:  DEALER-NAME  (Assertable)
  Source:  MAZDA-PARTS
  Default Value:  HAYWARD-CA {ALPHABET}
MEMBER slot:  PREFERENCE  (Assertable)
  Source:  MAZDA-PARTS
  Default Value:  MAZDA-WEST {ALPHABET}
Hit any key to continue:
```

Listings 10-3 and 10-4 indicate the difference between parts required for two types of cars. In Listing 10-3, the superclass of the WAGON class is MAZDA-PARTS. WAGON inherits the two common characteristics of MAZDA-PARTS: PREFERENCE and DEALER-NAME. Because DOCUMENTATION and ICON have not changed, they are inherited from the basic class (used as the origin of any root class, such as MAZDA-PARTS). WAGON has a common characteristic to be passed down to its subclass, COMMON-PARTS, which has default values of BATTERY, TIRE, and ENGINE. More common characteristics can be added to the slot of the class. Listing 10-4 illustrates information regarding one of the third layers in MAZDA-PARTS.

**Listing 10-3**
***The WAGON class of MAZDA-PARTS***

```
Documentation: parts for mazda wagons
Superclass: MAZDA-PARTS
Subclasses: NIL
Units: NIL
MEMBER slot:  PREFERENCE  (Assertable)
  Source:  MAZDA-PARTS
  Default Value:  MAZDA-WEST {ALPHABET}
MEMBER slot:  DEALER-NAME  (Assertable)
  Source:  MAZDA-PARTS
  Default Value:  HAYWARD-CA {ALPHABET}
MEMBER slot:  DOCUMENTATION  (Not Assertable)
  Source:  BASIC-CLASS
  Default Value:  {STRING}
```

```
MEMBER slot:  ICON  (Not Assertable)
  Source:  BASIC-CLASS
  Default Value:  TEXT-STRING {(MEMBER *ICON-LIST*)}
MEMBER slot:  COMMON-PARTS  (Assertable)
  Source:  WAGON
  Default Value:  (BATTERY TIRE ENGINE) {(ALPHABET ICON)}
Hit any key to continue:
```

**Listing 10-4**
***The SEDAN class of MAZDA-PARTS***

```
Documentation: mazda sedan class of cars
Superclass: MAZDA-PARTS
Subclasses: NIL
Units: NIL
MEMBER slot:  PREFERENCE  (Assertable)
  Source:  MAZDA-PARTS
  Default Value:  MAZDA-WEST {ALPHABET}
MEMBER slot:  DEALER-NAME  (Assertable)
  Source:  MAZDA-PARTS
  Default Value:  HAYWARD-CA {ALPHABET}
MEMBER slot:  DOCUMENTATION  (Not Assertable)
  Source:  BASIC-CLASS
  Default Value:  {STRING}
MEMBER slot:  ICON  (Not Assertable)
  Source:  BASIC-CLASS
  Default Value:  TEXT-STRING {(MEMBER *ICON-LIST*)}
MEMBER slot:  COMMON-PARTS  (Assertable)
  Source:  SEDAN
  Default Value:  (BATTERY LIGHTS TANK) {(ALPHABET ICON)}
Hit any key to continue:
```

The fourth layer of classes—for example, FUEL SYSTEM ELEMENTS—can have subclasses if the complexity of the element deserves further subclassification. Otherwise, a unit (also called an entity) can be created to compile all information about this element.

## *Create Units*

The sequential menus for creating units are *UNIT, CREATE.* A sample unit is created for FUEL-PUMP. The characteristics of FUEL-PUMP include all features inherited from MAZDA-PARTS, WAGON to FUEL-SYSTEM, plus all characteristics belonging to FUEL-PUMP only. FUEL-PUMP's own characteristics include:

- Current inventory level
- Optimal inventory level

- Minimum order size
- Availability
- Repair frequency
- Customer complaint frequency
- Best source, name, telephone number, terms, and conditions
- Least desired source, name, telephone number, terms, and conditions
- Cost
- Discount
- Storage space required
- Location of storage
- Substitute

These characteristics can be edited, deleted, and added with ease. A sample FUEL-PUMP inventory is shown in Listing 10-5.

**Listing 10-5**
***A partial unit for FUEL-PUMP***

```
  Source:  BASIC-CLASS
  Value:  fuel pumps used for wagons {STRING}
OWN slot:  ICON  (Not Assertable)
  Source:  BASIC-CLASS
  Value:  NIL {(PREDICATE VALID-ICON)}
OWN slot:  CURRENT-INVENTORY-LEVEL  (Assertable)
  Source:  FUEL-PUMP
  Value:  20 {EXPRESSION}
OWN slot:  OPTIMAL-INVENTORY-LEVEL  (Assertable)
  Source:  FUEL-PUMP
  Value:  2 {EXPRESSION}
OWN slot:  MINIMUM-ORDER  (Assertable)
  Source:  FUEL-PUMP
  Value:  20 {EXPRESSION}
OWN slot:  AVAILABILITY  (Assertable)
  Source:  FUEL-PUMP
  Value:  3-MONTH {EXPRESSION}
OWN slot:  REPAIR-FREQUENCY  (Assertable)
  Source:  FUEL-PUMP
  Value:  10-PER-MONTH {EXPRESSION}
Hit any key to continue:
```

## *Create Unstructured Facts/Data*

Unstructured facts/data cannot be represented in the format of either classes or units, but may be stored into either the unstructured knowledge data base or in the variable data base. Facts/data can be "pushed" into the knowledge base using either the menu of *ASSERT* or *STASH.* A fact is *asserted* into the unstructured knowledge base when a forward chaining mechanism is performed to trigger any rules whose antecedent matches the fact, to check the validity of the fact or the rule. The user is prompted for the certainty factor. A fact is *stashed* into the knowledge base when no forward chaining is performed. The user is also prompted for the certainty factor.

Facts can be expressed as random propositions, such as `(Customer 1 'DAVID)`, or propositions connected by logical connectors, such as `OR` and `AND`:

```
(OR ( Customer 1 'DAVID) ( Customer 2 'LISE))

(AND ( Customer 1 'DAVID) ( Customer 2 'EILEEN))

(NOT ( Customer 3 'EMILY))
```

User-defined variables are stored in the variable data base. A variable can be created, deleted, or edited. To create a variable, the menus of *Variable* and *Create* are clicked sequentially. Variable name, value, and certainty factor are prompted for input by the user. For example, a variable of `ECON-INDICATORS` can be created because it is not related to the hierarchy of parts but is important to the sale of Mazda parts:

- Variable name: `ECON-INDICATORS`
- Value: (86.9 99.8)
- Certainty: (0.6)

The resultant variable stored in the variable base and the input format are shown in Figure 10-2.

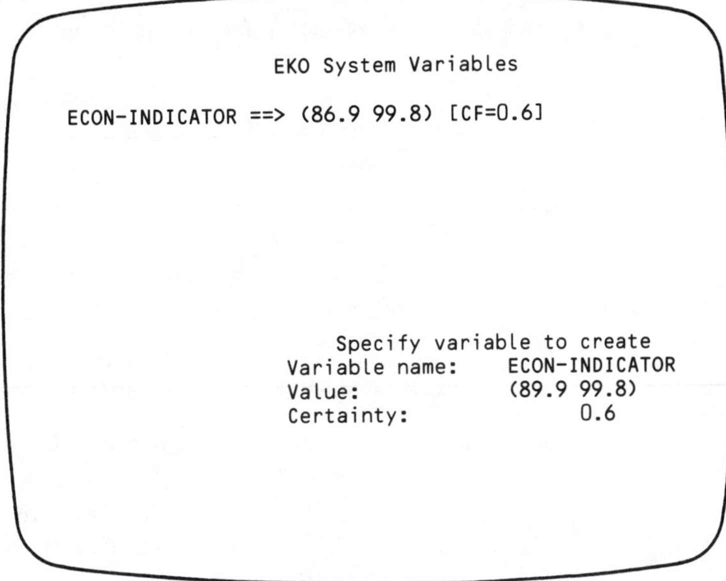


**Figure 10-2**
***Creating a variable, ECON-INDICATOR***

## *Create Rules for Inventory Control*

Rules, which are the source of the reasoning power for optimum inventory control of `Mazda-parts`, can be created by first creating a rule class and then creating the rules under each rule class. In creating a rule class, the name and document of the rule class are prompted by the EKO. When a rule is created, the name of the rule and the class it belongs to, as well as the explanation, premise, and conclusion, are prompted. Facts (data) in classes, units, or the unstructured knowledge base can be used to establish either the basis for the premise and/or conclusion.

Rules are required to connect the relevent pieces of information stored in the frame structure (classes and units), and the logic structure (unstructured knowledge base and the variable data base). For rapid search, rules are grouped into rule classes. A rule class is created using the menu of *Create Rule Class*, from which *enter name of rule class to create* is prompted. For example, *ORDER-PARTS-RULES* is entered as the root rule class and the documentation is then prompted, as shown in Figure 10-3.

Figure 10-3 shows the partial structure of the rule classes, such as ORDER-PARTS-RULES in 10-3a and the documentation of ORDER-PARTS-RULES in 10-3b. *Create Rules* is ordered to create a rule that is attached to a rule class. To specify facts in the premise and conclusion of a rule, two types of expressions can be used: the abbreviated English representation language (AER) or the predicate calculus representation (PC), to specify facts relating to units, classes, and variables. The AER expression is first presented, followed by the correspondent PC expression after a ==> sign.

- *Class facts*—A class's own slots and subclasses can be specified in the formats:

  Own slots — To specify a fact about the own slot value of a class, use:

  *the <slot name> of all <class-name> is <slot-value>==> (<slot-name> <class-name> <value>)*

  Subclasses — To specify a fact about the membership of a class in another, use:

  *all <class-name 1> are <class-name 2> ==> (Subclass <class-name 1> <class-name 2>)*

- *Unit Facts*—The value of unit slots and the membership of the unit in a class can be specified in the following formats:

  Slot values — To specify a fact about the slot value of a unit, use:

  *the <slot name> of <unit-name> is <value>==> (<slot-name> <unit name> <value>)*

  Class membership — To specify a fact about the class of a unit, use:

*<unit-name> is a type-of <class-name>*
*==> (in-class <unit-name> <class-name>)*

- *Variable Facts*—To specify a fact about the value of a variable, use: *<variable-name> is <variable-value> ==> (value <variable-name> <variable-value>)*

```
Choose rule-class to display
        BASIC-RULE-CLASS
        ORDER-PARTS-RULES
        REGULAR-ORDERING
```

*a. Partial Structure of the Rule Classes*

```
Expert Knowledge Organizer
                ORDER-PARTS-RULES:

Documentation: the rules to determine when to order parts
Superclass: BASIC-RULE-CLASS
Subclasses: (REGULAR-ORDERING)
Rules: NIL
```

*b. Documentation of the Rule Class ORDER-PARTS-RULES*

**Figure 10-3**
***Structure of a rule class***

These expression formats are employed to establish rules that are organized toward a final goal and a set of corresponding subgoals. Let us assume that the goal of ***Mazda-parts*** inventory control is to maximize customer satisfaction with a minimum cost in the inventory. The correspondent subgoals are shown in Figure 10-4.

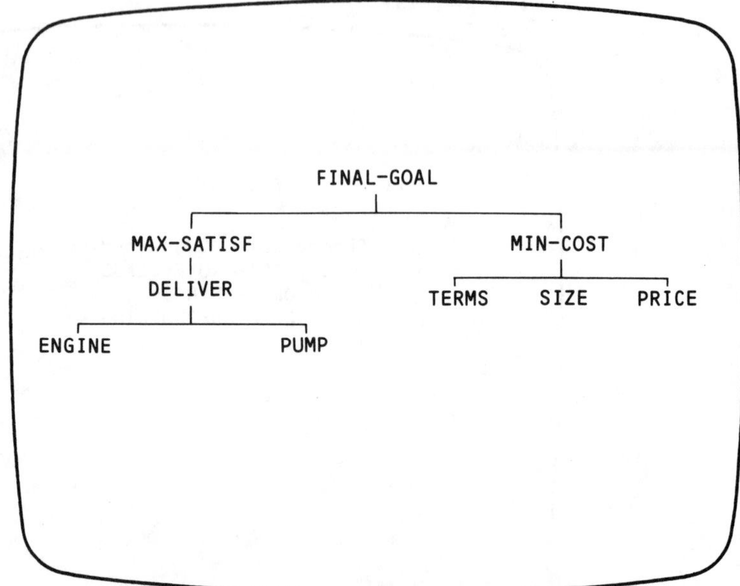


**Figure 10-4**
***Partial goals and subgoals of the Mazda inventory control system***

The rules for maximum satisfaction and minimum cost are

Maximum satisfaction

- Engine.delivery < 10 days
- Fuel pump.delivery <one day

Minimum cost

- Delivery >5 days
- Terms >30 days
- Order size <3 pieces
- Cost?

The formats discussed previously can be used to write some of these rules. The rule class for these rules is REGULAR-ORDERING. The final goal can be expressed in AER as follows:

```
IF (AND (Maximum-Satisfaction is True) (Minimum-Cost is
    True)
THEN (Inventory-Control is successful)
```

The subgoal of `Maximum-Satisfaction` can then be expressed as follows:

```
IF (AND (the Delivery of Engine of all WAGON is <10-days)
    (the Delivery of Fuel-Pump is <1-day)
THEN  (Maximum-Satisfaction is True)
```

Note the difference in expression for engine delivery and fuel pump delivery. `The Delivery of Engine` is a slot of a class, WAGON, which is inherited by all of its subclasses; however, `the Delivery of Pump` is a slot of a unit, Fuel-Pump. The subgoal of `Minimum-Cost` can be expressed in a similar manner. More detail is needed under each of the subgoals discussed so that the relationship of all activities in the operations of the *`Mazda-parts`* inventory control are fully represented.

### *Advise the User on Parts Inventory Control*

To provide the user with advice on parts inventory control, you can use the following commands:

`Achieve-goal` To answer a particular query.

`Assert` To assert a new fact into the knowledge base by performing a forward chaining mechanism.

`Justify` To justify the last conclusion (goal).

`Achieve-goal` can be used to achieve a goal such as `(Maximum-Satisfaction $X)`. EKO takes the command and achieves this goal through backward chaining. `Assert` is used to assert a new fact using forward chaining—for example, `(Minimum-Cost $200/order)`. `Justify` can be used after `Achieve-Goal` is performed, to trace the reasoning process.

## Using the Batch Mode of EKO

EKO may be slightly modified to write programs that run in a batch mode. Instead of receiving commands and input from the mouse (if any) and keyboard, in batch mode operation EKO needs to support the following keywords:

Knowledge base commands

1. `Create-unit`

   Keywords supported: `name, class assert?, slot`
2. `Delete-unit`
3. `Create-class`

   Keywords supported: `name, superclass, doc.`(documentation), `slots`
4. `Delete-class`
5. `Create-rule`

Keywords supported: `name rule-class, premise, conclusion, action, certainty, askable?`

6. `Delete-rule`
7. `Create-rule-class`

   Keywords supported: `name, superclass`
8. `Delete-rule-class`

Reasoning commands (similar to user command in the interactive mode)

1. `Assert`
2. `Achieve-Goal`
3. `Justify`

Listing 10-6 shows a sample program *`Create-Rule`*. Listing 10-7 shows a sample program written for running in the batch mode, which performs the same tasks as those discussed in the interactive mode.

**Listing 10-6**
***Create-Rule, a sample program to make the EKO a batch mode operation***

```
; Program Directed Rule Creation and Deletion
(defun Create-Rule (rule-name &rest keys-and-vals)
  "Supports keywords :name, :class, :premise, :conclusion,
    :action
  :certainty, :askable?"
  (let ((rule-class (or (second (member :class keys-and-
     vals))
                        'basic-rule-class)))
    (when (member rule-name *rule-list*)
      (when-debug "Rule ~A exists, replacing it..." rule-
    name)
      (delete-rule rule-name))
    (push-last rule-name (unit-rules (eval rule-class)))
    (push-last rule-name *rule-list*)
    (set rule-name (make-unit :name rule-name :class rule-
     class :type :rule))
    (inherit-slots rule-class rule-name)
    (dolist (rule-slot                '(explanation premise
     conclusion action certainty askable))
      (let ((value (second (member (keywordize rule-slot)
     keys-and-vals))))
        (when value
          (set-unit-slot-value rule-name rule-slot
     value))))))
(defun Delete-Rule (rule-name)
  (let ((rule-obj (eval rule-name)))
```

```
(pull rule-name *rule-list*)
(pull rule-name (unit-rules (eval (rule-class rule-
 obj))))))
```

**Listing 10-7**
***Partial batch mode program for the Mazda inventory control system***

```
#¦
 this file sets up a Mazda Parts Inventory Control System
  We need multiple superclasses to implement nomenclature
     fully.
¦#
(create-class 'Mazda-parts :doc "to control the inventory of
Mazda parts for a dealer"
               :slots
               '((dealer-name :type-restriction :alphabet
                   :default-value Hayward-Ca)
                 (preference :type-restriction :alphabet
                   :default-value Mazda-west))
(create-class 'wagon :doc "parts for Mazda wagons"
               :superclass 'mazda-parts
               :slots '((common-parts :type-restriction
     :(alphabet icon)
                :default-value (battery tire engine))
(create-class 'sedan :doc "Mazda sedan class of cars"
               :superclass 'mazda-parts
               :slots '((common-parts :type-restriction
     :(alphabet icon)
                :default-value (battery lights tank))
(create-class 'fuel-system :doc "Mazda wagon fuel system"
               :superclass 'wagon

;*****************************************************

(create-entity 'fuel-pump :class 'fuel-system :preference
     Mazda-east)
(create-entity 'fuel-cut-valve :class 'fuel-system
     :preference Mazda-west)

;*****************************************************

(create-rule-class 'regular-ordering :doc "Rules to
                determine when to order parts"
(create-rule 'customer-satisfaction :class 'regular-ordering
               :explanation "customer service goal"
               :premise '(and (Maximum-Satisfaction is
     True)
                              (Minimum-Cost is true))
```

**Listing 10-7 (cont.)**

```
                :conclusion '(Inventory-Control is
    successful))
(create-rule 'maximum-satisfaction :class 'regular-ordering
                :explanation "indicating maximum
                       satisfaction of the customers"
                :premise '(and (the tank.delivery of all
    wagon is
                      <10-days) (the delivery of FUEL-PUMP is
    <1-day))
                :conclusion '(Maximum-Satisfaction is True))

;**************************************************

;(achieve-goal '(Maximum-Satisfaction $x))
;(assert '(Minimum-Cost $200/order))
```

# Blackjack—Building a Training Tool

Expert systems can be developed as training tools to provide instructions to less experienced personnel, as does DELTA (developed by General Electric and discussed in Chapter 9). In this section, the problem of the game blackjack is used to develop an expert system prototype called Blackjack Assistant. Personal Consultant and M.1 are used to implement the prototype, to demonstrate the difference between these tools.

Blackjack is one of the most popular forms of casino gambling. It is an extremely simple game. Most people know how to play it, but only a very few experts can beat the dealer. Blackjack is essentially a card game between the dealer and the players. The purpose of the game is to get a count total as close as possible to 21 without exceeding 21, and to accumulate more points than the dealer at the same time. The game is played as follows. Play starts to the dealer's left and moves clockwise. Each player places a bet and then receives two cards face down ("hole" cards). The dealer receives one card face down and another card face up ("up" card). The player can choose either 1 or 11 as the value of an ace. All face cards are counted as tens and the value of the other cards is their face value. A hand that contains an ace is called a "soft" hand, if counting the ace as 11 does not cause the total to exceed 21. All others are called "hard" hands.

When the first two cards dealt to a player are an ace and a 10-value card, the player has a "blackjack." If the player has a blackjack and the dealer does not, the player generally wins 1.5 times his original bet. If the dealer has a blackjack, all players not having blackjack lose their bets. In most casinos, if both a player and the dealer have blackjacks, no money changes hands.

Each player examines his cards and decides whether to "stand" (not receive any more cards) or to "hit" (receive more cards) from the dealer. If the player's count exceeds 21, the player "busts" and loses his bet. After each player has drawn his cards, the dealer turns over his hole card. If the dealer's total is less than 17, he must draw another card and continue to draw until his total is 17 or higher. If the dealer busts, he pays all players who have not busted the amount of their bets. Otherwise, the dealer collects from players whose totals are less than his and pays players whose totals are higher than his but not more than 21. If a player and a dealer tie, no money changes hands in most casinos.

Three variations on this process are splitting pairs, doubling down, and insurance. First, if the player's two cards are identical (that is, a pair) the player has the option of "splitting" the pair. This entails treating the two cards as the first card in two separate hands. To exercise this option, the player must place an amount identical to his original bet to form a new hand. He then receives a second card for each of the two new hands and play continues, with the exception that the player now is in control of two hands. Two additional rules are that if the player splits aces, he receives only one more card, and cannot split a hand more than once.

Second, the player may choose to "double down." Doubling down entails doubling the original bet and receiving only one additional card. Third, if the dealer's up card is an ace, players have the alternative to buy "insurance" before play begins. To exercise this option, the player must put up a side wager of less than or equal to one-half of his original bet. If the dealer has a blackjack, the player's hand is dealt with accordingly, but he wins twice the amount of his side wager. If the dealer does not have a blackjack, the player loses his side wager and play resumes.

# *Applying Selection Rules to Blackjack*

The selection rules (necessary and sufficient conditions) discussed in Chapter 9 are used to determine the applicability of expert system technology to the game of blackjack.

## Necessary Conditions

The two criteria to be asserted as necessary conditions are

1. *Is the problem area well bounded and understood?* The problem of the game of blackjack is well bounded. The number of outcomes of the cards is limited and the result of the game depends on conditional probability functions. Most people understand the game even though they may not have the knowledge and experience of beating the dealer. Various books are available to increase the odds of winning the game.
2. *Is at least one human expert available to explain the knowledge required for the expert system being built?* A limited number of good players are available. Books are also available that detail strategies

that provide the knowledge for the expert system prototype. For example, the book authored by Edward O. Thorp explains strategies for splitting, doubling down, hitting, and standing [2].

## Sufficient Conditions

At least three sufficient conditions exist for the game of blackjack:

1. *Is the expert advice critical?* Expert advice makes a difference between winning and losing money when one gambles in casinos. It is not unusual for a person to lose several hundred dollars each visit to most casinos. The expert advice may increase the odds of winning.
2. *Is the expert advice costly?* The value of expert advice can be considered an opportunity cost that would occur if the advice were not sought. The opportunity cost could be very high if one lost a large sum of money in playing blackjack. Apparently, most casual gamblers do not seek expert advice.
3. *Is the game a routine, detail-dependent, decision-making process?* The game of blackjack involves a routine decision-making process. In each game, many factors must be considered if the dealer is to be beaten. A training tool that simulates the real-game situation and instructs the player on winning strategies will undoubtedly increase his ability to consider these factors more rapidly and accurately.

# *Applying Expert System Technology to Blackjack*

The game of blackjack requires a consolidation of game strategies outlined by experts, probability calculation, and rules of thumb of experienced players who have undertaken the game under pressure in the casino's smoky game room. Several game strategies illustrate the process of building a prototype for the problem.

A preliminary strategy that takes into account only the cards the player is currently holding and the dealer's up card was developed by Edward O. Thorp. The strategy is simply a set of tables that advises the player on how to make decisions about splitting, doubling down, hitting, and standing. It ignores any information concerning previously dealt cards. The strategy is summarized below.

***Splitting cards***—When the player has a pair, the first decision he may make is whether or not to split it. *Chart a* in Figure 10-5, labeled "Pair Splitting," details the advice. To find the splitting recommendation for a particular situation, simply find the row in the chart that corresponds to the hand the player is holding. Then move horizontally to the column that corresponds to the dealer's up card. The recommendation is determined by the shading of the cell that corresponds to the intersection of the selected row and column. If the cell is shaded, splitting the pair is recommended. In the strategy, for example, splitting 4 only if the dealer's up card is a 5 is recommended, as shown by arrow "a" in the illustration.

***Doubling down***—The next decision the player may make is whether or not to double down. *Chart b*, labeled "Hard Doubling," outlines the strategy for doubling down with hard hands. *Chart c*, labeled "Soft Doubling," outlines the strategy for doubling down with soft hands. These charts are read in the same fashion as the "Pair Splitting" chart, with the exceptions explained in footnotes. Thus the player should, for example, double down a soft 18 (You Have A and 7) against a dealer's 5 (arrow "a" in chart c).

***Hitting or standing***—After the split and double-down decisions have been made, the player may decide whether to take a hit or to stand. *Chart d*, labeled "Standing Numbers," shows the strategy for hard and soft hands.

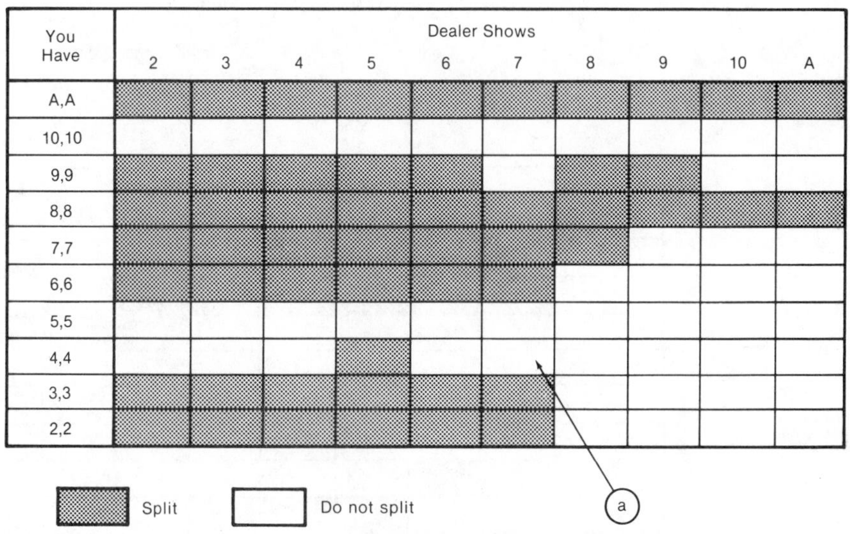


*a. Pair Splitting*

| You Have | 2 | 3 | 4 | 5 | 6 | 7 | 8 | 9 | 10 | A |
|---|---|---|---|---|---|---|---|---|---|---|
| | | | | Dealer Shows | | | | | | |
| 11 | | | | | | | | | | |
| 10 | | | | | | | | | | |
| 8 | | | | | | | | | | |
| 9 | | | | * | * | | | | | |

Double down    Do not double down

* Double down except with 6,2.

*b. Hard Doubling*

**Figure 10-5**
***Preliminary strategy in the game of blackjack***

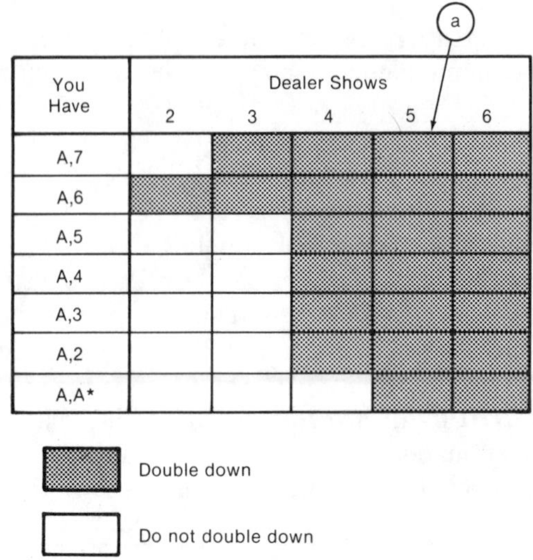


*Double down with A,A only if aces cannot be split.

*c. Soft Doubling*

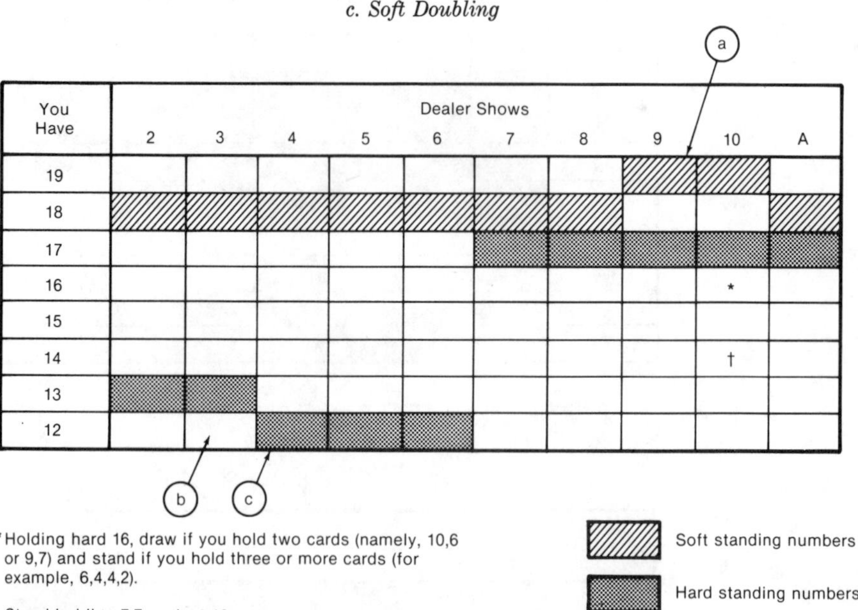

a
You Have
Dealer Shows
2
3
4
5
6
7
8
9
10
A
19
18
17
16
15
14
13
12
*
†
b
c
*Holding hard 16, draw if you hold two cards (namely, 10,6 or 9,7) and stand if you hold three or more cards (for example, 6,4,4,2).
† Stand holding 7,7 against 10.
Soft standing numbers
Hard standing numbers


*d. Standing Numbers*

**Figure 10-5 Cont.**

This chart is read differently from the previous charts. Cells shaded with crosshatching represent soft standing numbers; cells shaded in grey represent hard standing numbers. A standing number is defined as the lowest total at which the player is to stand against a specific dealer's up card. Thus the player is directed to stand if his total is greater than or equal to the standing number shown in the chart; otherwise, he is directed to hit, with some exceptions footnoted in the chart. For example, a player with a soft 19 (A counted as 11) should stand against a dealer's 9 (shown with arrow "a" in the chart). A player with a hard 12 should hit against a dealer's 3 but stand against a dealer's 4 (shown with arrows "b" and "c" in the chart). If the player's total is not shown on the chart, he should take a hit regardless of the dealer's up card.

# *Implementation of the Expert System Prototype*

Two tools are used to build the expert system (Blackjack Assistant) prototype for the blackjack problem: Personal Consultant and M.1.

The general theme of the Blackjack Assistant prototype is to enable the player (user) to let the system know his first two cards and the dealer's up card and then receive recommendations on how to play the game. The consultation can be performed repeatedly to the point where the user receives the benefit of simulation and becomes more knowledgeable in playing cards. Note that the game of blackjack is used only for illustration, not for teaching gambling skills.

## Using Personal Consultant

Personal Consultant, developed and maintained by Texas Instruments, employs a modified version of EMYCIN, an expert system shell (empty MYCIN) originated at Stanford University in 1980. Personal Consultant is a rule-structured tool and uses backward chaining to achieve a goal. It uses Abbreviated Rule Language (ARL) to provide a convenient format for writing functions in rules. For example, the ARL input for Rule 2 in Listing 10-8 is as follows:

```
Premise:   (FIRST-CARD <11 AND SECOND-CARD <12)
Action:    (TOTAL =(FIRST-CARD +SECOND-CARD))
```

The ARL form is then translated into IQLISP language below:

```
Premise:   (AND (LESSP* (VAL1 CNTXT FIRST-CARD) 11)
           (LESSP* (VAL1 CNTXT SECOND-CARD) 12)
Action     (DO-ALL
           (CONCLUDE CNTXT TOTAL
           (PLUS (VAL1 CNTXT FIRST-CARD)
           (VAL1 CNTXT SECOND-CARD)) TALLY 1000))
```

TALLY 1000 indicates that the certainty factor is 100 percent. Its value ranges from −1000 to +1000.

**Listing 10-8**
***Sample rules for Blackjack Assistant implemented in Personal Consultant (Rules 2,4,5,7,8,9,18)***

```
    Rule Group  BASIC-STRATEGYRULES
RULE002 [BASIC-STRATEGYRULES]
-------
If 1) the first card in your hand is less than 11, and
   2) the second card in your hand is less than 12,
Then it is definite (100%) that the count total of the
     cards in your hand is [ the first card in your
     hand plus the second card in your hand ].
PREMISE:  ($AND (LESSP* (VAL1 CNTXT FIRST-CARD) 11)
             (LESSP* (VAL1 CNTXT SECOND-CARD) 12))
ACTION:  (DO-ALL
            (CONCLUDE CNTXT TOTAL
              (PLUS (VAL1 CNTXT FIRST-CARD)
                (VAL1 CNTXT SECOND-CARD)) TALLY 1000))
RULE003 [BASIC-STRATEGYRULES]
-------
If 1) the first card in your hand is less than 12, and
   2) the second card in your hand is less than 11,
Then it is definite (100%) that the count total of the
     cards in your hand is [ the first card in your
     hand plus the second card in your hand ].
PREMISE:  ($AND (LESSP* (VAL1 CNTXT FIRST-CARD) 12)
             (LESSP* (VAL1 CNTXT SECOND-CARD) 11))
ACTION:  (DO-ALL
            (CONCLUDE CNTXT TOTAL
              (PLUS (VAL1 CNTXT FIRST-CARD)
                (VAL1 CNTXT SECOND-CARD)) TALLY 1000))
RULE004 [BASIC-STRATEGYRULES]
-------
If 1) the first card in your hand is 11, and
   2) the second card in your hand is 11,
Then it is definite (100%) that the count total of the
     cards in your hand is 2.
PREMISE:  ($AND (SAME CNTXT FIRST-CARD 11)
             (SAME CNTXT SECOND-CARD 11))
ACTION:  (DO-ALL (CONCLUDE CNTXT TOTAL 2 TALLY 1000))
RULE005 [BASIC-STRATEGYRULES]
-------
If 1) the first card in your hand is 1, or
   2) the first card in your hand is 11, or
   3) the second card in your hand is 1, or
   4) the second card in your hand is 11,
Then it is definite (100%) that your hand contains one or
     more aces.
```

```
PREMISE:  ($AND
            ($OR (SAME CNTXT FIRST-CARD 1)
              (SAME CNTXT FIRST-CARD 11)
              (SAME CNTXT SECOND-CARD 1)
              (SAME CNTXT SECOND-CARD 11)))
ACTION:  (DO-ALL (CONCLUDE CNTXT SOFT YES TALLY 1000))
RULE006 [BASIC-STRATEGYRULES]
-------
If 1) the first card in your hand is greater than 1, and
   2) the first card in your hand is less than 11, and
   3) the second card in your hand is greater than 1, and
   4) the second card in your hand is less than 11,
Then it is definite (100%) that your hand contains one or
     more aces is not true.
PREMISE:  ($AND (GREATERP* (VAL1 CNTXT FIRST-CARD) 1)
           (LESSP* (VAL1 CNTXT FIRST-CARD) 11)
           (GREATERP* (VAL1 CNTXT SECOND-CARD) 1)
           (LESSP* (VAL1 CNTXT SECOND-CARD) 11))
ACTION:  (DO-ALL (CONCLUDE CNTXT SOFT NO TALLY 1000))
RULE007 [BASIC-STRATEGYRULES]
-------
If the count total of the cards in your hand is 2,
Then it is definite (100%) that your hand contains one or
     more aces.
PREMISE:  ($AND (SAME CNTXT TOTAL 2))
ACTION:  (DO-ALL (CONCLUDE CNTXT SOFT YES TALLY 1000))
RULE008 [BASIC-STRATEGYRULES]
-------
If 1) 1) the first card in your hand is 1, and
      2) the second card in your hand is 1, or
   2) 1) the first card in your hand is 2, and
      2) the second card in your hand is 2, or
   3) 1) the first card in your hand is 3, and
      2) the second card in your hand is 3, or
   4) 1) the first card in your hand is 4, and
      2) the second card in your hand is 4, or
   5) 1) the first card in your hand is 5, and
      2) the second card in your hand is 5, or
   6) 1) the first card in your hand is 6, and
      2) the second card in your hand is 6, or
   7) 1) the first card in your hand is 7, and
      2) the second card in your hand is 7, or
   8) 1) the first card in your hand is 8, and
      2) the second card in your hand is 8, or
   9) 1) the first card in your hand is 9, and
      2) the second card in your hand is 9, or
   10) 1) the first card in your hand is 10, and
       2) the second card in your hand is 10, or
```

**Listing 10-8 (cont.)**

---

```
   11) 1) the first card in your hand is 11, and
       2) the second card in your hand is 11,
Then it is definite (100%) that your hand consists of
      two of a kind.
PREMISE:  ($AND
             ($OR
               ($AND (SAME CNTXT FIRST-CARD 1)
                 (SAME CNTXT SECOND-CARD 1))
               ($AND (SAME CNTXT FIRST-CARD 2)
                 (SAME CNTXT SECOND-CARD 2))
               ($AND (SAME CNTXT FIRST-CARD 3)
                 (SAME CNTXT SECOND-CARD 3))
               ($AND (SAME CNTXT FIRST-CARD 4)
                 (SAME CNTXT SECOND-CARD 4))
               ($AND (SAME CNTXT FIRST-CARD 5)
                 (SAME CNTXT SECOND-CARD 5))
               ($AND (SAME CNTXT FIRST-CARD 6)
                 (SAME CNTXT SECOND-CARD 6))
               ($AND (SAME CNTXT FIRST-CARD 7)
                 (SAME CNTXT SECOND-CARD 7))
               ($AND (SAME CNTXT FIRST-CARD 8)
                 (SAME CNTXT SECOND-CARD 8))
               ($AND (SAME CNTXT FIRST-CARD 9)
                 (SAME CNTXT SECOND-CARD 9))
               ($AND (SAME CNTXT FIRST-CARD 10)
                 (SAME CNTXT SECOND-CARD 10))
               ($AND (SAME CNTXT FIRST-CARD 11)
                 (SAME CNTXT SECOND-CARD 11))))
ACTION:  (DO-ALL (CONCLUDE CNTXT PAIR YES TALLY 1000))
RULE009 [BASIC-STRATEGYRULES]
-------
If 1) 1) the first card in your hand is 1, and
      2) the second card in your hand is not 1, or
   2) 1) the first card in your hand is 2, and
      2) the second card in your hand is not 2, or
   3) 1) the first card in your hand is 3, and
      2) the second card in your hand is not 3, or
   4) 1) the first card in your hand is 4, and
      2) the second card in your hand is not 4, or
   5) 1) the first card in your hand is 5, and
      2) the second card in your hand is not 5, or
   6) 1) the first card in your hand is 6, and
      2) the second card in your hand is not 6, or
   7) 1) the first card in your hand is 7, and
      2) the second card in your hand is not 7, or
```

```
    8) 1) the first card in your hand is 8, and
       2) the second card in your hand is not 8, or
    9) 1) the first card in your hand is 9, and
       2) the second card in your hand is not 9, or
   10) 1) the first card in your hand is 10, and
       2) the second card in your hand is not 10, or
   11) 1) the first card in your hand is 11, and
       2) the second card in your hand is not 11,
Then it is definite (100%) that your hand consists of
     two of a kind is not true.
PREMISE:  ($AND
             ($OR
               ($AND (SAME CNTXT FIRST-CARD 1)
                 (NOTSAME CNTXT SECOND-CARD 1))
               ($AND (SAME CNTXT FIRST-CARD 2)
                 (NOTSAME CNTXT SECOND-CARD 2))
               ($AND (SAME CNTXT FIRST-CARD 3)
                 (NOTSAME CNTXT SECOND-CARD 3))
               ($AND (SAME CNTXT FIRST-CARD 4)
                 (NOTSAME CNTXT SECOND-CARD 4))
               ($AND (SAME CNTXT FIRST-CARD 5)
                 (NOTSAME CNTXT SECOND-CARD 5))
               ($AND (SAME CNTXT FIRST-CARD 6)
                 (NOTSAME CNTXT SECOND-CARD 6))
               ($AND (SAME CNTXT FIRST-CARD 7)
                 (NOTSAME CNTXT SECOND-CARD 7))
               ($AND (SAME CNTXT FIRST-CARD 8)
                 (NOTSAME CNTXT SECOND-CARD 8))
               ($AND (SAME CNTXT FIRST-CARD 9)
                 (NOTSAME CNTXT SECOND-CARD 9))
               ($AND (SAME CNTXT FIRST-CARD 10)
                 (NOTSAME CNTXT SECOND-CARD 10))
               ($AND (SAME CNTXT FIRST-CARD 11)
                 (NOTSAME CNTXT SECOND-CARD 11))))
ACTION:  (DO-ALL (CONCLUDE CNTXT PAIR NO TALLY 1000))
RULE018 [BASIC-STRATEGYRULES]
-------
If 1) your hand consists of two of a kind, and
   2) the count total of the cards in your hand is 18, and
   3) the dealer's up card is greater than 7, and
   4) the dealer's up card is less than 10,
Then 1) it is definite (100%) that the following is one of
        the preliminary set of recommendations : SPLIT, and
     2) it is definite (100%) that the following is one of
        the reasons behind my recommendations : Split nines
        if the dealer shows 8 or 9..
PREMISE:  ($AND (SAME CNTXT PAIR YES) (SAME CNTXT TOTAL 18)
            (GREATERP* (VAL1 CNTXT DEALER-CARD) 7)
```

**Listing 10-8 (cont.)**

```
            (LESSP* (VAL1 CNTXT DEALER-CARD) 10))
ACTION:  (DO-ALL
             (CONCLUDE CNTXT RECOMMENDATION SPLIT TALLY
              1000)
             (CONCLUDE CNTXT REASON "Split nines if the
              dealer shows 8 or 9." TALLY 1000))
RULE019 [BASIC-STRATEGYRULES]
-------
If 1) your hand consists of two of a kind, and
   2) the count total of the cards in your hand is 16,
Then 1) it is definite (100%) that the following is one of
        the preliminary set of recommendations : SPLIT, and
     2) it is definite (100%) that the following is one of
        the reasons behind my recommendations : Always
        split eights..
PREMISE:  ($AND (SAME CNTXT PAIR YES) (SAME CNTXT TOTAL
           16))
ACTION:  (DO-ALL
             (CONCLUDE CNTXT RECOMMENDATION SPLIT TALLY
              1000)
             (CONCLUDE CNTXT REASON "Always split eights."
             TALLY 1000))
RULE052 [BASIC-STRATEGYRULES]
-------
If 1) the preliminary set of recommendations is not SPLIT,
     and
   2) the preliminary set of recommendations is not
      DOUBLE-DOWN, and
   3) the preliminary set of recommendations is not HIT,
Then it is definite (100%) that the final recommendation
     for your hand is STAND.
PREMISE:  ($AND (NOTSAME CNTXT RECOMMENDATION SPLIT)
              (NOTSAME CNTXT RECOMMENDATION DOUBLE-DOWN)
              (NOTSAME CNTXT RECOMMENDATION HIT))
ACTION:  (DO-ALL
             (CONCLUDE CNTXT FINAL-RECOMMENDATION STAND
             TALLY 1000))
```

Like most rule-based tools, a knowledge base built in a specific format is the only thing needed for developing an expert system. A knowledge base built in Personal Consultant contains contexts, parameters, and rules. A *context* is a structural unit used to separate areas or sections in the knowledge base. Basically, contexts are organizational units of information or knowledge for a specific problem. Each context has a set of *parameters* associated with it. Parameters are facts or pieces of information that can be used to obtain conclusions or recommendations. If facts are stored in parameters, the knowledge used to manipulate those facts and reach conclusions is organized into *rules*.

The three types of parameters that need to be defined in the system are

- `Sysvars` of two kinds: `DOMAIN`, with value equal to the name of the expert system, Blackjack Assistant 1.0; and `TREEROOT`, representing the most basic element in the structure, with value equal to `BASIC-STRATEGY`, the only context defined in this version. `DOMAIN` and `TREEROOT` are shown in Listing 10-9.
- `Parmgroups` of two different kinds: `BASIC-STRATEGY-PARMS`, containing all parameter names defined in the system. Ten different parameters are defined in the context BASIC-STRATEGY—for example, `PAIR` and `CONTEXTTYPES`—enumerating all contexts present in the system. The value of `CONTEXTTYPES` is `BASIC-STRATEGY`, as shown in Listing 10-9.
- `Rulegroups`, collecting all rules present in the system `BASIC-STRATEGYRULES` (all names of rules associated with the Basic-Strategy context, such as Rule 002), shown in Listing 10-9.

**Listing 10-9**
***System parameters for Blackjack Assistant implemented in Personal Consultant***

```
    System parameters
DOMAIN [SYSVARS]
------
Value:  "Blackjack Assistant 1.0"
TREEROOT [SYSVARS]
--------
Value:  BASIC-STRATEGY
    System parameters
BASIC-STRATEGYRULES [RULEGROUPS]
-------------------
CONTEXT:  (BASIC-STRATEGY)
SVAL:  (basic-strategy)
CTRANS:  "basic-strategys"
Value:  (RULE002 RULE003 RULE004 RULE005 RULE006 RULE007
         RULE008 RULE009 RULE010 RULE015 RULE016 RULE017
         RULE018 RULE019 RULE020 RULE021 RULE022 RULE023
         RULE024 RULE025 RULE026 RULE027 RULE028 RULE029
         RULE030 RULE031 RULE032 RULE033 RULE034 RULE035
         RULE036 RULE037 RULE038 RULE039 RULE040 RULE041
         RULE042 RULE043 RULE044 RULE045 RULE046 RULE047
         RULE048 RULE049 RULE050 RULE051 RULE052)
    System parameters
```

**Listing 10-9 (cont.)**

```
BASIC-STRATEGY-PARMS [PARMGROUPS]
--------------------
Value:  (THE-CONSULTATION-IS-OVER PAIR RECOMMENDATION
     REASON
         FINAL-RECOMMENDATION FIRST-CARD SECOND-CARD TOTAL
         DEALER-CARD SOFT)
CONTEXTTYPES [PARMGROUPS]
------------
Value:  (BASIC-STRATEGY)
```

Once system parameters have been defined, the two parameter groups, BASIC-STRATEGY-PARMS and CONTEXTTYPES, are then defined. BASIC-STRATEGY-PARMS classifies rules into groups for speedy search. A sample program is shown in Listing 10-10. CONTEXTTYPES defines GOALS and INITIALDATA to direct the search path of the expert system, also shown near the end of Listing 10-10. The parameters in the initial data list receive first priority when the consultation starts (in our case, the user is queried about the value of the parameters: FIRST-CARD, SECOND-CARD and DEALER-CARD). On the other hand, the goal parameters are set as such by the system and drive the consultation.

**Listing 10-10**
***Parameter groups for Blackjack Assistant implemented in Personal Consultant***

```
    Parameter Group  BASIC-STRATEGY-PARMS
DEALER-CARD [BASIC-STRATEGY-PARMS]
-----------
TRANS:  (the dealer's up card)
PROMPT:  (What is the dealer's card?
            (Ace = 1 or 11 , face cards = 10))
ASKFIRST:  T
EXPECT:  (1 2 3 4 5 6 7 8 9 10 11)
USED-BY:  (RULE015 RULE017 RULE018 RULE020 RULE021 RULE022
           RULE027 RULE028 RULE029 RULE030 RULE031 RULE032
           RULE033 RULE037 RULE038 RULE039 RULE040 RULE041
           RULE042 RULE043 RULE047 RULE048 RULE024 RULE025
           RULE026 RULE034 RULE035 RULE036 RULE044 RULE045
           RULE046)
FINAL-RECOMMENDATION [BASIC-STRATEGY-PARMS]
--------------------
TRANS:  (the final recommendation for your hand)
EXPECT:  (SPLIT DOUBLE-DOWN HIT STAND)
USED-BY:  (RULE010)
```

```
UPDATED-BY:  (RULE048 RULE049 RULE050 RULE051 RULE052)
FIRST-CARD [BASIC-STRATEGY-PARMS]
----------
TRANS:  (the first card in your hand)
PROMPT:  (What is the value of your first card?
          (Ace = 1 or 11 , face cards = 10))
ASKFIRST:  T
EXPECT:  (1 2 3 4 5 6 7 8 9 10 11)
CONTAINED-IN:  (RULE002 RULE003)
USED-BY:  (RULE002 RULE003 RULE004 RULE005 RULE006 RULE037
           RULE038 RULE039 RULE040 RULE008 RULE009 RULE026)
PAIR [BASIC-STRATEGY-PARMS]
----
TRANS:  (your hand consists of two of a kind)
DICTIONARY:  (PARAMETER NAME)
USED-BY:  (RULE015 RULE017 RULE018 RULE019 RULE020 RULE021
           RULE022 RULE047 RULE048 RULE016)
UPDATED-BY:  (RULE008 RULE009)
REASON [BASIC-STRATEGY-PARMS]
------
TRANS:  (the reasons behind my recommendations)
LEGALVALS:  TEXT
MULTIVALUED:  T
UPDATED-BY:  (RULE015 RULE017 RULE018 RULE019 RULE020
              RULE021 RULE022 RULE027 RULE028 RULE029
              RULE030 RULE031 RULE032 RULE033 RULE037
              RULE038 RULE039 RULE040 RULE041 RULE042
              RULE043 RULE047 RULE016 RULE023 RULE024
              RULE025 RULE026 RULE034 RULE035 RULE036
              RULE044 RULE045 RULE046)
RECOMMENDATION [BASIC-STRATEGY-PARMS]
--------------
TRANS:  (the preliminary set of recommendations)
LEGALVALS:  (SPLIT DOUBLE-DOWN HIT STAND)
MULTIVALUED:  T
USED-BY:  (RULE049 RULE050 RULE051 RULE052)
UPDATED-BY:  (RULE015 RULE017 RULE018 RULE019 RULE020
              RULE021 RULE022 RULE027 RULE028 RULE029
              RULE030 RULE031 RULE032 RULE033 RULE037
              RULE038 RULE039 RULE040 RULE041 RULE042
              RULE043 RULE047 RULE016 RULE023 RULE024
              RULE025 RULE026 RULE034 RULE035 RULE036
              RULE044 RULE045 RULE046)
SECOND-CARD [BASIC-STRATEGY-PARMS]
-----------
TRANS:  (the second card in your hand)
PROMPT:  (What is the second card in your hand?
          (Ace = 1 or 11 , face cards = 10))
```

**Listing 10-10 (cont.)**

```
ASKFIRST:  T
EXPECT:  (1 2 3 4 5 6 7 8 9 10 11)
CONTAINED-IN:  (RULE002 RULE003)
USED-BY:  (RULE002 RULE003 RULE004 RULE005 RULE006 RULE037
           RULE038 RULE039 RULE040 RULE008 RULE009 RULE026)
SOFT [BASIC-STRATEGY-PARMS]
----
TRANS:  (your hand contains one or more aces)
USED-BY:  (RULE027 RULE028 RULE029 RULE030 RULE031 RULE032
           RULE033 RULE041 RULE042 RULE043 RULE016 RULE023
           RULE024 RULE025 RULE026 RULE034 RULE035 RULE036
           RULE044 RULE045 RULE046)
UPDATED-BY:  (RULE005 RULE006 RULE007)
THE-CONSULTATION-IS-OVER [BASIC-STRATEGY-PARMS]
------------------------
TRANS:  (The consultation is over)
UPDATED-BY:  (RULE010)
TOTAL [BASIC-STRATEGY-PARMS]
-----
TRANS:  (the count total of the cards in your hand)
EXPECT:  (2 3 4 5 6 7 8 9 10 11 12 13 14 15 16 17 18 19 20
          21)
USED-BY:  (RULE007 RULE010 RULE015 RULE017 RULE018 RULE019
           RULE020 RULE021 RULE022 RULE027 RULE028 RULE029
           RULE030 RULE031 RULE032 RULE033 RULE041 RULE042
           RULE043 RULE047 RULE048 RULE023 RULE024 RULE025
           RULE026 RULE034 RULE035 RULE036 RULE044 RULE045
           RULE046)
UPDATED-BY:  (RULE002 RULE003 RULE004)
    Parameter Group  CONTEXTTYPES
BASIC-STRATEGY [CONTEXTTYPES]
--------------
TRANS:  (the basic strategy)
UNIQUE:  T
DISPLAYRESULTS:  T
GOALS:  (TOTAL SOFT PAIR RECOMMENDATION REASON
         FINAL-RECOMMENDATION THE-CONSULTATION-IS-OVER)
INITIALDATA:  (FIRST-CARD SECOND-CARD DEALER-CARD)
RULETYPES:  (BASIC-STRATEGYRULES)
PARMGROUP:  BASIC-STRATEGY-PARMS
PRINTID:  BASIC-STRATEGY-
PROMPTEVER:  (This is the Blackjack Assistant expert
              adviser for the card game of Twenty-One, best
              known as Blackjack. After asking you some
              simple questions, I will try to formulate a
```

```
set of possible recommendations, from which I
will select a final suggestion for play based
primarily on E.O. Thorp's Basic Strategy, as
outlined in his 1966 book: Beat the Dealer.)
```

---

Finally, the rules can be represented in simple or multiple logical statements. An example of a simple rule is the following (see rule 7 in Listing 10-8):

> IF the total in your hand is 2,
> THEN it is true that you have two aces.

A more complex rule can be formed by considering multiple statements in either the IF part and/or the THEN part of the rule, chained by logical connectors—AND, OR, NOT—as shown in RULE 18 of Listing 10-8.

Two notes on approaches to building the prototype are in order. First, since Personal Consultant is a backward chaining tool, the final goal and subgoals need to be identified. The final goal of Blackjack Assistant is that the consultation session is over; that is, no question needs to be answered. Second, many rules are written to define terms such as `PAIR` (Rule 8 and 9) and `SOFT` (Rule 5) as shown in Listing 10-8. No frame or logic structure is available to define these terms.

To consult the expert system prototype initially, you need to install Personal Consultant using the following procedure:

1. Insert the Personal Consultant Expert System Development Tools diskette into drive A.
2. Type the MS-DOS command:

   **COPY A:*.***

   Press the ⟨ENTER⟩ key.
3. When the `C>` prompt appears, repeat steps 1 and 2 for the following diskettes: Knowledge Bases, Software Migration Utilities, and IQLISP.
4. Type **PCGEN** and press the ⟨ENTER⟩ key. A copyright notice of IQLISP appears on the screen, and the names of the files that the system will need are displayed.
5. Once these file names are entered, the following prompt appears: `IS YOUR SYSTEM EQUIPPED WITH AN 8087 COPROCESSOR?` Answer this question **Y** or **N** and press the ⟨RETURN⟩ key.
6. When the process is finished, the following message appears: `PC.SYS is complete.`
7. To access the Personal Consultant program, place the *ORIGINAL* Personal Consultant Expert System Development Tools diskette in drive A and type **PC**. Press the ⟨ENTER⟩ key.
8. Select the knowledge base, BLACKJACK.KB.

9. Select the menu GO.
10. Select the 1st card: 4.
11. Select the 2nd card: 4.
12. Select the dealer's up card: 7.

The results of the session are shown in the box below. These recommendations conform with those shown in charts a and d of Figure 10-5.

**Results of a Sample Session for Blackjack Assistant Implemented in Personal Consultant**

```
   Knowledge Base :: Beat the Dealer 2.0

 The count total of the cards in your hand is as
follows:  8
 Your hand contains one or more aces is not true.
 Your hand consists of two of a kind.

 The preliminary set of recommendations is as follows:
HIT

 The reasons behind my recommendations are as follows:
Hit a hard
 16 or less if the dealer shows more than 6.

 The final recommendation for your hand is as follows:
HIT.
 The consultation is over.

      ... end   --  press RETURN


  Up   Down   CF Unknwn    Done  ---    Why   How    Help
Undo   Stop
  F1     F2   F3     F4    F5     F6   F7      F8    F9
F10    ESC
 F1-help F2-save F3-new file F4-import data F9-expand
F10-contract Esc-exit
```

## Using M.1

M.1, developed and maintained by Teknowledge, Inc. and also derived from MYCIN, employs a backward chaining inference engine that seeks to achieve goals that have been defined. Knowledge representation in M.1 consists of facts, rules, meta facts, and one or more goals. Two elements are required in building the knowledge base of the prototype: control structure and knowledge structure.

The *control structure* is in charge of the definition and specification of the elements in the system that drive the consultation. This includes the user interface, which obtains the initial data, the display of the final recommendation to the user, and all the intermediate reasoning necessary to attain the ultimate goal, which is to help the user play a whole hand of blackjack following a "winning" strategy.

The following M.1 commands are used:

`prefix/infix` — Defines commonly used terms and English words as operators in the system. For example:

```
* prefix hand

* infix for
```

`initialdata` — Specifies parameters whose values the system attempts to determine initially. Only one parameter is used:

```
*initialdata=[The consultation is
     over].
```

(This is the goal of the system; that is, if the system can prove that the value of this parameter is true, then M.1 returns control to the general prompt and a new consultation may start.)

`noautomaticquestion` — Indicates those parameters whose values the system attempts to deduce first from the knowledge base, querying the user only if the inference engine cannot reach a conclusion. For example:

```
*noautomaticquestion (the
     recommendation for hand N).
```

`multivalued` — Indicates the parameter in the system that may have different values simultaneously. For example:

```
*multivalued (reason for hand N).
```

`question` — Expresses the way the system queries the user for the value(s) of a particular parameter. For example:

```
*question (first-card) = 'What is your
     first card?'
```

| | |
|---|---|
| `legalvals` | Specifies valid options associated with each question. For example, for the previous question inquired:<br>`*legalvals (first-card) =integer(1,11)` |
| `configuration` | Facilitates the user interface. For example:<br>`*configuration (banner)=[welcome to Blackjack Assistant....]`<br>`configuration usually appears at the end of the program.` |
| `disable` | Avoids the possibility of system modification by the user. For example:<br>`*disable (show).` |

Further examples of these commands are given in Listing 10-11.

**Listing 10-11**
***Partial listing of Blackjack Assistant, implemented in M.1***

```
/* This knowledge-based system tries to model a small expert
     system for the game of Twenty One, best known as
     Blackjack.            */
/*
/*
     */
/*  The following words are used as operators in Blackjack
     Assistant:            */
prefix hand.
prefix has.
prefix the.
prefix player.
prefix suggestion.
prefix final.
infix for.
infix with.
infix to.
infix of.
infix after.
initialdata = [the consultation is over].
noautomaticquestion(the recommendation for hand N).
multivalued(the recommendation for hand N).
multivalued(reason for hand N).
legalvals(soft) =[yes, no].
legalvals(pair) =[yes, no].
legalvals(the recommendation for hand N)=[split, double-
                                          down, hit, stand].
```

```
legalvals(the final recommendation for hand N)=[split,
     double-down,
                                                        hit,
     stand].
legalvals(first-card)=integer(1,11).
legalvals(second-card)=integer(1,11).
legalvals(next-card to hand N)=integer(1,11).
legalvals(playing after hand N)= [yes,no].
legalvals(dealer-card)=integer(2,11).
/* The following set of rules reflects the basic strategy
     developed by E.O.Thorp in his well-known book: Beat the
     Dealer (1966)     */
/*
     */
rule-1: if total for hand N = T and
           T < 22 and
            the final recommendation for hand N is known and
            player informed of suggestion N and
            not (the final recommendation for hand N =
            stand) and not (playing after hand N)
          then hand N is complete.
rule-15: if total for hand N = T and
            T > 21 and
            display([nl,
             'Sorry, it seems that you are over 21. Maybe
     next time.',
             nl])
          then hand N is complete.
rule-16: if the final recommendation  for hand N = stand and
            player informed of suggestion N and
            display([nl,
            'If you follow my advice, you should stand
     firmly.',nl])
          then hand N is complete.
rule-2:  if nexthand to M = N and
            hand N is complete
          then hand M is complete.
rule-3:  if M + 1 = N
          then nexthand to M = N.
rule-4:  if M > 1 and
            M - 1 = N
          then previoushand to M = N.
rule-5:  if hand 1 is complete and
            display(['The consultation is over.', nl])
          then the consultation is over.
rule-6:  if first-card = X and
            second-card = Y and
            not (X = 11) and
```

**Listing 10-11 (cont.)**

```
                 X + Y = T
              then total for hand 1 = T.
rule-17:   if first-card = X and
                 second-card = Y and
                 not (Y = 11) and
                 X + Y = T
              then total for hand 1 = T.
rule-93:   if first-card = 11 and
                 second-card = 11
              then total for hand 1 = 2.
rule-7:    if first-card = 1
              then soft = yes.
rule-8:    if first-card = 11
              then soft = yes.
rule-9:    if second-card = 1
              then soft = yes.
rule-10:   if second-card = 11
              then soft = yes.
rule-11:   if first-card = X and
                 second-card = Y and
                 not (X = 1) and
                 not (X = 11) and
                 not (Y = 1) and
                 not (Y = 11)
               then soft = no.
rule-12:   if total for hand 1 = 2
              then soft = yes.
rule-13:   if first-card = X and
                 second-card = Y and
                 X = Y
              then pair = yes.
rule-14:   if first-card = X and
                 second-card = Y and
                 not (X = Y)
              then pair = no.
rule-18:   if first-card = 6 and
                 second-card = 2 and
                 dealer-card = 5
              then exception-62 = yes.
/*
    */
/* Rules associated to the SPLITTING-THE-PAIR reasoning.
/*
    */
rule-52:   if soft = yes and
```

```
           pair = yes
        then reason for hand 1 = 'Always split aces.'.
rule-53: if pair = yes and
           total for hand 1 = 18 and
           dealer-card = D and
           D < 7
        then reason for hand 1 =
        'Split nines if the dealer shows less than seven.'.
rule-54: if pair = yes and
           total for hand 1 = 18 and
           dealer-card = D and
           D > 7 and
           D < 10
        then reason for hand 1 =
        'Split nines if the dealer shows 8 or 9.'.
rule-55: if pair = yes and
           total for hand 1 = 16
        then reason for hand 1 = 'Always split eights.'.
rule-56: if pair = yes and
           total for hand 1 = 14 and
           dealer-card = D and
           D < 9
        then reason for hand 1 =
        'Split sevens if the dealer shows less than 9.'.
rule-57: if pair = yes and
           total for hand 1 = 12 and
           dealer-card = D and
           D < 8
        then reason for hand 1 =
        'Split sixes if the dealer shows less than 8.'.
rule-58: if pair = yes and
           total for hand 1 = 8 and
           dealer-card = 5
        then reason for hand 1 =
        'Split fours against a dealers five.'.
rule-59: if pair = yes and
           total for hand 1 = T and
           T > 3 and
           T < 7 and
           dealer-card = D and
           D < 8
        then reason for hand 1 =
         'Split twos and threes if the dealer shows less
     than 8.'.
/*
     */
/* Rules recommending the DOUBLING-DOWN option.
     */
```

**Listing 10-11 (cont.)**

```
/*
     */
rule-60: if soft = no and
            total for hand 1 = 11
         then the recommendation for hand 1 = double-down.
rule-61: if soft = no and
            total for hand 1 = 10 and
            dealer-card = D and
            D < 10
          then the recommendation for hand 1 = double-down.
rule-62: if soft = no and
            total for hand 1 = 9 and
            dealer-card = D and
            D < 7
         then the recommendation for hand 1 = double-down.
rule-63: if soft = no and
            total for hand 1 = 8 and
            exception-62 = no and
            dealer-card = D and
            D > 4 and
            D < 7
         then the recommendation for hand 1 = double-down.
rule-64: if soft = yes and
            total for hand 1 = T and
            T < 9 and
            dealer-card = D and
            D > 4 and
            D < 7
         then the recommendation for hand 1 = double-down.
rule-65: if soft = yes and
            total for hand 1 = T and
            T > 2 and
            T < 8 and
            dealer-card = 4
         then the recommendation for hand 1 = double-down.
rule-66: if soft = yes and
            total for hand 1 = T and
            T > 6 and
            T < 8 and
            dealer-card = 3
         then the recommendation for hand 1 = double-down.
rule-67: if soft = yes and
            total for hand 1 = 7 and
            dealer-card = 2
         then the recommendation for hand 1 = double-down.
```

```
rule-118: if not (the recommendation for hand N = split) and
             not (the recommendation for hand N = double-
             down) and not (the recommendation for hand
             N = hit)
          then the final recommendation for hand N = stand.
/*
     */
/*  The following code is added to the previous knowledge to
     prepare it for the end-user utilization.  */
/*
     */
/*
     */
/*  To improve the user-interface:
     */
configuration(banner) = [nl, nl, nl,
'                  WELCOME TO Blackjack Assistant !!!!!',
     nl, nl,
'                  I THINK YOU WOULD ENJOY PLAYING BLACKJACK
     WITH ME.',nl,
'                  UNFORTUNATELY, AT THE PRESENT STAGE OF
     DEVELOPMENT,'
, nl,
'                  YOU CANNOT TAKE ME WITH YOU TO THE
    CASINO, BUT BE', nl,
'                  PATIENT, IT IS ONLY A MATTER OF
     TIME......',nl,
nl,
' To start a consultation just type:"go." to the M.1
     prompt.',nl,
' NOTE:  when you answer the questions associated to a
     consultation',
nl,
' type a period "." at the end of your input. It is the only
     way that',
nl,
' the system knows when you did answer a question.  Don't be
     afraid,',
nl,
' put a period after your answers, and everything will be
     O.K. ',
nl,
' Remember, if you want to know the reason why the system is
     asking',
nl,
' you a particular question, guess what?, answer "WHY."
    (dont forget',
nl,
```

**Listing 10-11 (cont.)**

```
' the period !!).',nl,
'                                GOOD LUCK !!!!!',nl,nl].
/*
      */
/* To assure that the system may not be modified:
      */
/*
      */
/*    disable(show).     */
disable(savecache).
disable(add).
disable(adda).
disable(addz).
disable(remove).
disable(find).
/*
      */
```

The *knowledge structure* contains the representation of the basic strategy in the form of simple IF-THEN rules. Among these rules we can differentiate several types:

- *Control Rules*—These rules indicate how the system achieves its goal, specifying subgoals at all levels that drive the consultation. Examples of this type of rule are rules 1, 2, 15, and 16 from Listing 10-11.
- *First-Level Deduction Rules*—Given the initial information, the system tries to reach conclusions to be used at a higher level of deduction. Examples of this type of rule are rules 6 through 14 and rules 17 and 18 from Listing 10-11—knowing the values for the first two cards, conclude the values for `total`, `pair`, `soft`, and `exceptions`.
- *Second-Level Deduction Rules*—This set of rules contains the actual implementation of the basic strategy to play blackjack. In other words, given the values obtained at the previous level, the system suggests the set of recommendations and the final recommendation to play. Examples are rules 52 through 59 as shown in Listing 10-11, which make recommendations for splitting a pair.

To consult the Blackjack Assistant prototype implemented in M.1, follow this procedure:

1. Put the diskette containing M.1 and the knowledge base for the prototype, BJ, into Drive A.

2. Type **A:**
3. Type **M1 BJ.**
4. Type **GO.** after an M1 prompt. Be sure to terminate all responses to the M1 prompt with a period (.).
5. Follow the instructions in the M1 prompt.

A sample consultation session is shown in the box below. The result shown reveals similar recommendations.

**Results of a Sample Consultation with Blackjack Assistant Implemented in M.1**

```
M.1> go.
What is your first-card?
>> 4.
What is the second-card in your hand?
>> 4.
What is the dealers up card?
>> 7.


The possible suggestions to play are:
    the recommendation for hand 1 = hit (100%) because
rule-81.

The rules I applied are:
    reason for hand 1 = Hit a hard 16 or less if the
dealer shows more than 6. (100%) because rule-89.

My recommendation to play now is the following
    the final recommendation for hand 1 = hit (100%)
because rule-117. Do you want to continue playing under
my advice?
>> y.

What is the value of your next-card?

>> 8.


The possible suggestions to play are:
    the recommendation for hand 2 = hit (100%) because
rule-81.

The rules I applied are:
    reason for hand 2 = Hit a hard 16 or less if the
dealer shows more than 6. (100%) because rule-89.

My recommendation to play now is the following
    the final recommendation for hand 2 = hit (100%)
```

```
because rule-117. Do you want to continue playing under
my advice?
>> 2.

Execution. "2" is not a legal response.
(Error 218)
Your response must be chosen from the following:
yes, no.
Do you want to continue playing under my advice?
>> y.
What is the value of your next-card?
>> 2.


The possible suggestions to play are:
    the recommendation for hand 3 = stand (100%) because
rule-102.

The rules I applied are:
    reason for hand 3 = Stand on a hard 17 or better
against dealers more than 6. (100%) because rule-110.

My recommendation to play now is the following
    the final recommendation for hand 3 = stand (100%)
because rule-118. If you follow my advice, you should
stand firmly.
The consultation is over.
```

# Transportation Configurer—Accumulating and Disseminating Knowledge

Transportation represents a complex system problem that is fully comprehended by a very small but vitally important number of experts and that is critical to the economic utilization of national resources. Conventional algorithms such as linear programming transportation solutions cannot meet the needs of the complex issues in discontinuity of regulations, inter- and intracompetitions, and resulting impacts of resource allocation. The knowledge used in the transportation sector is subsequently bound within a closed and well-defined domain, and is frequently applied to solve repetitive problems such as scheduling, regulations, and truck load configurations. Rules of thumb exist with these few experts who are approaching retirement. Equipment operation, traffic control and maintainance are some of the areas that are now performed by relatively inexperienced personnel. The consequence of this situation is significant operational loss and risk of accidents. If the knowledge of the small group of experts could be accumulated and passed on to less experienced operators, transportation operation would be safer and more cost effective.

The three areas that are suitable applications for AI/ES technology are (1) heavy vehicle configuration, (2) transportation planning, and (3) freight train operation and maintenance. We will discuss briefly the three areas and then use a heavy vehicle configuration problem to demonstrate the application of AI/ES technology.

The first area is heavy vehicle configuration. Trucking is a multibillion dollar per year business. Because of the necessity of ensuring highway safety and protecting the investment in roadway and bridge structures, each jurisdiction has its own regulations of weights and dimensions of trucks permitted to operate to meet local conditions. For example, to improve trucking operation efficiency, it was suggested that the implementation of a uniform regulatory environment in Canada would result in improved system efficiencies of 1–5 percent, estimated savings of $210 million to $1 billion annually [3]. A knowledge-based system is thus desired to address heavy vehicle configuration to current weight and dimension regulations.

The heavy vehicle configuration problem is used as an example to explain how a suitable expert system application area is determined, how the technology is applied, and what an expert system looks like after implementation.*

Transportation planning involves complex tradeoffs among modes of transport. For the ground-based transportation infrastructure, the choice is among airplane, bus, train, or ship. Each mode of transport has advantages and disadvantages and the balance among these modes changes over time. The same is true for a national airspace system in which investments for ground-based and satellite-based navigation systems compete. Various disciplines are required to make an optimum choice. The disciplines required for a satellite system alone include orbital mechanics, signal processing, computer science, and radio frequency propagation. No one person can possess all of the expertise necessary to make intelligent decisions. An intelligent knowledge-based fusion system that contains all of the knowledge required for various disciplines is desirable for expediting the speed of and reducing the cost of making major planning decisions.

A long freight train is a classical control system. It presents a complex load metering problem to the operator when he accelerates and it becomes potentially unstable when the operator brakes to slow down or stop. It presents a problem in acceleration because the operator wishes to prevent wasteful and abrasive wheel slip; it also presents a problem in braking if the brakes are applied too heavily or too quickly. The problem is almost intrac-

*Special thanks go to Gregory L. Campbell and Dale M. Nesbitt of Decision Focus, Inc. (Los Altos, CA) for providing necessary materials and an expert system prototype on transportation [3]. These materials and prototype were results of a project sponsored by the Roads and Transportation Association of Canada (Ottawa, Canada).

table by conventional control algorithms. However, an experienced locomotive engineer handles these variables intuitively every day. The engineer understands the interrelationships among the track, the locomotives, changing loads, weather, traffic conditions, and many other facts, and adjusts them for cost-effective and safe operation of a freight train. In other words, the experienced locomotive engineer is an expert operator who has been on the road for twenty or thirty years. His experience can be accumulated to enable the less experienced engineer to become experienced more quickly. The same reasoning can be applied to troubleshooting in maintenance and traffic control.

## *Applying Selection Rules To Test the Heavy Vehicle Configuration Problem*

The selection rules (necessary and sufficient conditions) discussed in Chapter 9 are used to determine the applicability of expert system technology to the heavy vehicle configuration problem.

### Necessary Conditions

The two questions to be tested for necessary conditions are

1. *Is the application (problem) area well bounded and understood?* The overall problem area of trucking regulations is well bounded because the number of regulations is bounded and the history of these regulations can be traced. The problem of evaluating the benefit of changes in heavy vehicle regulations is also well bounded because it can be described concretely even though the problem is complex.

   The overall problem is well understood even though it is difficult to formulate and solve due to its complexity and the interdependency among various affected parties. Some aspects of the problem, such as economics and vehicle dynamics, are well understood. Certain other aspects, such as impact on highways, are understood with a high degree of uncertainty.
2. *Is there at least one human expert available to explain the knowledge required for the expert system being built?*

   A small group of experts is available who are well versed in the regulations governing weight and dimension of heavy vehicles, and their impacts on highways and economics. Because each state, province, or territory prescribes its own regulations, different experts may be needed for each locality.

## Sufficient Conditions

At least three sufficient conditions are met for the heavy vehicle configuration problem. These conditions are discussed in their order of importance:

1. *Is the expert advice critical?* As discussed previously, the value of the problem is estimated to be between $200 million and $1 billion for Canada [3]. Accurate expert advice (evaluation of the problem) is critical to the trucking industry and other impacted sectors.
2. *Is the expert advice costly?* The expert advice is costly because the small group of experts who are well versed in regulations and their impacts are highly trained and expensive. Most of them are experienced lawyers and legislators.
3. *Does the problem involve routine, detail-dependent decision making?* The analysis of the problem—that is, the determination of optimal conformity of heavy vehicle weights and dimensions—is very repetitive since many alternatives and assumptions need to be considered. Situations change with time, and today's optimal solution may not be optimal in a few years.

# *Applying Expert System Technology to the Heavy Vehicle Configuration Problem*

The heavy vehicle configuration problem requires the optimal use of expert system technology and conventional algorithms. The two areas that particularly require expert system technology are solving the truck fleet operation problem and determining vehicle dynamics using available data, algorithms, and models (such as that available at the University of Michigan).

The most promising application of expert system technology to the configuration problem appears to be an intelligent assistant to regulators and trucks provided in the form of information regarding

- Regulations
- Physical feasibility
- Vehicle dynamics
- Economics
- Pavement
- Bridges

The system would guide the user through the correct application of knowledge to solve a specific trucking problem and answer one or more of the following questions:

1. Is a vehicle legal in relevant jurisdictions?
    - State
    - Provinces
    - Territories

2. Is a vehicle physically feasible?
    - Can the combination actually be configured as specified?
    - Can the vehicle be loaded to its allowed weight?
3. What are a vehicle's dynamic characteristics?
    - What are the tracking characteristics of the vehicle?
    - What is the vehicle's tendency to roll?
    - Does rearward amplification pose a problem for the vehicle?
    - What is the braking distance of the vehicle?
4. What are the economic characteristics of the vehicle?
    - How many cubic meters of capacity does the vehicle have?
    - How many kilograms (tons) of load can it carry?
    - How much does it cost to purchase and operate?
    - What is its fuel consumption?
5. What impact would the vehicle have on a bridge?
    - Is a particular bridge strong enough and wide enough to carry the vehicle?
    - How much wear would the vehicle produce on the bridge surface and structure?

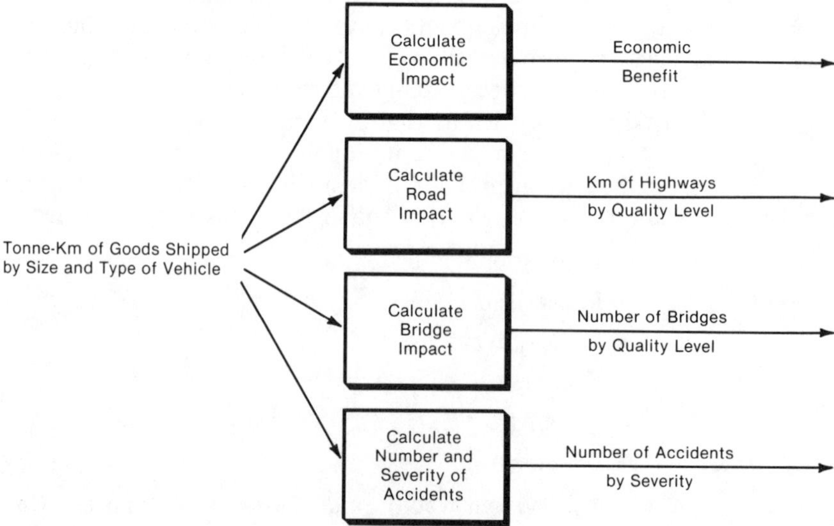


**Figure 10-6**
***Determining impacts of trucking sector response with an expert system***

The structure of the expert system is shown in Figure 10-6. Regulators could use this expert system to modify regulatory parameters, experiment with various legal vehicle configurations, and evaluate applications for specific permits. Truckers could use the system to find the most economic and legal vehicle for a particular haul. Other users, such as vehicle designers and legislators, could use the system for other purposes and save many hours of time now spent in sifting through batches of documents to search for applicable regulations.

## *Implementation of the Expert System Prototype*

The expert system prototype can be implemented conveniently using an Expert Knowledge Organizer. Frames can be used to represent regulations, vehicles, commodities, pavement, and bridge descriptions. Rules can be used to represent conditions and heuristic knowledge. Logic can be used to represent the remaining unstructured data. However, a prototype implemented in Micro-Expert (available from McGraw-Hill Publishing Company) is discussed here to provide the perspective for using a new tool, Micro-Expert, whose representation language is the rule structure only.

Micro-Expert provides a user interface and the inference engine. The user interface provided by Micro-Expert allows an expert system to accept questions, to provide results, and to explain the sequence of reasoning that has been used to solve the problem under consideration. The questions and results are written in plain text. The explanation facility is driven by the questions *why* and *how*. In answer to the question *why*, the system prints the rule in the knowledge base that corresponds the answer to the question. In response to the question *how*, the system shows the facts and rules used to determine a given conclusion. The inference engine is a backward chaining type. It works backward from a goal specified by the user to the facts and rules needed to prove or disprove the goal.

The expert system prototype (configuration prototype) developed contains regulation knowledge bases for one Canadian province, Ontario. The prototype can be used to accomplish the task of applying complex regulations to determine the legality of a heavy truck (the first function shown in Figure 10-6).

The knowledge base consists of two types of rules:

1. Rules defining provincial regulations
2. Rules defining vehicle configurations

The vehicle configurations include the following vehicles (shown in Figure 10-7):

A = straight truck

B = truck + trailer

C = tractor + semitrailer

D = tractor + semitrailer + trailer (A-train)

E = tractor + semitrailer + semitrailer (western B-train)—7 axle

F = tractor + semitrailer + semitrailer (triple axle B-train)—8 axle

G = tractor + semitrailer + trailer (C-train)

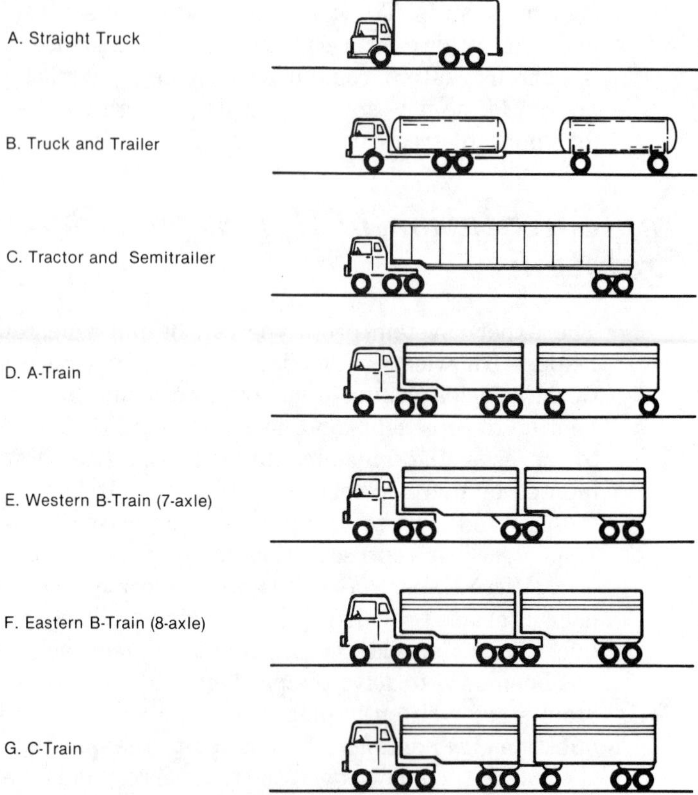


**Figure 10-7**
***Types of heavy vehicles included in the expert system prototype***

The following weight and dimension regulations are included:

1. Dimensions

   Height
   Width
   Length

2. Weights

   Tire loads
   Axle loads
   Gross vehicle and combination weight

Width exceptions to rules are also encoded.

The flowchart of the configuration prototype, shown in Figure 10-8, is fairly simple. The configuration prototype asks the user to identify a consultation goal that can be selected from the eight goals shown (for example, finished, allowed, etc.) and the truck type. Then the prototype checks the

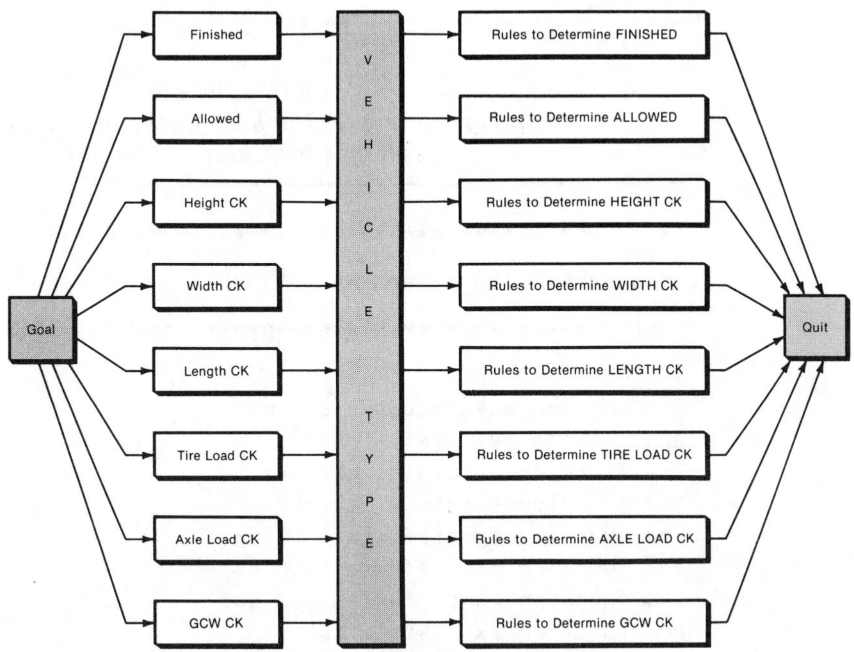


**Figure 10-8**
***Flowchart of heavy vehicle configuration prototype***

relevant rule group to respond to user questions such as *what* and *why*. It quits when the user prompts the command *quit*. As in any backward chaining system, any statement in the conclusion of a rule can be selected as the final goal. Some major goals are:

| | |
|---|---|
| *Finished* | Check all rules. |
| *Allowed* | Check rules until all are checked or until one rule is violated. |
| *Height CK* | Check vehicle height. |
| *Width CK* | Check vehicle width. |
| *Length CK* | Check vehicle length. |
| *Tire load CK* | Check tire loads. |
| *Axle load CK* | Check axle loads. |
| *GCW CK* | Check gross combination weight. |

Take a look at the following branch from the flowchart in Figure 10-8:

> Goal → Tire Load CK → Vehicle Type → Rules to Determine Tire Load CK

To function properly, this branch requires three programs:

- Master rule to determine FINISHED
- VEHICLE TYPE to determine proper vehicle type
- Rules to check TIRE LOAD

Sample programs to accomplish this task are shown in Listing 10-12.

**Listing 10-12**
***Sample programs for the heavy vehicle configuration prototype for Ontario, Canada***

---

```
************************************************************

 Master Rule to determine FINISHED

************************************************************

1
if function exists(vehicle type)
and function exists(allowed)
and function exists(height ck)
and function exists(width ck)
and function exists(length ck)
and function exists(tire load ck)
and function exists(axle load ck)
and function exists(gcw ck)
then finished is yes

************************************************************

 VEHICLE TYPE is prompted from user
 The following are direct consequences of VEHICLE TYPE

************************************************************

2
if vehicle type is a
then has_a truck is yes
and has_a tractor is no
and num trailer is 0
and num semi is 0
and is_a combination is no

3
if vehicle type is b
then has_a truck is yes
and has_a tractor is no
and num trailer is 1
and num semi is 0
and is_a combination is yes

4
if vehicle type is c
then has_a truck is no
and has_a tractor is yes
```

```
and num trailer is 0
and num semi is 1
and is_a combination is yes

5
if vehicle type is d
then has_a truck is no
and has_a tractor is yes
and num trailer is 1
and num semi is 1
and is_a combination is yes

6
if vehicle type is e
then has_a truck is no
and has_a tractor is yes
and num trailer is 0
and num semi is 2
and is_a combination is yes

7
if vehicle type is f
then has_a truck is no
and has_a tractor is yes
and num trailer is 0
and num semi is 2
and is_a combination is yes

8
if vehicle type is g
then has_a truck is no
and has_a tractor is yes
and num trailer is 1
and num semi is 1
and is_a combination is yes

************************************************************

 Rules to determine TIRE LOAD CK

************************************************************

78
if function exists(number of axles)
and tire load 1 ck is ok
and tire load 2 ck is ok
and tire load 3 ck is ok
and tire load 4 ck is ok
and tire load 5 ck is ok
```

**Listing 10-12 (cont.)**

```
and tire load 6 ck is ok
and tire load 7 ck is ok
and tire load 8 ck is ok
and tire load 9 ck is ok
then tire load ck is ok

79
if tire load 1 ck is not ok
then tire load ck is not ok

80
if tire load 2 ck is not ok
then tire load ck is not ok

81
if tire load 3 ck is not ok
then tire load ck is not ok

82
if tire load 4 ck is not ok
then tire load ck is not ok

83
if tire load 5 ck is not ok
then tire load ck is not ok

84
if tire load 6 ck is not ok
then tire load ck is not ok

85
if tire load 7 ck is not ok
then tire load ck is not ok

86
if tire load 8 ck is not ok
then tire load ck is not ok

87
if tire load 9 ck is not ok
then tire load ck is not ok

88
if function compare(number of axles, '<', '9')
then tire load 9 ck is ok
```

```
and axle load 9 is 0
and axle-unit num 9 is 0
and spacing 89 is 0
and load sharing 89 is no

89
if function compare(number of axles, '<', '8')
then tire load 8 ck is ok
and axle load 8 is 0
and axle-unit num 8 is 0
and spacing 78 is 0
and load sharing 78 is no

90
if function compare(number of axles, '<', '7')
then tire load 7 ck is ok
and axle load 7 is 0
and axle-unit num 7 is 0
and spacing 67 is 0
and load sharing 67 is no

91
if function compare(number of axles, '<', '6')
then tire load 6 ck is ok
and axle load 6 is 0
and axle-unit num 6 is 0
and spacing 56 is 0
and load sharing 56 is no

92
if function compare(number of axles, '<', '5')
then tire load 5 ck is ok
and axle load 5 is 0
and axle-unit num 5 is 0
and spacing 45 is 0
and load sharing 45 is no

93
if function compare(number of axles, '<', '4')
then tire load 4 ck is ok
and axle load 4 is 0
and axle-unit num 4 is 0
and spacing 34 is 0
and load sharing 34 is no

94
if function compare(number of axles, '<', '3')
then tire load 3 ck is ok
```

**Listing 10-12 (cont.)**

```
and axle load 3 is 0
and axle-unit num 3 is 0
and spacing 23 is 0
and load sharing 23 is no

95
if function compare (tire width 1, '>', '150')
and function compare (tire load 1, '>', '11')
then tire load 1 ck is not ok

96
if function compare (tire width 1, '>', '150')
and function compare (tire load 1, '<=', '11')
then tire load 1 ck is ok

97
if function compare (tire width 1, '<=', '150')
and function compare (tire load 1, '>', '9')
then tire load 1 ck is not ok

98
if function compare (tire width 1, '<=', '150')
and function compare (tire load 1, '<=', '9')
then tire load 1 ck is ok

99
if function compare (tire width 2, '>', '150')
and function compare (tire load 2, '>', '11')
then tire load 2 ck is not ok

100
if function compare (tire width 2, '>', '150')
and function compare (tire load 2, '<=', '11')
then tire load 2 ck is ok

************************************************************

 Prompts for data

************************************************************

prompt vehicle type
What type of vehicle do you want to check (enter letter)?
A = straight truck
B = truck + trailer
C = tractor + semitrailer
```

```
D = tractor + semitrailer + trailer (A - train)
E = tractor + semitrailer + semitrailer (western B - train)
    - 7 axle
F = tractor + semitrailer + semitrailer (triple axle B -
     train) - 8 axle
G = tractor + semitrailer + trailer (C - train)

numeric prompt vehicle height
What is the maximum height of your vehicle or its load
     (meters)?

numeric prompt vehicle width
What is the maximum width of the vehicle (meters)?

numeric prompt truck length
What is the length of the truck (meters)?
```

---

The program *Rules to determine TIRE LOAD CK* has fifty-three rules excluding those that are called from other functions such as TIRE LOAD. Many of these rules can be eliminated if frames are used to organize regulations and vehicle characteristics.

To consult the heavy vehicle configuration prototype, use the following procedure:

1. Put the diskette containing Micro-Expert and the knowledge base for the prototype into Drive A.
2. Type **A:**
3. Type **microexp**
4. Answer the question prompted by Micro-Expert by typing **ONTARIO**
5. Answer other Micro-Expert prompts as shown in the box below.

The results, also shown in the box below, indicate the vehicle is too tall.

**Results of a Sample Consultation with the Heavy Vehicle Configuration Prototype for Ontario, Canada**

```
What is the final goal for this consultation? allowed

What is the maximum height of your vehicle or its load
(meters)? why

The system is trying to find a value for ALLOWED using
rule no 9.
Rule 9
```

```
IF
 1) HEIGHT CK                IS OK
 2) WIDTH CK                 IS OK
 3) LENGTH CK                IS OK
 4) TIRE LOAD CK             IS OK
 5) AXLE LOAD CK             IS OK
 6) GCW CK                   IS OK
THEN
 7) ALLOWED                  IS YES

Press <Space Bar> to continue.

What is the maximum height of your vehicle or its load
(meters)? 5.4


Conclusion :
HEIGHT CK                IS NOT OK

Press <Space Bar> to continue.

Conclusion :
ALLOWED                  IS NO

Press <Space Bar> to continue.

The following facts have been determined :
 1) ALLOWED                  IS NO
 2) HEIGHT CK                IS NOT OK
 3) VEHICLE HEIGHT           IS 5.4

Do you want to perform another consultation with this
knowledge base (Y/N)
```

# Issues of Expert System Delivery

The issues of expert system delivery in the PC environment are slightly different from those for AI workstations and mainframe computers because PC expert systems tend to be smaller and less complicated. The main issues include user friendliness, convenience, usefulness, maintenance, and training.

## User Friendliness

User friendliness is the most important criterion for winning user acceptance and overcoming any resistance to using and accepting the system as an office aid. Two important features identified with user friendliness are (1) ease in getting into the system without training and (2) convenience in daily or occasional use without cumbersome memorization of operational procedures. With menus, helps, graphics, and explanations, expert systems should be easier to get into and more convenient to use either routinely or occasionally than conventional software packages. In input queries during consultations and in output explanations stating consultation results, the following guidelines need to be observed carefully:

- Questions and explanations presented should be in the user's jargon.
- Explanations should be tailored to the user's level of expertise and adjusted accordingly.
- A reservoir of alternative questions or explanations should be available for use if the user fails to understand the initial set.

## Convenience (Compatibility with the Working Environment)

Convenience to the user or compatibility with the working environment is generally overlooked by the developer until the expert system is field tested. The example of DELTA illustrates the point vividly. DELTA was designed for use by repair mechanics in railroad shops. DELTA calls for a hardened VAX computer, a videodisk player, a color terminal, and a printer. The cables connecting these individual units often become a formidable problem after a few relocations—that is, transfers to other sites or even minor relocations in the same site.

When a system is designed, it is essential that convenience to the user be carefully measured to prevent unexpected deficiencies. The following issues need to be assessed:

- Does the system call for complex facilities?
- Is an attempt made to use existing equipment in the working environment; for example, personal computers?
- Does the system require a complicated assembly?
- Can the system tolerate abuse by the intended/unintended user?
- Does the system require substantial additional effort on the part of the user to either carry or use it?

## Usefulness of Products

Usefulness of products is the primary concern of many system designers because it is the objective of expert systems. Products include decisions recommended, advice given, actions suggested, and training received by new users. Many PC expert system packages are compared with junior specialists or aides, such as loan officers, in their performance. Three useful strategies are:

- Target the performance of the system under development first at the level of aides or junior specialists.
- Improve system performance to the level most suitable for the application after the system has been accepted.
- The usefulness of a product is determined by the user, so be open to the user's suggestions.

Usefulness of an expert system may also imply accuracy of its advice—that is, accuracy of the conclusions and reasoning that the system offers to the user. Conclusions should not be too vague to be useful; however, expert systems often provide the user with approximate, heuristic decisions or advice, and thus it is difficult to assume the conclusions are accurate in the sense of numerical computation. Not all system designers are concerned about whether their expert systems reason correctly—that is, whether they arrive at decisions in human expert-like manner, as long as the products they offer are appropriate. However, the correctness of the reasoning mechanism of an expert system in some applications should receive as much emphasis as the conclusions themselves (for example, in bank loan applications where possible legal implications are entailed).

## Maintenance

Maintenance may include improvement, expansion, and extension of an expert system including: minor refinements, major refinements, expansion of coverage to a new related task, and extension of the task definition.

- *Minor refinements* add knowledge to improve the expert system's performance on an existing subtask.
- *Major refinements* add knowledge to enable the expert system to perform a new subtask.
- *Expansion of coverage to new, related equipment* expands the coverage of the expert significantly to include new equipment types.
- *Extension of the task definition* extends to include new capacities of the expert system.

The first type of improvement is usually given as the reason for adding knowledge to an expert system, namely to polish its performance. With XCON, however, of the more than 2,500 rules added to the original 777 rules over four years (January 1, 1980 through January 1, 1984), the recorded data indicates that slightly more than 10 percent were added to make minor improvements, such as obtaining more complete knowledge on a subtask; 35 percent were added to provide capabilities needed to deal with new DEC computer types, such as PDP-11/23, VAX-11/730, and MICRO-PDP11; and up to 15 percent were added to extend the definition of XCON's task (for example, to extend the definition of customer orders from "single-CPUs" to "multiple-CPUs").

The four types of maintenance tasks may vary slightly for different expert systems. One point to be emphasized is that appropriate maintenance not only updates the expert system but also assures the user's satisfaction.

### *Training*

Training in the use of large, complex expert systems and tools has been crucial because many earlier versions of these systems and tools were not designed with the user in mind. For most PC expert systems and tools, training is less of a problem. A good training plan may be essential if a new expert system is to be widely used. The training requirement should not be more extensive than that required for WordStar or LOTUS 1-2-3, if the expert system is designed to include sufficient user friendliness in system input and output.

## Summary

- The three application areas that are discussed include expert knowledge organization, training tools, and transportation configuration.
- The four tools used in this chapter are Expert Knowledge Organizer, Personal Consultant, M.1, and Micro-Expert.
- Various components of tools, which are discussed in Chapters 7 and 8, can be used to build expert system tools to meet a particular application requirement.
- Both interactive and batch mode can be implemented for an expert system tool.
- Personal Consultant and M.1 are used to build a training tool, Blackjack Assistant, to demonstrate the difference between tools.
- The heavy vehicle configuration prototype provides a demonstration of the feasible application of expert system technology to transportation problems.
- The main issues of expert system delivery include user friendliness, convenience, usefulness, maintenance, and training.

# References

[1] Baldur Systems Corporations, *Product Description of Baldur IQ 100: The Intelligent Data Communications Shell* (Hayward, CA, 1987).

[2] Edward O. Thorpe, *Beat the Dealer* (New York: Vintage Books, 1976).

[3] G. Sparks, G. Campbell, et al., "The Feasibility of Applying Knowledge-based System Technology to Heavy Vehicle Configuration Problems" (prepared for Roads and Transportation Association of Canada by Decision Focus, Inc., Los Altos, CA, November 1986).

# Appendixes

# A

# LISP Commands

This appendix lists the commands (functions, macros, and variables) of two LISP packages:

- Golden Common LISP (distributed by Gold Hill Computers of Cambridge, MA)
- muLISP-82 (distributed by Microsoft Corporation of Bellevue, WA).

Golden Common LISP, frequently referred to in the text as GCLISP, is a Common LISP package that has implemented most of the Common LISP features. MuLISP is a LISP dialect that contains a Common LISP primitives library. Only the commands that may be frequently used in AI/expert system development are listed here.

## Frequently-Used GCLISP Commands

| Command | Page Number in Reference Manual[1] | Command | Page Number in Reference Manual[1] |
|---|---|---|---|
| %contents | 221 | *** | 174 |
| %ioport | 222 | *prompt* | 175 |
| %pointer | 222 | *query-io* | 178 |
| %structure-size | 222 | *read-base* | 184 |
| %sysint | 223 | *standard-input* | 177 |
| * | 116, 174 | *standard-output* | 177 |
| *& | 118 | *terminal-io* | 178 |
| ** | 174 | *trace-output* | 178 |

| Command | Page Number in Reference Manual[1] | Command | Page Number in Reference Manual[1] |
|---|---|---|---|
| + | 115, 173 | caddr | 140 |
| +& | 118 | cadr | 138 |
| ++ | 173 | car | 137 |
| +++ | 173 | case | 64 |
| - | 115, 174 | catch | 79 |
| -& | 118 | cd | 203 |
| 1+ | 117 | cdaar | 140 |
| 1- | 117 | cdadr | 140 |
| abs | 120 | cdar | 138 |
| acons | 152 | cddar | 141 |
| adjoin | 151 | cdddr | 141 |
| allocate | 215 | cddr | 139 |
| alpha-char-p | 127 | cdr | 138 |
| and | 44 | ceiling | 122 |
| append | 144 | cerror | 205 |
| apply | 56 | char | 162 |
| applyhook | 172 | char-bit | 131 |
| apropos | 212 | char-bits | 130 |
| apropos-list | 213 | char-code | 129 |
| aref | 157 | char-equal | 129 |
| array | 14 | char-lessp | 129 |
| array-length | 158 | char-name | 131 |
| arrayp | 39 | char-upcase | 130 |
| ash | 125 | character | 10 |
| assoc | 153 | characterp | 38 |
| atan | 121 | close | 180 |
| atom | 36 | close-all-files | 180 |
| autoload | 203 | closure | 18, 81 |
| backtrace | 210 | closurep | 40 |
| block | 65 | code-char | 130 |
| both-case-p | 128 | coerce | 24 |
| boundp | 49 | commonp | 41 |
| break | 205 | compiled-function | 18 |
| butlast | 147 | compiled-function-p | 40 |
| caaar | 139 | cond | 64 |
| caadr | 139 | cons | 13, 141 |
| caar | 138 | consp | 37 |
| cadar | 139 | continue | 207 |

| Command | Page Number in Reference Manual[1] | Command | Page Number in Reference Manual[1] |
|---|---|---|---|
| copy-alist | 145 | eval | 170 |
| copy-array-contents | 161 | evalhook | 171 |
| copy-list | 145 | evenp | 112 |
| copy-symbol | 97 | every | 135 |
| copy-tree | 145 | exec | 220 |
| cos | 121 | exit | 219 |
| decf | 117 | exp | 119 |
| declare | 92 | export | 105 |
| defconstant | 32 | expt | 119 |
| defmacro | 90 | fasload | 203 |
| defparameter | 32 | fboundp | 50 |
| defstruct | 167 | file-info | 202 |
| defun | 31 | file-namestring | 199 |
| defvar | 32 | fill-pointer | 159 |
| delete | 135 | find-package | 102 |
| delete-file | 201 | find-symbol | 105 |
| delete-if | 136 | first | 142 |
| describe | 211 | fixnum | 9 |
| digit-char-p | 128 | flatc | 191 |
| directory | 203 | flatsize | 191 |
| directory-namestring | 199 | float | 10, 121 |
| do | 67 | floatp | 38 |
| do* | 68 | floor | 122 |
| do-all-symbols | 109 | format | 191 |
| do-external-symbols | 109 | funcall | 57 |
| do-symbols | 108 | function | 18, 48 |
| doc | 208 | functionp | 40 |
| documentation | 208 | gc | 216 |
| dolist | 69 | gclisp | 218 |
| dos | 219 | gensym | 98 |
| dotimes | 69 | get | 94 |
| dribble | 212 | get-decoded-time | 213 |
| ed | 212 | | |
| endp | 142 | get-output-stream-string | 179 |
| eq | 41 | get-properties | 96 |
| eql | 42 | getf | 95 |
| equal | 43 | go | 75 |
| error | 205 | identify | 215 |

| Command | Page Number in Reference Manual[1] | Command | Page Number in Reference Manual[1] |
|---|---|---|---|
| if | 61 | make-array | 156 |
| ifn | 62 | make-list | 144 |
| ignore-errors | 206 | make-package | 101 |
| import | 106 | make-pathname | 197 |
| in-package | 102 | make-stack-group | 84 |
| incf | 117 | make-string-input-stream | 179 |
| integer | 9 | | |
| integerp | 38 | make-string-output-stream | 179 |
| intern | 104 | | |
| keywordp | 99 | make-symbol | 97 |
| labels | 61 | makunbound | 52 |
| lambda-list | 209 | mapc | 71 |
| last | 143 | mapcan | 73 |
| ldiff | 147 | mapcar | 70 |
| length | 133 | mapcon | 73 |
| let | 59 | mapl | 72 |
| let* | 60 | maplist | 71 |
| list | 13, 144 | max | 114 |
| list* | 144 | member | 150 |
| list-all-packages | 104 | member-if | 151 |
| list-length | 142 | merge-pathnames | 196 |
| listener | 172 | min | 114 |
| listp | 37 | minusp | 111 |
| load | 202 | mod | 123 |
| log | 119 | multiple-value-bind | 78 |
| logand | 124 | multiple-value-list | 77 |
| logbitp | 125 | multiple-value-progl | 77 |
| logeqv | 124 | multiple-value-setq | 78 |
| logior | 123 | name-char | 131 |
| lognot | 124 | named-structure-p | 168 |
| logtest | 125 | named-structure-symbol | 169 |
| logxor | 124 | namedstring | 199 |
| loop | 67 | nbutlast | 147 |
| lsh | 126 | nconc | 145 |
| macro | 91 | ncons | 141 |
| macro-function | 89 | neq | 42 |
| macroexpand | 91 | neql | 42 |
| macroexpand-1 | 91 | nil | 34 |

| Command | Page Number in Reference Manual[1] | Command | Page Number in Reference Manual[1] |
|---|---|---|---|
| not | 44 | progv | 61 |
| nreverse | 134 | psetq | 52 |
| nth | 142 | push | 146 |
| nthcdr | 143 | pushnew | 146 |
| null | 13, 36 | quote | 47 |
| number | 9 | rassoc | 153 |
| numberp | 37 | read | 187 |
| oddp | 111 | read-byte | 189 |
| open | 200 | read-char | 188 |
| or | 45 | read-from-string | 188 |
| package | 16 | read-line | 187 |
| package-name | 102 | read-preserving-whitespace | 187 |
| package-nicknames | 103 | remf | 96 |
| package-use-list | 103 | remove | 135 |
| packagep | 39 | remove-if | 135 |
| pairlis | 152 | remprop | 95 |
| parse-directory-namestring | 196 | rename-file | 201 |
| parse-namestring | 195 | rest | 143 |
| pathname | 16, 195 | return | 66 |
| pathname-device | 198 | return-from | 66 |
| pathname-directory | 198 | reverse | 134 |
| pathname-name | 198 | room | 211 |
| pathname-type | 198 | round | 123 |
| pathnamep | 197 | rplaca | 148 |
| plusp | 111 | rplacb | 149 |
| pop | 147 | rplacd | 148 |
| power | 1 | second | 143 |
| pprint | 190 | select-page | 220 |
| prin1 | 189 | send | 181 |
| princ | 190 | set | 52 |
| print | 189 | set-char-bit | 132 |
| probe-file | 201 | set-macro-character | 185 |
| prog | 74 | set-syntax-from-char | 184 |
| prog* | 75 | setf | 54 |
| prog1 | 58 | setq | 5, 51 |
| prog2 | 59 | shadow | 107 |
| progn | 58 | signum | 120 |

| Command | Page Number in Reference Manual[1] | Command | Page Number in Reference Manual[1] |
|---|---|---|---|
| sin | 120 | symbol-package | 99 |
| snoc | 149 | symbol-plist | 95 |
| some | 134 | symbol-value | 49 |
| sort | 136 | symbolp | 36 |
| special-form-p | 50 | t | 34 |
| sqrt | 120 | tailp | 151 |
| stack-group | 19 | tan | 121 |
| stack-group-p | 41 | terpri | 190 |
| stack-group-preset | 84 | third | 143 |
| stack-group-resume | 86 | throw | 80 |
| stack-group-return | 86 | time | 211 |
| stack-group-unwind | 85 | trace | 209 |
| standard-char | 11 | truncate | 122 |
| standard-char-p | 127 | type-of | 25 |
| step | 210 | typep | 35 |
| stream | 17 | unless | 63 |
| string | 15, 166 | unread-char | 188 |
| string-append | 165 | untrace | 210 |
| string-char | 12 | upper-case-p | 128 |
| string-equal | 163 | use-package | 107 |
| string-left-trim | 165 | values | 76 |
| string-lessp | 163 | values-list | 77 |
| string-right-trim | 165 | vector | 14, 157 |
| string-search | 164 | vector-pop | 160 |
| string-search* | 164 | vector-push | 159 |
| stringp | 38 | vectorp | 39 |
| structure | 17 | when | 63 |
| sublis | 150 | with-open-file | 200 |
| subseq | 133 | write-byte | 191 |
| subst | 149 | write-char | 190 |
| subtypep | 35 | y-or-n-p | 193 |
| sxhash | 155 | yes-or-no-p | 193 |
| symbol | 12 | zerop | 111 |
| symbol-function | 49 | ¦ | 6 |
| symbol-name | 97 | | |

# Frequently-Used muLISP Commands

| Command | Page Number in Reference Manual[2] | Command | Page Number in Reference Manual[2] |
|---|---|---|---|
| and | 10 | gcd | 21 |
| append | 4 | get | 13 |
| apply | 33 | getd | 15 |
| ascii | 19 | greaterp | 8 |
| assoc | 13 | lambda | 35 |
| atom | 7 | length | 18 |
| caaar | 2 | length | 19 |
| caadr | 2 | lessp | 9 |
| caar | 2 | linelength | 29 |
| cadar | 2 | linelength | 31 |
| caddr | 2 | list | 4 |
| cadr | 2 | load | 40 |
| car | 1 | loop | 36 |
| cdaar | 3 | lprinter | 30 |
| cdadr | 3 | member | 8 |
| cdar | 2 | memory | 41 |
| cddar | 3 | minus | 20 |
| cdddr | 3 | minusp | 7 |
| cddr | 2 | movd | 16 |
| cdr | 1 | name | 7 |
| clrscrn | 42 | nconc | 6 |
| cond | 36 | nil | 7 |
| cons | 4 | nlambda | 35 |
| cursor | 42 | not | 10 |
| difference | 20 | null | 7 |
| divide | 21 | numberp | 7 |
| driver | 37 | oblist | 5 |
| echo | 26 | or | 10 |
| echo | 30 | orderp | 9 |
| eq | 8 | pack | 18 |
| equal | 8 | plus | 20 |
| eval | 32 | plusp | 7 |
| even | 7 | pop | 12 |
| findstring | 17 | prin1 | 30 |
| flag | 14 | prin1 | 27 |
| flagp | 14 | print | 30 |

| Command | Page Number in Reference Manual[2] | Command | Page Number in Reference Manual[2] |
|---|---|---|---|
| print | 28 | remprop | 13 |
| prog1 | 37 | reverse | 4 |
| push | 12 | rplaca | 6 |
| put | 13 | rplacd | 6 |
| putd | 15 | save | 40 |
| quote | 32 | set | 11 |
| quotient | 20 | setq | 11 |
| radix | 29 | spaces | 28 |
| ratom | 23 | substring | 17 |
| rds | 22 | system | 41 |
| rds | 26 | t | 7 |
| read | 23 | tconc | 5 |
| read | 26 | terpri | 28 |
| readch | 22 | time | 42 |
| readch | 26 | times | 20 |
| readp | 24 | unpack | 18 |
| reclaim | 38 | wrs | 27 |
| reclaim | 38 | wrs | 30 |
| remainder | 20 | zerop | 7 |
| remflag | 14 | | |

# References

[1] Gold Hill Computers, *Golden Common LISP Reference Manual*, version 1.01 (Cambridge, MA, 1985).

[2] The Software Warehouse, *The muLISP/muSTAR-82 Artificial Intelligence Development System Reference Manual for the IBM Personal Computer* (Honolulu, HI, 1982).

# B

# Prolog Commands

This appendix lists frequently-used commands (predicates) for two Prolog packages:

- Prolog-86 (distributed by Solution Systems, South Weymouth, MA) [1]
- Turbo Prolog (distributed by Borland International, Scotts Valley, CA) [2]

## Prolog-86 Commands

| Command | Page Number in User's Guide[1] | Command | Page Number in User's Guide[1] |
|---|---|---|---|
| ! | 88 | <= | 86 |
| = | 107 | >= | 86 |
| -> | 89 | , | 86 |
| + | 85 | ; | 86 |
| - | 85 | ¦ | 86 |
| * | 85 | arg | 107 |
| / | 85 | ascii | 112 |
| ^ | 85 | ask | 100 |
| =, == | 85 | assert | 91 |
| /= | 86 | asserta | 91 |
| < | 86 | assertz | 91 |
| > | 86 | atom | 105 |

| Command | Page Number in User's Guide[1] | Command | Page Number in User's Guide[1] |
|---|---|---|---|
| atomic | 106 | print | 100 |
| char | 108 | prompt | 100 |
| clause | 109 | putc | 103 |
| close | 98 | ratom | 99 |
| concat | 109 | read | 98 |
| consult | 93 | read_from_this_file | 96 |
| eof | 98 | repeat | 87 |
| fail | 87 | retract | 92 |
| file | 94 | retractall | 92 |
| findall | 90 | save | 94 |
| functor | 106 | see | 95 |
| getc | 102 | seeing | 95 |
| integer | 106 | seen | 96 |
| is | 84 | skip | 103 |
| length | 110 | tab | 104 |
| listing | 113 | tell | 97 |
| load | 94 | telling | 97 |
| mod | 85 | told | 97 |
| name | 108 | trace | 113 |
| nl | 102 | true | 87 |
| nonvar | 105 | unload | 94 |
| not | 87 | untrace | 115 |
| numbervars | 110 | var | 104 |
| op | 110 | write | 101 |
| pp | 113 | | |
| prin | 101 | | |

## Turbo Prolog Commands

Standard Turbo Prolog commands are listed alphabetically. The name and the parameters (in parentheses) of each command are presented. All arithmetic operation commands appear on pages 64 and 65 of the "Owner's Handbook"[2]; commands for other operations appear on pages 183–194.

## *Arithmetic Operations*

+
-
*
/
<
<=
=
>
>=
<>
><
bitand(X,Y,Z)
bitor(X,Y,Z)
bitnot(X,Z)
bitxor(X,Y,Z)
bitleft(X,N,Y)
bitright(X,N,Y)
X mod Y
X div Y
abs(X)
cos(X)
sin(X)
tan(X)
arctan(X)
exp(X)
ln(X)
log(X)
sqrt(X)

## *Other Operations*

asserta(<fact>)
assertz(<fact>)
attribute(Attr)
back(Step)
beep
bois(InterruptNo,RegsIn,
RegsOut)
bound(Variable)
char_int(CharParam,
IntParam)
clearwindow
closefile(SymbolicFileName)
consult(DOSFileName)
cursor(Row,Column)
cursorform(Startline,
Endline)
date(Year,Month,Day)
deletefile(DOSFileName)
dir(Pathname,
FileSpecString,DosFileName)
disk(DosPath)
display(String)
dot(Row,Column,Color)
edit(InputString,
OutputString)
editmsg(InStr,OutStr,
LeftHeader,RightHeader,
Message,
HelpFileName,Position,Code)
eof(SymbolicFileName)
existfile(DosFileName)
exit
fail
field_attr(Row,Column,
Length,Attr)
field_str(Row,Column,
Length,String)
filepos(SymbolicFileName,
FilePosition,Mode)
file_str(DosFileName,
StringVariable)
findall(Variable,<atom>,
ListVariable)

flush(SymbolicFileName)
forward(Step)
free(Variable)
frontchar(String,FrontChar,RestString)
frontstr(NumberOfChars,String1,StartStr,String2)
fronttoken(String,Token,RestString)
graphics(ModeParam,Palette,Background)
isname(StringParam)
left(Angle)
line(Row1,Col1,Row2,Col2,Color)
makewindow(WindowNo,ScrAttr,FrameAttr,Header,Row,Col,Height,Width)
membyte(Segment,Offset,Byte)
memword(Segment,Offset,Word)
nl
not(<atom>)
openappend(SymbolicFileName,DosFileName)
openmodify(SymbolicFileName,DosFileName)
openread(SymbolicFileName,DosFileName)
openwrite(SymbolicFileName,DosFileName)
pencolor(Color)
pendown
penup
portbyte(PortNo,Value)
ptr_dword(StringVar,Segment,Offset)
readchar(CharVariable)
readdevice(SymbolicFileName)
readint(IntVariable)
readln(StringVariable)
readreal(RealVariable)
readterm(Domain,Term)
removewindow
renamefile(OldDosFileName,NewDosFileName)
retract(<fact>)
right(Angle)
save(DosFileName)
scr_attr(Row,Col,Attr)
scr_chr(Row,Column,Char)
shiftwindow(WindowNo)
sound(Duration,Frequency)
storage(StackSize,HeapSize,TrailSize)
st_chr(StringParam,CharParam)
str_int(StringParam,IntParam)
str_len(String,Length)
str_real(StringParam,RealParam)
system(DosCommandString)
text
time(Hours,Minutes,Seconds,Hundredths)
trace(Status)
upper_lower(StringInUpperCase,StringInLowerCase)
window_attr(Attr)
window_str(ScreenString)
write(e1,e2,e3,. . . .,eN)
writedevice(SymbolicFileName)
writef(FormatString,Arg1,Arg2,Arg3,. . . .)

## References

[1] Micro-AI, *Prolog-86 User's Guide and Reference Manual*, version 2.01 (Rheem Valley, CA, 1985).

[2] Borland International, Inc., *Turbo Prolog: Owner's Handbook* (Scotts Valley, CA, 1986).

# C

# Smalltalk Classes and Methods

This appendix details the hierarchy of Smalltalk/V classes, defines those classes, and discusses methods. Classes and methods are described on pages 253 to 504 of the Smalltalk user's guide [1].

## Hierarchy of Smalltalk Classes

- Object
  - Behavior
    - Class
    - MetaClass
  - BitBlt
    - CharacterScanner
    - Pen
      - Animation
      - Commander
  - Boolean
    - False
    - True
  - ClassBrowser
  - ClassHierarchyBrowser
  - ClassReader
  - Collection
    - Bag
    - IndexCollection

```
            FixedSizeCollection
               Array
               Bitmap
               ByteArray
                  CompiledMethod
                  FileControlBlock
               Interval
               String
                  Symbol
            OrderedCollection
               Process
               SortedCollection
      List
         EmptyList
      Set
         Dictionary
            IdentityDictionary
               MethodDictionary
            SystemDictionary
         SymbolSet
      Compiler
         LCompiler
      Context
      CursorManager
         NoMouseCursor
      DemoClass
      Directory
      DiskBrowser
      Dispatcher
         GraphDispatcher
         PointDispatcher
         ScreenDispatcher
         ScrollDispatcher
            ListSelector
            TextEditor
               PromptEditor
            TopDispatcher
      DispatchManager
```

- DisplayObject
  - DisplayMedium
    - Form
      - DisplayScreen
      - SelectorForm
  - DisplayString
  - InfiniteForm
- File
- Inspector
  - Debugger
  - DictionaryInspector
- Magnitude
  - Association
  - Character
  - Date
  - Number
    - Float
    - Fraction
    - Integer
      - LargeNegativeInteger
      - LargePositiveInteger
      - SmallInteger
  - Time
- Menu
- Message
- Pane
  - SubPane
    - GraphPane
    - ListPane
    - TextPane
  - TopPane
- Pattern
  - WildPattern
- Point
- Prompter
- Rectangle
- Stream
  - ReadStream

WriteStream
ReadWriteStream
FileStream
TerminalStream
StringModel
TextSelection
UndefinedObject

## Definition of Classes

***Animation*** A collection of pens representing the objects being animated.

***Array*** A collection of objects accessed through a fixed range of integer indexes as the external keys.

***Association*** Provides the means of associating two objects known as the key/value pair, and defines the protocol to manipulate them.

***Bag*** A collection of unordered elements in which duplicates are allowed.

***Behavior*** The abstract class that defines and implements the common protocol for all classes in Smalltalk.

***BitBlt*** Groups together all basic graphics operations.

***Boolean*** An abstract class that defines the common protocol for logical values.

***ByteArray*** A fixed-size, indexable sequence of integers in the range 0 through 255.

***Character*** The protocol for all characters in the system (ASCII codes from 0 to 255).

***CharacterScanner*** Converts characters represented by ASCII values into displayable bit patterns.

***Class*** The superclass of all classes (that is, metaclasses) in Smalltalk.

***ClassBrowser*** Implements a window on all methods for a single class.

***ClassHierarachyBrowser*** Implements a window on all classes in Smalltalk/V.

***ClassReader*** Supports Smalltalk source code reading and installation (compilation) from a stream, and writing to a stream.

***Collection*** The superclass of all collection classes; collections are the basic data structures used to store objects in groups.

***Commander*** Governs an *Array* of pens.

***CompiledMethod*** Produced by the Smalltalk/V compiler and interpretively executed by the Smalltalk/V virtual machine.

***Compiler*** Converts Smalltalk source code to compiled methods and evaluates Smalltalk expressions.

***Context*** Contains method temporaries and arguments and describes blocks of code (enclosed in square brackets).

***CursorManager*** Contains the bit pattern to display a cursor shape.

***Date*** Represents a particular day since the start of the Julian calendar.

***Debugger*** A window application that allows the debugging of a *Process* in two different windows: a single-pane walkback window and a four-pane debugger window.

***DemoClass*** Contains methods for demonstrating graphics.

***Dictionary*** A collection of key/value pairs of objects that are stored as a set of associations.

***DictionaryInspector*** Implements a window on a dictionary, which allows the entries of a dictionary to be viewed and changed.

***Directory*** Represents a DOS directory with a device letter and a path name string.

***DiskBrowser*** Implements a window on the complete directory hierarchy on a disk.

***Dispatcher*** An abstract class that provides the common protocol for its subclasses.

***DispatchManager*** Schedules windows by providing messages for adding and removing windows and displaying all windows.

***DisplayMedium*** An abstract class without any instance variables.

***DisplayObject*** An abstract class that provides the common protocol for transferring a rectangular block of characters from the receiver display object to a *DisplayMedium.*

***DisplayScreen*** A special kind of form whose bit map address and size is determined by the display adapter.

***False*** A single instance, false, that represents logical falsehood.

***File*** Provides sequential or random access to a DOS file.

***FileControlBlock*** An array of bytes whose structure is defined by DOS.

***FileStream*** Allows streaming over the characters of DOS files for read and write access.

***FixedSizeCollection*** An abstract class for all indexable fixed-size collections.

***Float*** Defines the protocol to perform arithmetic operations on floating point numbers.

***Font*** Defines the bit map patterns and characteristics of characters necessary for display.

***Form*** Contains a bit map and other instance variables to describe the bit map as a two-dimensional array of bits.

***Fraction*** Defines the protocol to perform arithmetic operations on rational numbers.

***GraphDispatcher*** Handles the user input directed to a *GraphPane.*

***GraphPane*** Allows the user to do generalized graphic drawing in the pane.

***IdentityDictionary*** A collection of key/value pairs of objects that are stored in two parallel *Array* structures.

***IndexedCollection*** An abstract class providing the common protocol for all indexable *Collection* subclasses.

***Inspector*** Implements a window on an object, which allows the instance variables to be viewed and changed for that object.

***Integer*** An abstract class used to compare, count, and measure instances of its subclasses representing integral numbers.

***Interval*** Represents mathematical progressions.

***LargeNegativeInteger*** Defines the data structure for instances of integral numbers less than −16384.

***LargePositiveInteger*** Defines the data structure for instances of integral numbers greater than 16383.

***LCompiler*** Converts Prolog source code to compiled methods.

***ListPane*** Provides functions to display and scroll a portion of the data held by the pane.

***Magnitude*** An abstract class used to compare, count, and measure instances of its subclasses.

***Menu*** Defines the protocol for an application to present a menu of items to the user.

***Message*** Defines a data structure with an *Array* of message arguments and a message selector to describe a Smalltalk message.

***MetaClass*** The class of all metaclasses in Smalltalk (for example, of *Array*).

***MethodDictionary*** A special kind of identity dictionary used to describe the compiled methods for each class.

***NoMouseCursor*** Contains the bit pattern needed to display a cursor shape.

***Number*** An abstract class used to compare, count, and measure instances of its numerical subclasses.

***Object*** The superclass of all classes defining the protocol common to all objects.

***OrderedCollection*** A dynamic array, stack or queue.

***Pane*** An abstract class that provides the common protocol for all its subclasses; a subarea of a window.

***Pattern*** Contains a finite-state pattern to match against another object.

***Pen*** Provides a turtle graphics type of interface.

***Point*** Represents a position in two dimensions.

***PointDispatcher*** Defines or modifies a rectangle on the screen.

***Process*** Contains a copy of the hardware stack for the purpose of saving the state of the current process which may later be resumed.

***PromptEditor*** Processes input for its associated *TextPane* in a *Prompter.*

***Prompter*** A window with one *TextPane*, which allows an application to pose a question and solicit an answer from the user.

***ReadStream*** Allows streaming over an indexed collection of objects for read access, but not write access.

***ReadWriteStream*** Allows streaming over an indexed collection of objects for read and write access.

***Rectangle*** Represents a rectangular area described by an origin (upper left corner) and a corner (lower right corner) point.

***ScreenDispatcher*** Processes the user input directed to the background window.

***ScrollDispatcher*** An abstract class that processes scrolling-related inputs from either the keyboard or the mouse.

***SelectorForm*** Provides the bit map image of the text selector, which denotes the insertion point in a *TextPane.*

***Set*** Represents an unordered collection of unique objects with no external keys.

***SmallInteger*** Defines additional protocol for numbers in the range of −16384 to +16383.

***SortedCollection*** Contains elements sorted according to the two argument blocks of code known as the sort blocks (sortBlock).

***Stream*** Used to access files, devices and internal objects as a sequence of characters or other objects.

***String*** A fixed-size, indexable sequence of characters (ASCII codes from 0 to 255).

***StringModel*** A text holder that assists the *TextEditor* class by performing editing functions on the text it contains.

***SubPane*** An abstract class that provides the functions common to the *ListPane* and *TextPane* classes.

***Symbol*** A fixed-size sequence of characters guaranteed to be unique throughout the system.

***SymbolSet*** A set used to record all symbol instances.

***SystemDictionary*** Contains all global variables.

***TerminalStream*** Defines the streaming protocol to and from the terminal.

***TextEditor*** Processes input for its associated *TextPane.*

***TextPane*** Provides functions to display and scroll a portion of the text held by the pane.

***TextSelection*** Remembers the two points of a selection in the *TextPane*, and understands all messages for manipulating the selection.

***Time*** Represents a particular time of day to the nearest second.

***TopDispatcher*** Processes input for its associated *TopPane.*

***TopPane*** Responsible for all operations related to its entire window.

***True*** A single instance, true, that represents logical truth.

***UndefinedObject*** A single instance, nil, used to identify undefined values.

***WildPattern*** Contains a finite-state pattern for efficient matching, which includes at least one wild card character.

***WriteStream*** Allows streaming over an indexed collection of objects for write access, but not read access.

## Brief Discussion of Methods

Methods are like function definitions in other languages. They determine an object's behavior and performance. When a message is sent to an object, a method is called and evaluated, and an object is returned as a result. You can use methods created by the developer in each class or create your own and associate them with a given class. A library of available methods in Smalltalk/V is shown in Appendix 4 of the Smalltalk/V user's guide [1].

## References

[1] Digitalk, Inc., *Smalltalk/V: Tutorial and Programming Handbook* (Los Angles, 1986).

# D

# Expert Systems and Tools

Besides the AI/expert system programming language packages detailed in Chapters 4, 5, and 6, a number of languages and development tools and systems are available for the PC environment. This appendix provides a summary of these tools and systems, including:

- Description, hardware requirements, software requirements, cost (subject to changes by vendor), and contact of commonly-used (easy-to-obtain brochures) tools
- Tables of AI languages, tools, and expert systems currently available
- Tools and expert systems frequently mentioned in the AI literature

## Commonly-Used Tools

The information contained in this section is based mostly on information provided by developers of the products and not on my own experience using the products, except for those described in Chapters 4, 5, 6, and 10. This section is divided into three subsections. The first subsection contains summaries of expert system tools for IBM personal computers; the second contains summaries of tools available for the Apple Macintosh; and the third subsection contains summaries of tools that run on both IBM and Macintosh personal computers. Within each section, summaries are placed alphabetically.

### *Tools for IBM Personal Computers*

#### *APES 1.1*

DESCRIPTION: APES 1.1 is an augmented version of Prolog specifically designed for developing expert systems. It retains the flexibility of Prolog while providing the modules common to many expert systems.

HARDWARE REQUIREMENTS: IBM PC

SOFTWARE REQUIREMENTS: Micro-Prolog 3.1, which is included in the purchase price

COST: $425 (academic discount available)

CONTACT: Programming Logic Systems, Inc.
31 Crescent Drive
Milford, CT 06460
(203) 877-7988

### *ES/P Advisor*

DESCRIPTION: ES/P Advisor is an expert system shell for rapid development of demonstration and prototype expert systems. Knowledge is represented by simple production rules. Uncertain knowledge cannot be directly handled. Language hooks to Prolog are supported. ES/P Advisor is written in Prolog.

HARDWARE REQUIREMENTS: IBM PC/XT with a minimum of 128K RAM

SOFTWARE REQUIREMENTS: PC-DOS

COST: $895
$626.50 for academic institutions

CONTACT: Expert Systems International
1150 First Avenue
King of Prussia, PA 19406
(215) 337-2300

### *Expertech*

DESCRIPTION: Expertech is a "software laboratory" consisting of an integrated collection of expert system tutorials, case studies, online teaching programs, and expert systems building tools. Expertech includes eight rule-based expert system shells. A forward chaining and a backward chaining shell has been implemented in each of LISP, Prolog, dBASE II and Pascal. The emphasis of Expertech is on educating the user about expert system technology.

HARDWARE REQUIREMENTS: IBM PC/XT with a minimum of 256K RAM

COST: $475 (no academic discount available)

CONTACT: Intelliware, Inc.
4676 Admiralty Way, Suite 401
Marina del Rey, CA 90291
(213) 827-1334

### *Expert Ease*

DESCRIPTION: Expert Ease is an expert system tool that uses inductions made from examples to generate rules. Uncertain knowledge cannot be represented, and Expert Ease doesn't support hooks to other languages. Expert Ease is written in Pascal.

HARDWARE REQUIREMENTS: IBM PC with a minimum of 128K RAM

SOFTWARE REQUIREMENTS: PC-DOS

COST: $695 per package, retail
$278 per package for academic institutions

CONTACT: Human Edge Software, Inc.
2445 Faber Place
Palo Alto, CA 94303
(415) 493-1593

### *EXSYS 3.0*

DESCRIPTION: EXSYS is an expert systems development tool implementation for the IBM PC. EXSYS uses a backward chaining inference mechanism and simple production rules for knowledge representation. Uncertain knowledge is handled through the use of simple probability measures or through uncertainty factors. EXSYS can execute external programs and can pass its results to external programs as well. EXSYS is written in C.

HARDWARE REQUIREMENTS: IBM PC/AT with at least 256K RAM

SOFTWARE REQUIREMENTS: MS-DOS 2.0 or higher

COST: $395 per package, retail (no academic discount available)

CONTACT: EXSYS, Inc.
P. O. Box 75158, Contract Station 14
Albuquerque, NM 87194
(505) 836-6676

### *GCLISP*

DESCRIPTION: GCLISP is a Common LISP package that implements most features available in Common LISP. GCLISP has two versions. One is for the regular PC user and the other is for the expert system developer (286 developer) using the IBM AT machines. See Chapters 3 and 4 for more information.

HARDWARE REQUIREMENTS: The PC version requires 512K RAM; the 286 developer requires at least 2M RAM.

SOFTWARE REQUIREMENTS: PC-DOS

COST: The PC version is sold for $495; the developer is sold for $1,195.

CONTACT: Gold Hill Computers
163 Harvard Street
Cambridge, MA 02139
(800) 242-LISP

### *Insight-1 and -2*

DESCRIPTION: Insight-1 is a knowledge engineering software tool that provides an environment in which to design, create, and run prototype expert systems. Insight-1 represents knowledge as simple production rules, and allows both forward and backward chaining. Insight-1 uses "confidence weighting" to represent uncertain knowledge, and supports hooks to Pascal.

Insight-2 is an enhanced version of Insight-1, for more serious applications. Expert systems developed with Insight-2 can interface to external programs.

HARDWARE REQUIREMENTS: Insight-1 requires an IBM PC/XT/AT with at least 128K RAM; Insight-2 requires at least 256K RAM.

SOFTWARE REQUIREMENTS: MS-DOS 2.0 or higher

COST: Insight-1 $95; Insight-2 $485

CONTACT: Level Five Research, Inc.
503 Fifth Ave.
Indialantic, FL 32903
(305) 729-9046

### *KDS*

DESCRIPTION: KDS is an expert system tool that uses inductions made from examples to generate rules. Uncertain knowledge cannot be represented. KDS supports both forward and backward chaining, can execute external programs, utilizes user-developed code, and can take input from external programs. KDS is written 100 percent in assembly language.

HARDWARE REQUIREMENTS: IBM PC with at least 256K RAM

SOFTWARE REQUIREMENTS: PC-DOS

COST: $795 for the development module, retail
$495 for the playback (inference engine) module, retail
A 20 percent discount is available to academic institutions.

CONTACT: KDS Corporation
934 Hunter Road
Wilmette, IL 60091
(312) 251-2621

### *KES*

DESCRIPTION: KES is a family of software tools for developing, implementing, and supporting expert systems. KES uses production rules and frames to represent knowledge. Certainty factors are used to represent uncertain knowledge. Hooks to other languages are not supported.

HARDWARE REQUIREMENTS: The IBM PC/XT version of KES requires the 8087 math coprocessor and at least 640K RAM.

SOFTWARE REQUIREMENTS: KES requires IQLISP, which must be purchased separately from Integral Quality in Seattle, Washington, (206) 527-2918.

COST: $4,000. A 75 percent discount is available to academic institutions. Training is available at a cost of $1,200 per student.

CONTACT: Software Architecture and Engineering, Inc.
1500 Wilson Boulevard, Suite 800
Arlington, VA 22209
(703) 276-7910

### *Micro-Expert*

DESCRIPTION: Micro-Expert is a rule-based expert system development tool that provides the user interface and the inference engine. The user interface is equipped to allow the user to entertain questions, obtain results, and explain the sequence of reasoning used. For details, see Chapter 10.

HARDWARE EQUIPMENT: 256K RAM

SOFTWARE REQUIREMENTS: PC-DOS

COST: $99 (includes book)

CONTACT: McGraw-Hill Publishing
1221 Avenue of the Americas
New York, NY 10020
(212) 512-2000

### *Micro-Prolog*

DESCRIPTION: Micro-Prolog is a microcomputer implementation of Prolog, a logic-based programming language suitable for use in expert systems, robotic control, language processing, and other artificial intelligence applications. It incorporates advanced pattern matching, generalized record structuring, list manipulation, assertional data base, and backtracking search strategy mechanisms.

HARDWARE REQUIREMENTS: 640K RAM and one disk drive

SOFTWARE REQUIREMENTS: PC-DOS
COST: $250 (academic discount available)
CONTACT: Programming Logic Systems, Inc.
31 Crescent Drive
Milford, CT 06460
(203) 877-7988

### *M.1*

DESCRIPTION: According to the manual, "M.1 is a knowledge engineering tool that provides training, exploration, and proof-of-concept capabilities for investigating applications of knowledge engineering . . . M.1 is used to design, build, and run stand-alone knowledge systems." Its backward chaining inference engine is based on that of MYCIN. M.1 offers explanation and debugging facilities, as well as a hook to C. Uncertain knowledge is represented by certainty factors.

HARDWARE REQUIREMENTS: IBM PC/XT/AT with one disk drive and at least 192K RAM

SOFTWARE REQUIREMENTS: Text editing program (such as the EDLIN program that accompanies MS-DOS)

COST: $5,000 (retail)
$1,250 for academic institutions

A four-day training course is available at a cost of $2,500 per student retail; $1,000 per student for academic institutions.

CONTACT: Teknowledge, Inc.
525 University Avenue
Palo Alto, CA 94301
(415) 327-6600

### *muLISP*

DESCRIPTION: muLISP is one of the earliest LISP packages for personal computers. It is not a Common LISP package, but contains a library of Common LISP primitives. Its functions can be linked to user-defined machine language subroutines. The commands available on muLISP are listed in Appendix A.

HARDWARE REQUIREMENTS: 48K RAM

SOFTWARE REQUIREMENTS: PC-DOS or CP/M

COST: $250

CONTACT: Microsoft Corporation
16011 Northeast 36 Way
Box 97017
Redmond, WA 98073
(206) 882-8088

### *Prolog-86*

DESCRIPTION Prolog-86 is an interpretive logic programming language to help the user learn and experiment with small problems. It is based on Clocksin's and Mellish's definitive work entitled, *Programming in Prolog*. For more information see Chapter 5.

HARDWARE REQUIREMENTS: 96K RAM

SOFTWARE REQUIREMENTS: PC-DOS or CP/M

COST: $95

CONTACT: MICRO-AI (Solution Systems)
541 Main Street, Suite 410
South Weymouth, MA 02190
(617) 337-6963

### *PROLOG-1 and -2*

DESCRIPTION: PROLOG-1 is a logic-based (as opposed to algorithm-based) programming language suitable for use in expert systems, robotic control, language processing, and other artificial intelligence applications. It incorporates advanced pattern matching, generalized record structuring, list manipulation, assertional data base, and backtracking search strategy mechanisms.

PROLOG-2 is a logic programming language environment that offers all the advantages of PROLOG-1, but allows for modules written in other languages as well. PROLOG-2 also runs about twice as fast as PROLOG-1.

HARDWARE REQUIREMENTS: IBM PC/XT with a minimum of 128K RAM
SOFTWARE REQUIREMENTS: MS-DOS
COST: PROLOG-1 costs $276.50 and PROLOG-2 costs $1,326 per package, for academic institutions.
CONTACT: Expert Systems International
1150 First Avenue
King of Prussia, PA 19406
(215) 337-2300

### *Personal Consultant*

DESCRIPTION: Personal Consultant is a set of programs and utilities that can be used to develop customized expert systems. Personal Consultant uses backward chaining logic in a rule-based environment. Both structural and factual knowledge can be explicitly represented. Uncertain knowledge is represented by the use of certainty factors. Personal Consultant offers extensive explanation and debugging facilities, as well as the capability of translating knowledge-based rules into plain English.

HARDWARE REQUIREMENTS: IBM PC/XT with one disk drive, a 10 megabyte hard disk, and 640K RAM

SOFTWARE REQUIREMENTS: PC-DOS 2.0 or higher and IQLISP 1.7 or higher

COST: $950. A 35 percent discount is available for academic institutions.

CONTACT: Texas Instruments, Inc.
12501 Research Blvd.
Austin, TX 78759
(512) 250-7111

### *Smalltalk-AT*

DESCRIPTION: Smalltalk-AT is a PC implementation of the original Smalltalk-80 developed at Xerox Palo Alto Research Center. It is an object-oriented programming language, featuring interactive debugger, inspectors, snapshotting, bit-mapped graphics, windows, and text editor.

HARDWARE REQUIREMENTS: IBM PC/AT, 1 megabyte of RAM memory, a mouse, and an EGA card

SOFTWARE REQUIREMENTS: DOS 3.0

COST: $995

CONTACT: Softsmarts, Inc.
4 Skyline Drive
Woodside, CA 94062
(415) 327-8100

### *Smalltalk/V*

DESCRIPTION: Smalltalk/V is an object-oriented language with features similar to Smalltalk-AT. For details of operation, see Chapter 6.

HARDWARE REQUIREMENTS: 512K RAM, an EGA card, and two disk drives

SOFTWARE REQUIREMENTS: PC-DOS 2.0

COST: $99

CONTACT: Digitalk, Inc.
5200 West Century Boulevard
Los Angeles, CA 90045
(213) 645-1082

### *Turbo Prolog*

DESCRIPTION: Turbo Prolog is a logic programming language. Turbo Prolog provides windows, simple menus, and point- and line-based graphics, in addition to the normal Prolog features. The commands available in Turbo Prolog are listed in Appendix C.

HARDWARE REQUIREMENTS: 384K RAM

SOFTWARE REQUIREMENTS: PC-DOS 2.0

COST: $95

CONTACT: Borland International, Inc.
4585 Scotts Valley Drive
Scotts Valley, CA 95066
(800) 742-1133

### *VP-Expert*

DESCRIPTION: VP-Expert is an expert system development tool that is built on C. It features simple backward and forward chaining, inductive front end, windows, text editor, and confidence factors.

HARDWARE REQUIREMENTS: IBM PC with 256K RAM and graphics card

SOFTWARE REQUIREMENTS: PC-DOS

COST: $99.95

CONTACT: Paperback Software International
2830 Ninth Street
Berkeley, CA 94710
(415) 644-2116

### *XSYS*

DESCRIPTION: XSYS is an expert system shell for the development of prototype expert systems. Knowledge is represented by simple production rules, and uncertainty is represented by certainty factors. Hooks to other languages are not supported.

HARDWARE REQUIREMENTS: IBM PC/XT/AT with at least 640K. The 8087 math coprocessor is required if certainty factors are to be supported.

SOFTWARE REQUIREMENTS: PC-DOS

COST: $995 (no discount available to academic institutions)

CONTACT: California Intelligence
912 Powell Street #8
San Francisco, CA 94108
(415) 391-4846

## *Tools for the Apple Macintosh*

### *ExperOPS5*

DESCRIPTION: OPS5 is a production system programming language. It uses a forward chaining inference mechanism to make conclusions based on known facts, and is thus best suited for data-driven applications. ExperOPS5 is an implementation of OPS5 in ExperLISP and offers no built-in explanation facilities or means of representing uncertainty.

HARDWARE REQUIREMENTS: ExperOPS5 requires a 512K Macintosh equipped with an external disk drive or a hard drive.

SOFTWARE REQUIREMENTS: ExperOPS5 requires ExperLISP version 1.03 or higher.

COST: $325 (ExperLISP required, $495 retail). No academic discount is available. No training or formal support is available. Updates are available for a nominal fee.

CONTACT: ExperTelligence, Inc.
559 San Ysidro Road
Santa Barbara, CA 93108
(805) 969-7871

### *MacKIT Level 1*

DESCRIPTION: The stated purpose of MacKIT is to "provide a reasonably priced tool to support the technology transfer of basic Knowledge Engineering skills to you . . . You will build your own knowledge systems to provide the productivity tools you require." MacKIT uses backward chaining inference on simple production rules and does not support variables or calculations of any type. Uncertain knowledge is represented as a variant of certainty factors.

HARDWARE REQUIREMENTS: MacKIT Level 1 requires a Macintosh 512K.

SOFTWARE REQUIREMENTS: A word processing program (e.g., MacWrite)

COST: $149. Updates are available for a nominal fee.

CONTACT: Knowledge System Environments, Inc.
201 S. York Road
Dillsburg, PA 17019
(717) 766-4496

### *Nexpert*

DESCRIPTION: Nexpert is an expert system development environment for the Macintosh. Nexpert represents knowledge by using a combination of simple production rules, contexts, and categories. Knowledge base structure can be represented either as a tree or a network. Nexpert supports backward chaining, forward chaining, or a combination of both. Nexpert automatically generates a graphic representation of the knowledge structure and supports both text and image associations with rules.

HARDWARE REQUIREMENTS: Nexpert requires a 512K Macintosh.

SOFTWARE REQUIREMENTS: None

COST: $5,000 (no academic discount available). Training is available for an additional fee.

CONTACT: Neuron Data, Inc.
444 High Street
Palo Alto, CA 94301
(415) 321-4488

## *Tools for Both IBM and Macintosh Computers*

### *OPS5+*

DESCRIPTION OPS5+ is a programming language principally designed to implement forward chaining production systems. Knowledge is represented by simple production rules, and control structure can be built into these rules as well. A development and debugging environment is included. OPS5+ is written in C and supports hooks to Lattice/Microsoft C (not included).

HARDWARE REQUIREMENTS: OPS5+ runs on an IBM PC/XT/AT with at least 640K RAM, the standard IBM graphics card, and a Mouse Systems mouse; or on an Apple Macintosh 512K.

SOFTWARE REQUIREMENTS: None

COST: $3,000 ($960 for academic institutions)

CONTACT: Artelligence, Inc.
14902 Preston Road, Suite 212-252
Dallas, TX 75240
(214) 437-0361

# PC Languages, Tools and Systems

**Table D-1**
***AI languages on PCs***

| Language | Applicable PC | Developer | Telephone |
|---|---|---|---|
| **LISP** | | | |
| BYSCO LISP | IBM AT | Levien Instrument | (703) 396-3345 |
| CLISP | IBM | Westcomp | (714) 982-1738 |
| Cromenco LISP | Z-80 | Cromenco | (415) 964-7400 |
| ExperLISP | Macintosh | ExperTelligence | (805) 969-7871 |
| GCLISP | IBM | Gold Hill Computers | (617) 492-2071 |
| IQLISP | IBM | Integral Quality | (206) 527-2918 |
| LISP/80 | IBM | Software Toolworks | (818) 986-4885 |
| LISP/88 | IBM | Norell Data Systems | (213) 748-5978 |
| muLISP | All | Soft Warehouse | (206) 455-8080 |
| TLC-LISP 86 | All | The LISP Company | |
| UO-LISP | IBM | Northwest Computer Algorithms | (213) 426-1893 |
| Waltz LISP | All | Pro Code Int'l | (800) LIP-4000 |
| XLISP | All | N.Y. Amateur Computer Club | (603) 924-9820 |
| **Prolog** | | | |
| Arity/Prolog | IBM | Arity | (617) 371-1243 |
| IF/Prolog | IBM | Interface Computer, W. Germany | 089/984444 |
| LPA Micro-Prolog | IBM | Logic Programming Assoc., UK | 01-874-0350 |
| MPROLOG | All | Logicware | |
| Micro-Prolog | IBM | Programming Logic Systems | (203) 877-7988 |
| PC-Prolog | IBM | SuInfologics AB, Stockholm, Sweden | |
| PROLOG-1 & -2 | IBM | Expert Systems Int'l | (215) 337-2300 |
| PROLOG V | IBM | Chalcedony Software | (619) 483-8513 |
| Prolog-86 | IBM | Solution Systems | (617) 337-6963 |
| Turbo Prolog | IBM | Borland Int'l | (408) 438-8400 |
| **Smalltalk** | | | |
| Smalltalk-AT | IBM | Softsmarts, Inc. | (415) 327-8100 |
| Smalltalk/V | IBM | Digitalk, Inc. | (213) 645-1082 |

**Table D-2**
***ES tools currently available on PCs***

| Tool | Applicable PC | Developer | Telephone | Notes |
|---|---|---|---|---|
| ADS | IBM | Aion | (415) 328-9595 | |
| Advisor | All | Ultimate Media | (415) 924-3644 | |
| APES | IBM | Logic Programming Assoc., UK | 01-874-0350 | |
| ES/P Advisor | IBM | Expert Systems Int'l | (215) 735-8510 | |
| EX-TRAN 7 | IBM | Intelligent Terminals, Scotland | 041-552-1353 | Induction |
| Expert Choice | IBM | Decision Support Software | (703) 442-7900 | |
| EXPERT 4 | IBM | Elsevier-Biosoft, UK | 02-23-31-5961 | |
| Expert Ease | IBM | Human Edge Software Corp. | (415) 431-9562 | Induction |
| EXSYS | IBM | EXSYS, Inc. | (505) 836-6676 | |
| 1st Class | IBM | Mountain View Press | (415) 961-4103 | |
| Inference Manager | IBM | Intelligent Terminals, Scotland | 041-552-1353 | Inference |
| Insight-1 & -2 | IBM | Level Five Research, Inc. | (305) 729-9046 | Linked to dBase |
| KDS | IBM | KDS Corp | (312) 251-2621 | |
| KES | IBM | Software A&E | (703) 276-7910 | |
| M.1 and M.1a | IBM | Teknowledge, Inc. | (415) 327-6600 | |
| MO-LRO | IBM | Conception et Realisation Industrielles de Logiciel, France | 1-776-34-37 | |
| MP-LRO | IBM | Conception et Realisation Industrielles de Logiciel, France | 1-776-34-37 | |
| Micro-Expert | IBM | McGraw-Hill Publishing | (212) 512-2000 | |
| Nexpert | Macintosh | Neuron Data | (415) 321-4488 | |
| OPS5 | IBM, Apple | Artelligence, Inc. | (214) 437-0361 | |
| Personal Consultant | TI, IBM | Texas Instruments | (512) 250-7111 | |
| Reveal | IBM | Tymshare UK Heiron House | 04862 26761 | |
| Rulemaster | IBM | Radian Corp. | (512) 454-4797 | |
| Savoir | IBM, HP | ISI, UK | 07-377-1327 | |
| TESS | IBM | Helix Expert Systems, UK | 01-248-1734 | |
| Think! | Apple II, Atari | UME | (805) 488-2972 | |
| TIMM-PC | IBM | General Research Corp. | (703) 893-5915 | Induction |
| Texpert | All | Texpert Systems | (713) 469-4068 | Linked to dBase |
| TOPS I | IBM | Dynamic Master Systems | (404) 565-0771 | Based on OPS5 |
| XSYS | IBM | California Intelligence | (415) 391-4846 | |
| Xi | IBM | Expertech House, UK | 0753-821321 | |

**Table D-3**
***Selected PC expert systems***

| System | Developer | Application Areas | Telephone | Notes |
|---|---|---|---|---|
| Capital Investment Expert Systems | Palladian Software | Capital investment | (617) 661-7171 | |
| Clout* | Microrim (Bellevue, WA) | Data base front end | | Linked to R:Base |
| Expert Choice | Decision Support Software | Decision support | (800) 368-2022 | Linked to Lotus 1-2-3 |
| GURU* | Micro Data Base Systems | Data base management | (317) 463-2581 | |
| HAL* | GNP Development (Pasadena, CA) | Spreadsheet front end | | Linked to Lotus 1-2-3 |
| HULK II | Brainstorm Computer Solutions, UK | Rule founder | 01 263 6926 | Also UNIX |
| Hypnotist | Intelligence Products, UK | Expert analysis on Lotus 1-2-3, Symphony | 016777583 | |
| Javelin* | Javelin Software (Cambridge, MA) | Data base management | | |
| Lightyear | Lightyear, Inc. | Decision analysis | (408) 985-8811 | |
| Manufacturing and Logistics Expert System | Palladian Software | Manufacturing and logistics | (617) 661-7171 | |
| Micro-Synthese | Ecole Nationale Superieure Chimie de Paris, France | Organic molecule | 133625235 | Apple II |
| Paradox* | Ansa Software (Belmont, CA) | Data base management | | |
| Parys | Business Information Techniques, UK | Personnel management | 0274736766 | |
| Plan Power | Applied Expert Systems (Cambridge, MA) | Financial planning | | |
| Q&A* | Symantec (Cupertino, CA) | Data base management | | |
| REVEAL* | McDonnell Douglas | Data management | (408) 446-7406 | |
| Superfile ACLS | Southdata, UK | Data base management | 017277564 | |
| WIZDOM XS | Software Int'l | Commercial and financial | (212) 627-4475 | |

*Natural language front ends that employ expert system technology

# Frequently-Mentioned Tools and Systems

**Table D-4**
***Frequently-mentioned tools***

| Tool | Representation Method | Developer |
|---|---|---|
| ACLS | Aid* | University of Edinburgh |
| ADVISE | Aid | University of Illinois |
| AIMDS | Frame based and procedure oriented | Rutgers University |
| AL/X | Rule based | Intelligent Terminals, Ltd. |
| ALICE | Logic based | Institute de Programmation (France) |
| AMORD | Rule based | MIT |
| APES | Logic based | Imperial College of London (UK) |
| APLICOT | Logic based | University of Tokyo |
| ARBY | Rule based | Yale University |
| ARS | Rule based | MIT |
| ART | Rule and frame based; procedure oriented | Inference Corporation |
| C | Procedure oriented | Bell Laboratories |
| Common LISP | Procedure oriented | Carnegie-Mellon University |
| CONCHE | Aid | University of Leeds |
| CSRL | Frame based | Ohio State University |
| DETEKR | Aid | Tektronix, Inc. |
| DPL | Frame based | MIT |
| DUCK | Logic and frame based | Smart Systems Technology |
| EMYCIN (a shell of MYCIN) | Rule based | Stanford University |
| ERS | Rule based | PAR Technology Corp. |
| ES/P Advisor | Rule based | Expert Systems Int'l. |
| ETS | Aid | Boeing Computer Services |
| Expert | Rule based | Rutgers University |
| Expert-2 | Rule based | Helion, Inc. |
| Expert Ease | Rule based (induction) | Human Edge Software |
| EXPRS | Rule based | Lockheed Palo Alto Research Lab |
| FIT | Logic based | University of Hamburg |
| FLAVORS | Object based | Symbolics |
| FRL | Frame based | MIT |
| GEN-X | Rule based | General Electric R & D Center |
| GLIB | Rule based | Tektronix, Inc. |
| GUESS/1 | Rule based | Virginia Institute/State University |
| HCPRVR | Logic based | University of Texas at Austin |
| HEARSAY-III | Rule based | Information Sciences Institute |
| HPRL | Frame based | Hewlett-Packard |

*Expert system building aids that help acquire and represent the human expert's/specialist's knowledge, or help design an expert system under development.

**Table D-4 (cont.)**

| Tool | Representation Method | Developer |
|---|---|---|
| HSRL | Logic and frame based | Robotics Institute, Carnegie-Mellon University |
| Insight-1, -2 | Rule based | Level Five Research |
| INTERLISP | Procedure oriented | Xerox Corporation |
| INTERLISP-D | Procedure oriented | Xerox Corporation |
| KANDOR | Frame based | Fairchild Lab for Artificial Intelligence Research |
| KAS (a shell of PROSPECTOR) | Rule based | SRI International |
| KC | Rule and frame based; object and procedure oriented | Carnegie Group |
| KEE | Rule and frame based; object and procedure oriented | Intellicorp |
| KES | Rule and frame based | Software A & E |
| KL-ONE | Frame based | Bolt, Beranek and Newman |
| KMS | Frame based | University of Maryland |
| KRYPTON | Frame based | Fairchild Lab for Artificial Intelligence Research |
| LES | Rule based | Lockheed Palo Alto Research Lab |
| LISP | Procedure oriented | MIT |
| LOOPS | Rule based; object and procedure oriented | |
| M.1 | Rule based | Teknowledge, Inc. |
| M.1 | Frame based | Teknowledge, Inc. |
| MARS | Rule based | Stanford University |
| MELD | Rule based | Westinghouse R & D Center |
| MORE | Aid | Carnegie-Mellon University |
| MRS | Rule and logic based | Stanford University |
| MUMPS | Procedure oriented | N/A |
| NETL | Frame based | MIT |
| OPS5 | Rule based | Carnegie-Mellon University; available from Verac Corp. and from DEC |
| OPS/83 | Rule based | Carnegie-Mellon University; available from Production Systems Technologies |
| OWL | Frame based | MIT |
| Personal Consultant | Rule based | Texas Instruments, Inc. |
| PICON | Rule and frame based; object oriented | LISP Machines, Inc. |
| PICON | Aid | LISP Machines, Inc. |
| PLUME | Aid | Carnegie Group, Inc. |
| PRISM | Rule based | IBM Palo Alto Scientific Center |
| Prolog | Logic based | Available from various vendors |
| PSL | Procedure oriented | University of Utah |
| PSYCHO | Rule based | Imperial Cancer Research Fund and Queen's Medical Center |
| RADIAL | Rule based; procedure oriented | Radian Corporation |

**Table D-4 (cont.)**

| Tool | Representation Method | Developer |
|---|---|---|
| RITA | Rule based | Rand Corporation |
| RLL | Frame based | Stanford University |
| ROGET | Aid | Stanford University |
| ROSIE | Rule based; procedure oriented | Rand Corporation |
| Rulemaster | Aid | Radian Corporation |
| S.1 | Rule and frame based; procedure oriented | Teknowledge, Inc. |
| SAIL | Procedure oriented | Stanford University |
| Savoir | Rule based | ISI (a joint venture between ISIS Systems Ltd., and ICI Ltd., UK) |
| SEEK | Aid | Rutgers University |
| Smalltalk | Object based | Xerox Palo Alto Research Center |
| SOAR | Rule based | Carnegie-Mellon University |
| SRL | Frame based | Robotics Institute, Carnegie-Mellon University |
| SRL+ | Rule, frame, and logic based; object oriented | Carnegie Group, Inc. |
| STROBE | Object based | Schlumberger-Doll Research |
| T.1 | Aid | Teknowledge, Inc. |
| TEIRESIAS | Aid | Stanford University |
| TIMM | Aid | General Research Corporation |
| UNIT PACKAGE | Frame based | Stanford University |
| ZETALISP | Procedure oriented | MIT |

**Table D-5**
***Frequently-mentioned expert systems***

| Expert System | Application | Developer/User |
|---|---|---|
| ACE | Diagnosis and debugging of telephone networks | Bell Laboratories of Whippany, New Jersey |
| ACES | Design map labeling | Developed by ESL |
| ATTENDING | Instructs medical students in anesthesiology | Yale University School of Medicine |
| BLUE BOX | Treats various forms of depression | Stanford University |
| CADHELP | Instructs in use of CAD subsystem for digital circuit design | University of Connecticut |
| CELLISTO | Project management | Carnegie Group |
| DELTA | Field service for diesel-electric locomotion troubleshooting | General Electric |
| DENDRAL | Infers molecular structure of unknown compounds | Stanford University |
| DIPMETER ADVISOR | Infers subsurface geological structure by interpreting dipmeter loop | Schlumberger-Doll Research |

**Table D-5 (cont.)**

| Expert System | Application | Developer/User |
|---|---|---|
| DRILLING ADVISOR | Corrects oil right "drill sticking" problem | Teknowledge in cooperation with Societe National Elf Aquitaine |
| EL | Performs a steady-state analysis of resistor-diode-transistor circuits | MIT |
| FOLIO | Assists portfolio managers in determining client investment goals and selecting portfolios | Stanford University |
| GA1 | Development experiments in DNA structure | Stanford University |
| HASP/SIAP | Interprets sonar sensor data to detect and identify ocean vessels | Joint effort of Stanford University and Systems Control Technology |
| I&W | Analyzes intelligence reports and predicts when and where armed conflict will occur | Joint effort by ESL and Stanford University |
| IDT | Locates defective units in PDP11/30 computers | DEC |
| INTERNIST | Diagnosis of disease | University of Pittsburgh |
| MUD | Troubleshoots drilling fluid problems | Carnegie-Mellon University in cooperation with NL Baroid |
| MYCIN | Assists in selection of appropriate antimicrobial therapy for patients | Stanford University |
| PALLADIO | Designs new VLSI circuits | Stanford University |
| PLANT/cd | Predicts degree of damage caused by cutworms | University of Illinois |
| PROSPECTOR | Aids geologists in their search for ore deposits | SRI International |
| PTRANS | Develops plans for assembling and testing the ordered computer system | DEC and Carnegie-Mellon University |
| PUFF | Diagnosis of presence and severity of lung diseases | Stanford University |
| REACTOR | Diagnosis and treatment of nuclear reactor accidents/abnormal events | EG&G Idaho |
| SECS | Synthesizes organic molecules | University of California at Santa Cruz |
| SPE | Interprets scanning densitometer data to diagnose inflammatory conditions | Rutgers University (incorporated in CliniScan and marketed by Helena Labs) |
| STEAMER | Instructs navy engineering students in steam plant propulsion operation | Naval Personal Research and Development Center in cooperation with Bolt, Beranek and Newman |
| TALIB | Electronics: automatically synthesizes integrated circuit layouts for nMOS cells | Carnegie-Mellon University |
| TATR | Develops plan for air targeteer to attack enemy airfields | Rand Corporation |

**Table D-5 (cont.)**

| Expert System | Application | Developer/User |
|---|---|---|
| TIMM/TUNER | Tunes VAX/VMS computers | General Research Corp. |
| TQMSTUNE | Fine tunes a triple quadruple mass spectrometer | Lawrence Livermore Labs |
| XCON | Configures VAX computers | Carnegie-Mellon University and DEC |
| XPS-E | Production planning | Carnegie Group |
| XSEL | Assists design/distribution selection | Carnegie-Mellon University and DEC |

# E

# Selected Expert System Companies

Advanced Decision Systems
201 San Antonio Circle, #286
Mountain View, CA 94049
TEL: (415) 941-3912

AI Decision Systems
8624 Via del Sereno
Scottsdale, AZ 85258
TEL: (602) 991-0599

Aion Corporation
101 University Avenue, 4th Floor
Palo Alto, CA 94301
TEL: (415) 328-9595

Apollo Computer, Inc.
330 Billerica Rd.
Chelmsford, MA 01824, MS 37
TEL: (617) 256-6600

Applicon (Schlumberger)
32 Second Avenue
Concord, MA 01803
TEL: (617) 272-7070

Applied Expert Systems (APEX)
5 Cambridge Center
Cambridge, MA 02142
TEL: (617) 492-7322

ARCO Resources Administration
Plano Employee Relations
P.O. Box 2819
Dallas, TX 75221

Arity Corporation
358 Baker Avenue
Concord, MA 01742
TEL: (617) 371-2422

Arthur D. Little
25 Acorn Park
Cambridge, MA 02140
TEL: (617) 864-5770

Artificial Intelligence Research Group
921 N. La Jolla Avenue
Los Angeles, CA 90046
TEL: (213) 656-7368

Artificial Intelligence Software S.r.1
Casella Postale 198-45100 Rovigo
Italy
TEL: 0425/27151

AT&T/Bell Laboratories
Crawford's Corner Road
Holmdel, NJ 07733
TEL: (201) 949-3000

Automated Reasoning Corporation
290 W. 12th Street, Suite 1-D
New York, NY 10014
TEL: (212) 206-6331

Battelle Columbus Laboratories
505 King Avenue
Columbus, OH 43201
TEL: (614) 424-7728

BDM Corporation
7915 Jones Branch Drive
McLean, VA 22102
TEL: (703) 821-5000

Boeing Computer Services
P.O. Box 24346/MS 7A-03
Seattle, WA 98124
TEL: (206) 763-5392

Bolt, Beranek and Newman, Inc.
10 Moulton Street
Cambridge, MA 02238
TEL: (617) 491-1850

Brattle Research Corporation
215 First Street
Cambridge, MA 02142
TEL: (617) 492-1982

Bynas Division, Uny Co., Ltd.
5F, Dai-Nagoya Bldg., 28-12,
3-Chome
Meieki, Nakamura-ku, Nagoya, 450
Japan
TEL: 052-581-7655

California Intelligence
912 Powell Street, Suite 8
San Francisco, CA 94108
TEL: (415) 391-4846

Carnegie Group, Inc.
Commerce Court and Station
Square
Pittsburgh, PA 15219
TEL: (412) 642-6900

Center for Machine Intelligence
2001 Commonwealth Blvd.
Ann Arbor, MI 48105

Cognitive Systems
234 Church Street
New Haven, CT 06510
TEL: (203) 773-0726

Computer Thought Corporation
1721 W. Plano Parkway, Suite 125
Plano, TX 75075
TEL: (214) 424-3511

Control Data Corporation
P.O. Box O
Minneapolis, MN 55440
TEL: (612) 853-6137

Decision Support Software
1300 Vincent Plain
McLean, VA 22101
TEL: (703) 442-7900

Digital Equipment Corporation
77 Technology Way
Westboro, MA 01580
TEL: (617) 366-8911

Digitalk, Inc.
5200 West Century Blvd.
Los Angeles, Ca 90045
TEL: (213) 645-1082

ESL, Inc.
495 Java Drive
Sunnyvale, CA 94088-3510
TEL: (408) 738-2888

ExperTelligence, Inc.
559 San Ysidro Road
Santa Barbara, CA 93108
TEL: (805) 969-7871

Expert Technologies, Inc.
2600 Liberty Avenue
Pittsburgh, PA 15230
TEL: (412) 355-0900

Expert-Knowledge Systems, Inc.
6313 Old Chesterbrook Road
McLean, VA 22101
TEL: (703) 734-6966

EXSYS, Inc.
P.O. Box 75158, Con. Station 14
Albuquerque, NM 87914
TEL: (505) 836-6676

Ford Aerospace and
Communications Corporation
Aeronutronic Division
Dept. A703-001
Ford Road
Newport Beach, CA 92660

Fountain Hills Software, Inc.
6900 E. Camelback Road,
Suite 1000
Scottsdale, AZ 85251
TEL: (602) 945-0261

General Motors Research
Laboratories
Computer Science Department
Warren, Michigan 48090-9057
TEL: (313) 575-3101

General Research Corporation
7655 Old Springhouse Road
McLean, VA 22102
TEL: (703) 893-5915

Gold Hill Computers
163 Harvard Street
Cambridge, MA 02139
TEL: (617) 492-2071

Gould Electronics
6901 West Sunrise Blvd.
Fort Lauderdale, FL 33313-4499
TEL: (303) 587-2900

Grumman-CTEC, Inc.
1355 Beverly Road, Suite 200
Dept. 13
McLean, VA 22101
TEL: (703) 448-0226

GTE Laboratories
Box A3, 40 Sylvan Road
Waltham, MA 02254

Hewlett-Packard Labs
1501 Page Mill Road
Palo Alto, CA 94304
TEL: (415) 857-5356

Honeywell, Inc.
1000 Boone Avenue North
Golden Valley, MN 55427
TEL: (612) 541-6579

Hughes Research Laboratories
3011 Malibu Canyon Road
Malibu, CA 90265

IBM
1501 California Avenue
Palo Alto, CA 94303-0821
TEL: (415) 855-3938

Iconics
8502 E. Via de Ventura
Scottsdale, AZ 85258
TEL: (602) 948-2600

IDC
5 Speen Street
Framingham, MA 01701
TEL: (617) 872-8200

Impak
P.O. Box 7148
Alexandria, VA 22307-0148

Inference Corporation
5300 W. Century Boulevard
Los Angeles, CA 90045
TEL: (213) 417-7997

Intellicorp
708 Laurel Street
Menlo Park, CA 94025
TEL: (415) 323-8300

Intelliware, Inc.
4676 Admiralty Way, Suite 401
Marina del Rey, CA 90291
TEL: (213) 305-9391

Interface Computer
Oberfohringer Strabe 24a + b
D-8000 Munchen 81
West Germany
TEL: 0 89/98 44 44

Jeffrey Perrone and Associates
3685 17th Street
San Francisco, CA 94114
TEL: (415) 431-9562

KDS Corporation
934 Hunter Road
Wilmette, IL 60091
TEL: (312) 251-2621

Knowledge Quest (search firm)
1210 Park Newport, #106
Newport Beach, CA 92660
TEL: (714) 760-2527

Level Five Research
503 Fifth Ave.
Indialantic, FL 32903
TEL: (305) 729-09046

Lithp Systems BV
Meervalweg 72
1121 JP Landsmeer
The Netherlands

Lockheed Software Technology Center
Department 700-20
P.O. Box 17100
Austin, TX 78760

Lucid, Inc.
1090 East Meadow Circle
Palo Alto, CA 94303
TEL: (415) 424-8855

MacKintosh Consulting
14395 Saratoga Avenue, Suite 150
Saratoga, CA 95027
TEL: (408) 867-9800

Martin Marietta Data Systems
98 Inverness Drive East, Suite 135 (P193)
Englewood, CO 80112
TEL: (303) 790-3404

McDonnell Douglas—Knowledge Engineering
20705 Valley Green Drive, VG2-BO1
Cupertino, CA 95014
TEL: (408) 446-6553

MDBS (Micro Database Systems)
P.O. Box 248
Lafayette, IN 47902
TEL: (317) 463-2581

Mitre Corporation
Burlington Road
Bedford, MA 01730
TEL: (617) 271-2000

Naval Underwater Systems Center
Personnel Staffing Division, A1
Newport, Rhode Island 02841-5047
TEL: (401) 841-3585

Palladian
41 Munroe Street
Cambridge, MA 02142
TEL: (617) 661-7171

Perceptronics
21111 Erwin Street
Woodland Hills, CA 91367
TEL: (818) 884-7572

Programming Logic Systems, Inc.
31 Crescent Drive
Milford, CT 06460
TEL: (203) 877-7988

Quintus Computer Systems, Inc.
2345 Yale Street
Palo Alto, CA 94306
TEL: (415) 494-3612

Radian Corporation
P.O. Box 9948
Austin, TX 78766
TEL: (512) 454-4797

Reasoning Systems
1801 Page Mill Road
Palo Alto, CA 94303
TEL: (415) 494-6201

Schlumberger-Doll Research
P.O. Box 307/Old Quarry Road
Ridgefield, CT 06877
TEL: (203) 431-5000

Scientific DataLink
850 Third Avenue
New York, NY 10022
TEL: (212) 838-7200

Semantic Microsystems
1001 Bridgeway, Suite 543
Sausalito, CA 94965
TEL: (415) 332-8094

Shell Development Company
Research Recruitment
P.O. Box 1380
Houston, TX 77001

SIL
50 Broad Street, 10th Floor
New York, NY 10004
TEL: (212) 747-9066, 7, 8

Silogic
6420 Wilshire Boulevard
Los Angeles, CA 90048
TEL: (213) 653-6470

Smart Systems Technology
6870 Elm Street, Suite 300
McLean, VA 22101
TEL: (703) 448-8562

Software Architecture & Engineering, Inc.
1500 Wilson Boulevard, Suite 800
Arlington, VA 22209
TEL: (703) 276-7910

Soft Warehouse
P.O. Box 11174
Honolulu, HI 96828-0174
TEL: (808) 734-5801

Sperry Corporation
Systems Management Group
Employment Department RB-522
12010 Sunrise Valley Drive
Reston, VA 22091

SRI International
333 Ravenswood Avenue
Menlo Park, CA 94025
TEL: (415) 326-6200

SU Infologics AB
Box 7733
S-103 95
Stockholm, Sweden

Syntelligence
1000 Hamlin Court
Sunnyvale, CA 94088
TEL: (408) 745-6666

Systems Designers Software, Inc.
444 Washington Street, Suite 407
Woburn, MA 01801
TEL: (617) 935-8009

Systems Research Laboratories, Inc.
Computer Systems Division
2800 Indian Ripple Road
Dayton, OH 45440-3639
TEL: (513) 426-6000

Teknowledge, Inc.
525 University Avenue
Palo Alto, CA 94301
TEL: (415) 327-6600

United Technologies Research Center
Silver Lane
East Hartford, CT 06108

Verac, Inc. (Applied Computer Science Group)
9605 Scranton Road, Suite 500
San Diego, CA 92121
TEL: (619) 457-5550

Software Engineering Group
517 N. Mountain Avenue
Upland, CA 91786-5016
TEL: (714) 982-1738

## *Publishers*

Addison-Wesley Publishing Co.
Reading, MA 01867
ATTN: Carolyn Berry

Cambridge University Press
32 East 57th Street
New York, NY 10022

Computational Intelligence
Distribution, R-88
National Research Council of Canada
Ottawa, Canada K1A 0R6

Electronic Trend Publications
10080 N. Wolfe Road, Suite 372
Cupertino, CA 95014
TEL: (408) 996-7416

Harper & Row
10 East 53rd Street, Suite 3D
New York, NY

John Wiley & Sons, Inc.
605 Third Avenue
New York, NY 10158
TEL: (800) 526-5368

Kluwer Academic Publishers
190 Old Derby Street
Hingham, MA 02043
TEL: (617) 749-5262

Morgan Kaufman Publishers, Inc.
Dept. A1, 95 First Street
Los Altos, CA 94022

Pitman Publishing, Inc.
1020 Plan Street
Marshfield, MA 02050
TEL: (617) 837-1331

The MIT Press
28 Carleton Street
Cambridge, MA 02142

W. W. Norton & Company, Inc.
500 Fifth Avenue
New York, NY 10010

Westcomp
Software Engineering Group
517 N. Mountain Avenue
Upland, CA 91786-5016

# Glossary

**Attribute** A property of an object.

**Best search** A search strategy in which a criterion is used to minimize search time.

**Bidirectional search** An inference method that combines forward chaining and backward chaining.

**Blackboard** A working memory accessible to independent knowledge sources and used by them to communicate with one another.

**Blackboard architecture** (Also HEARSAY architecture) An expert system design in which several independent knowledge sources each examine a common working memory (a "blackboard").

**Breadth-first search** A search strategy in which rules or objects on the same level of the hierarchy are examined before rules or objects on the next lower level.

**C** A programming language initially associated with the UNIX operating system.

**Certainty factor** A number that measures the certainty or confidence in a fact or rule.

**Deep knowledge** Knowledge of basic theories, first principles, axioms, or models, in contrast to surface knowledge.

**Declarative Knowledge** Facts about objects, events, or situations.

**Demon** A procedure activated by the chaining of values in a data base.

**Depth-first search** A search strategy in which a rule or object on the highest level is examined, followed by rules or objects immediately below that one (in contrast to breadth-first search).

**Domain** The application area of an expert system.

**Domain expert** A person with expertise in a particular domain.

**Expert system** A computer program containing knowledge and reasoning capability that imitates human experts in problem solving in a particular domain.

**Expert system building tool** The computer programming language and support package designed to build an expert system.

**Explanation facility** The component of an expert system that explains how solutions are reached and justifies the steps used to reach them.

**Forward chaining** An inference technique where the IF portions of rules are matched against facts to establish new facts.

**Frame** A knowledge representation method that associates an object with a collection of features (for example, facts, rules, defaults, and active values). Each feature is stored in a slot.

**Heuristic** A rule-of-thumb approach that suggests a procedure to solve a problem. A heuristic approach does not guarantee a solution to a specific problem.

**Induction system** An example-driven system that has a knowledge base consisting of examples.

**Inference** The process by which new facts are derived from known facts.

**Inference engine** The component of an expert system that controls its operation by selecting the rules to use, executing those rules, and determining when an acceptable solution has been reached.

**Inheritance** A process by which characteristics of one object are assumed to be characteristics of another in the same class.

**Knowledge acquisition** The process of identifying, interviewing, collecting, and refining knowledge.

**Knowledge base** The component of an expert system that contains the system's knowledge.

**Knowledge-based system** Another name for an expert system.

**Knowledge engineer** An AI programmer responsible for capturing and encoding human expert knowledge.

**Knowledge representation** The technique used to encode and store facts and relationships in a knowledge base.

**LISP** (*Li*st *P*rocessing) An AI programming language based on list processing, consisting of atoms and lists only.

**LISP machine** (Also "AI workstation") A single-user computer designed to facilitate the development of AI programs.

**Logic-based method** Programming technique that uses predicate calculus to structure the program.

**Logical inferences per second (LIPS)** A method of measuring the speed of computers, used for AI applications.

**Man-machine interface** See user interface.

**Model-based expert system** A type of expert system that is based on a model of the structure and behavior of the physical system it is designed to understand.

**Modus ponens** A basic rule of logic that asserts that if A implies B and if A is true, then B is also true.

**Monotonic reasoning** A reasoning technique based on the assumption that once a fact is determined, it cannot be altered during the course of the consultation process.

**Natural Language Interface (NLI)** A program that allows a user to communicate with a computer in the user's natural language, such as English.

**Nonmonotonic reasoning** A reasoning method that allows multiple approaches to reach the same conclusion and the retraction of facts or conclusions, given new information.

**Object** Physical or conceptual entities that have attributes. A collection of attributes or rules are organized around an object.

**Object-oriented programming** Programming technique based on the use of objects that communicate with one another by means of messages.

**Predicate calculus** A classical logic that uses functions and predicates to describe relations between individual entities. Each elementary unit in predicate calculus is called an object. Statements about objects are called predicates.

**Procedural knowledge** Information about courses of action.

**Procedure-oriented programming** Conventional programming techniques that use nested subroutines to organize and control program execution.

**Production rule** A rule in the form of an IF-THEN or CONDITION-ACTION statement.

**Prolog** (*Pro*gramming in *Log*ic) An AI programming language based on predicate calculus, which is popular in Europe and Japan.

**Rapid prototype** In expert system development, a prototype is an initial version of an expert system, usually a system with from 10 to 300 rules, used to demonstrate effectiveness of knowledge representation and inference strategies.

**Reasoning** The process of drawing inferences or conclusions, either by human experts or by expert systems.

**Representation** The method by which an expert system stores knowledge about a domain.

**Rule** A conditional statement of two parts. The first part, comprised of one or more IF clauses, establishes conditions that must be satisfied. The second part, comprised of one or more THEN clauses, is to be acted upon.

**Rule-based method** Programming technique using IF-THEN rules to perform forward or backward chaining.

**Search** The process of examining the set of possible solutions to a problem in order to find an acceptable solution.

**Search space** The set of all possible solutions to a problem that might be evaluated during a search.

**Semantic network** A method for representing associations between objects and events.

**Shell** See Tool.

**Skeletal system** A computer program designed for building expert systems. It is derived by removing all domain-specific knowledge from an existing expert system.

**Slot** A component in a frame that contains a specific attribute of an object.

**Smalltalk** An object-oriented programming language.

**Speech recognition** An area of AI research that attempts to enable computers to recognize words or phrases at human speed.

**Symbolic reasoning** Problem solving based on the application of strategies and heuristics to manipulate symbols, in contrast to traditional numerical processing.

**Tool** (Also "Shell") A short name for "expert system building tool," which is a computer software package that simplifies the effort of building expert systems.

**Tree structure** A way of representing knowledge as a connected graph where each node can branch into other nodes deeper in the structure.

**User interface** (Also "Man-machine interface") The component of an expert system that allows communication between the expert system and its user.

**Unit** A frame-like knowledge representation method using slots with values and procedures attached to them.

**Value** A quantity or quality that can be used to describe an attribute in a knowledge representation frame.

**Width-first search** A search strategy in which rules or objects on the same level are searched first before moving down to the next level.

**Working memory** The component of an expert system that is composed of all attribute-value relationships temporarily established while the consultation is in progress. Used mainly in OPS5.

# Selected Bibliography

## *Magazines and Journals*

*AI Expert*, San Francisco.

*IEEE Expert*, published by IEEE Computer Society.

*Computer Language*, San Francisco.

*AI Journal*, published by North-Holland.

*AI Magazine*, an informal quarterly magazine included with membership in the American Association for Artificial Intelligence (Menlo Park, CA).

*Proceedings of the IJCAI*, from the International Joint Conference on Artificial Intelligence, a bi-annual conference held in odd-numbered years.

*Proceedings of the AAAI*, from the American Association for Artificial Intelligence Conference, held annually.

## *Useful Books and Articles*

Aleksander, I. *Designing Intelligent Systems: An Introduction*, New York: UNIPUB, 1984.

Bachant, J. and J. McDermott. "R1 Revisited: Four Years in the Trenches," *The AI Magazine*, 5, no. 3 (Fall 1984).

Barr, A. and E. A. Feigenbaum, eds. *The Handbook of Artificial Intelligence*, Vol. 1, Vol. II. Los Altos, CA: William Kaufman, Inc., 1981.

Brachman, R. and H. Levesque, eds. *Readings in Knowledge Representation*. Los Altos, CA: Morgan Kaufman Publishers, 1985.

Brownston, L., R. Farrel, E. Kant, and N. Martin. *Programming Expert Systems in OPS5. An Introduction to Rule-Based Programming*. Reading, MA: Addison-Wesley, 1985.

Buchanan, B. G. and E. H. Shortliffe, eds. *Rule-Based Expert Systems: The MYCIN Experiments of the Stanford Heuristic Programming Project*. Reading, MA: Addison-Wesley, 1984.

Campbell, J. A., ed. *Implementations of Prolog*. New York: Halsted Press, 1984.

Charniak, E. and D. M. McDermott. *Introduction to Artificial Intelligence*. Reading, MA: Addison-Wesley, 1985.

Clancey, W. J. and E. H. Shortliffe. *Readings in Medical Artificial Intelligence: The First Decade.* Reading, MA: Addison-Wesley, 1984.

Clocksin, W. F. and C. S. Mellish. *Programming in Prolog.* New York: Springer-Verlag, 1984.

Coombs, M. J. *Development in Expert Systems.* London: Academic Press, 1984.

Danicic, I. *LISP Programming.* Boston: Blackwell Scientific Publications, 1983.

Davis, Randall. "Expert Systems: Where Are We? And Where Do We Go From Here?" *The AI Magazine,* 3, no. 2 (Spring 1982).

Davis, R. and D. B. Lenat. *Knowledge-Based Systems in Artificial Intelligence.* New York: McGraw-Hill International Book Co., 1982.

Emrich, M. L. *Energy Division, Expert Systems Tools and Techniques.* Prepared by Oak Ridge National Laboratory for the U.S. Department of Energy under contract No. DE-AC05-840R21400, August 1985.

Ennals, J. R. *Beginning Micro-Prolog* 2nd rev. ed. New York: Harper & Row, 1984.

Forsyth, R., ed. *Expert Systems: Principles and Case Studies.* New York: Methuen, 1984.

Gevarter, W. B. *Artificial Intelligence, Expert Systems, Computer Vision, and Natural Language Processing.* Park Ridge, NJ: Noyes Publications, 1984.

Glorioso, R. M. and F. C. C. Osorio. *Engineering Intelligence Systems: Concepts, Theory, and Applications.* Bedford, MA: Digital Press, 1980.

Harmon, P. and D. King. *Expert Systems: Artificial Intelligence in Business.* New York: John Wiley, 1985.

Hayes, J. E. and D. Michie, eds. *Intelligent Systems: The Unprecedented Opportunity.* New York: Halstead Press, 1983.

Hayes-Roth, F., A. Waterman, and D. B. Lenat, eds. *Building Expert Systems.* Reading, MA: Addison-Wesley, 1983.

Hu, D. *Expert Systems for Software Engineers and Managers.* New York: Chapman & Hall, 1987.

Johnson, T. *The Commercial Application of Expert System Technology.* London: Ovum Ltd., 1985.

Kelly, D. P. *Expert Consulting Systems in Construction Management Engineering.* Thesis, Department of Civil Engineering, Stanford University, California, 1984.

McDermott, John. "R1: The Formative Years," *The AI Magazine,* 2, no. 2 (Summer 1981).

McDermott, John, "R1: A Rule-Based Configurer of Computer Systems," *Artificial Intelligence* (1982).

Miller, R. D., ed. *The 1984 Inventory of Expert Systems.* Madison, GA: SEAI Institute and Fort Lee, NJ: Technical Insights, Inc., 1984.

Naylor, Chris. *Build Your Own Expert System.* Halstead Press, a division of John Wiley & Sons, 1983.

Negoita, C. V. *Expert Systems and Fuzzy Systems.* Menlo Park, CA: Benjamin/Cummings Pub. Co., 1985.

Polit, Stephen. "R1 and Beyond: AI Technology Transfer at DEC," *The AI Magazine*, 5, no. 4 (Winter 1985).

Reboh, R. *Knowledge Engineering Techniques and Tools for Expert Systems.* Software Systems Research Center, Linkoping University, Sweden, 1981.

Rich, E. *Artificial Intelligence.* New York: McGraw-Hill, 1983.

Sell, Peter S. *Expert Systems—A Practical Introduction.* MacMillan Publishers Ltd. (in Great Britain) and Halstead Press, a division of John Wiley & Sons, Inc. (in the U.S.), 1985.

Shafer, G. *Probability judgment in artificial intelligence and expert systems.* Working paper 165, School of Business, University of Kansas, 1984.

Sleeman, D. and J. S. Brown, eds. *Intelligent Tutoring Systems.* New York: Academic Press, 1982.

Steele, Guy L., Jr. *Common LISP Reference Manual.* Spice Project Internal Report. Pittsburgh: Carnegie-Mellon University, Digital Press, 1982.

Tversky, A. and D. Kahneman. "Judgment under uncertainty: heuristics and biases in D. Kahneman, P. Slovix, and A. Tversky," in *Judgment Under Uncertainty: Heuristics and Biases.* Cambridge: Cambridge University Press, 1982.

Waterman, Donald A. *A Guide to Expert Systems.* Reading, MA: Addison-Wesley, 1986.

Weiss, S. M. and C. A. Kuliwoski. *A Practical Guide to Designing Expert Systems.* Totwa, NJ: Rowman and Allanheld, 1984.

Winston, P. H. and B. K. P. Horn. *LISP.* 2nd ed. Reading, MA: Addison-Wesley, 1984.

Winston, P. H. and K. A. Prendergast, eds. *The AI Business: The Commercial Uses of Artificial Intelligence.* 2nd ed. Cambridge: MIT Press, 1984.

# Index